The Idea of *Cheng* (Sincerity/Reality) in the History of Chinese Philosophy

A Volume in
the ACPA Series of Chinese and Comparative Philosophy

Sponsored by the Association of Chinese Philosophers in America
http://www.acpa-net.org

The Idea of *Cheng* (Sincerity/Reality) in the History of Chinese Philosophy

Yanming An

Global Scholarly Publications, New York

A Volume in the ACPA Series of Chinese and Comparative Philosophy
Sponsored by the Association of Chinese Philosophers in America
http//www.acpa-net.org

Cover design by Xiao Hu

Published by

Global Scholarly Publications

ISBN: 1-59267-060-1

Distributed by

Global Scholarly Publications

220 Madison Avenue, Suite 11G
New York, NY 10016
www.gsp-online.org
books@gsp-online.org
Phone: (212) 679-6410 Fax: (212) 679-6424

To Professor Donald J. Munro —

My Teacher, Friend, and Colleague

Acknowledgements

This study began with a term paper written for Professor Donald J. Munro's seminar of *Ancient Chinese Philosophy* at the University of Michigan in the fall of 1992. There I developed two points. First, as a philosophical term, *cheng* in Xunzi denotes a general principle governing and regulating both humans and Nature. Secondly, its content can be summarized with a group of interrelated English terms: consistency, correspondence, and constancy. After this work, I wrote sequentially three short essays, dealing respectively with *cheng* in WANG Bi, GUO Xiang, and ZHU Xi.

Before starting my systematical training in Chinese philosophy, I had studied German Philosophy, especially philosophical Hermeneutics for many years. Wilhelm Dilthey's idea about the relation between "expression" (Ausdruck) and "lived experience" (Erlebnis) enabled me to realize soon that "consistency" etc. are actually not *cheng* itself, but things in the category of external "expression," which are caused by and reflect the inner state of *cheng*. Furthermore, I was inspired by Hans-Georg Gadamer's idea that all statements can be viewed as answers to certain questions, and a correct understanding of the question may help people apprehend the answer itself. In Mencius, who first used *cheng* as a philosophical concept, I identified the question to which *cheng* was applied to answer. The question is, how can people get "trust" from others, and how can they retain this "trust" forever? Put differently, the concept of *cheng* emerged because of people's needs to ensure the trust and its acquisition.

However, there are still a number of complicated problems waiting for their solution. *Cheng* was widely used by philosophers from various schools: Confucianism, Daoism, Legalism, and Buddhism, and for the issues concerning both human life and natural phenomena. The variety of uses makes *cheng* a concept "elusive" and even "unintelligible," as

Munro and ZHANG Dainian respectively phrased. Dilthey's other ideas directed me to put things in order. One of his major works is entitled "*The Formation of Historical World in the Human Sciences*." Following his line of thought, I substituted the "historical world with the "idea of *cheng*," the "human sciences" with the "history of Chinese philosophy," and preserved the double meaning of "formation:" a process to construct and the construction as its result. The conclusion is that, *cheng* as seen today is not a concept in a regular sense, but a conceptual unity with multiple dimensions and layers. Originating from people's basic concern about trust and its acquisition, *cheng* advances with continuous absorption of intellectual elements from various schools in a rather long period. The diversity of sources explains why it is "elusive" and "unintelligible," while the common interest from those schools implies that it may characterize Chinese philosophy in general. Thus, I planned to reveal the idea of *cheng* by tracing its evolution in the entire history of Chinese philosophy. I saw at this point that what I learned from Dilthey actually rooted in Hegel's idea: the reconciliation of history and logic, which has attracted me since the time when I was an undergraduate student at Fudan University, China. With the above knowledge, there came my dissertation.

It is the teaching career at Clemson University, especially a course of "Comparative Issues in Western and Eastern Philosophies," which I co-taught with Professor Todd May that enabled me to place *cheng* in the context of world civilizations, and to explore its universal significance by comparing and contrasting it with relevant ideas in Western philosophy. With the shifting of approach, this study became a work falling mainly in the category of "International Sinology," rather than that of traditional Chinese scholarship. By the term of "International Sinology," I mean an intellectual effort to put a typical Chinese topic such as *cheng,* in the context of world cultures, understanding and interpreting it in reference with the ideas from other cultures. It is "international" because what it seeks for is something universal to humankind as a whole; meanwhile it is "Sinology" because the topic and materials it concerned with come originally from China, and the methods applied are often distinctively Chinese. It is my belief that, along with China's increasing position into the world community economically and politically, this approach will become more and more popular in the field of Chinese learning in general, and Chinese philosophy in particular.

I am grateful to all the scholars whose contributions have been remarked in this study, especially the English translators of Chinese classics, including, but not limited to, James Legge, Arthur Waley, A. C. Graham, Wing-tsit Chan, Burton Watson, Thomas Cleary, and John Knoblock. Their translations saved me a tremendous work and, in many cases, corrected my understanding on original Chinese texts, although I often modified them here and there for various reasons.

Also, I would like to say thanks especially to six distinguished scholars who greatly helped for the final completion of this study. Professor Theodore de Boer at the University of Amsterdam and Professor Rudolf Makkreel at Emory University respectively guided me reading through Gamader and Dilthey. Professor LI He at the Institute of Philosophy, Chinese Academy of Social Sciences and Professor Geling Shang at Grand Valley State University brought to this study many valuable insights through our regular discussions on *cheng* and other related issues. Professor Todd May at Clemson University stimulated me to think about the relation between several Western concepts and their Chinese counterparts. In addition, I am much indebted to Professor Peimin Ni at Grand Valley State University for his standing as both the manuscript editor of this study and the editor of ACPA book series to which this study belongs. He identified its original manuscript as potentially publishable, challenged me to improve my arguments, and worked with me closely to make this study more readable. These remind me of many touching stories from ancient time in which friends assist each other solely for the pursuit of truth.

My deepest gratitude goes to Professor Munro. With an encouraging grade of A+ on my first paper, he convinced me of the desirability of taking *cheng* as a long time project. He discussed with me on a weekly basis, from the time when I was writing the three short essays until the completion of my dissertation. Before this study reached its final form, he read the manuscript, and helped me by introducing new materials, challenging my arguments, and even refining my English expression. His eyes are sharp, his suggestions are constructive, and most importantly, he doesn't compromise his criticism to the "politeness" in a negative sense. Checking through this final version now, I can recognize how much I have learned from him, and how many places in which he put his thinking, time, and energy. I am truly moved. In addition to confirming the norm in academia that, despite all the intellectual debts I owe to Professor Munro, the fault in this study belongs to me, not to him, I would emphasize whole-heartedly that this study would be of much less value if there were no help from him.

Yanming An
Clemson, South Carolina
August 19, 2005

Table of Contents

Introduction

The idea of *cheng* 誠 occupies a key position in Chinese culture. It has been widely used by Chinese thinkers of all fields from the Pre-Qin 秦 period (221-214 B.C.E.) until today. LI Ao 李翺 (772-841), a philosopher in the Tang 唐 dynasty (618-907), describes it as the nature of the sage. It stands as a source of light from which come individual enlightenment and social harmony (Li 1963, 551). CHEN Tingchuo 陳廷綽 (1853-1892), a literary critic in the Qing 清 Dynasty (1616-1912), characterizes it as the ultimate reason for the creation of DU Fu's 杜甫 (712-770) brilliant poetry and HAN Yu's 韓愈 (768-824) magnificent prose (CHEN Tingchuo, 211). In modern times, JIANG Jieshi 蔣介石 (1887-1975), a political and military leader of the Nationalist Party, regards *cheng* as "the first principle for the well-being of both a man and a country" (Jiang 1937, 29). These claims indicate a belief that *cheng* represents a universally valid power for positive consequence in all areas of a society.

At the same time, *cheng* is a complicated notion. Mencius 孟子 (around 372-289 B.C.E.) defines it as the "Way of Heaven," an ideal goal that we humans should strive to reach by means of moral cultivation (*Mengzi*, 4A12). The author of *Centrality and Commonality* (*Zhongyong* 《中庸》) explains its attribute with two metaphorical terms, "ceaselessness" (*buxi* 不息) and "no duplicity" (*bu'er* 不貳) (*Zhongyong*, 34). CHENG Yi 程頤 (1033-1107) names it as the "principle of reality" (*shili* 實理) that determines a thing to be as itself (Cheng and Cheng, 1161). Finally, ZHU Xi 朱熹 (1130-1200) expounds it with three terms, "truth (*zhen* 真), reality (*shi* 實), and no irregularity (*wuwang* 無妄)" (Zhu 1983, 31). With the first glance, these uses seem so disconnected with each other that it is difficult to identify a central meaning that holds them together. Because of this, *cheng* often looks like a philosophical puzzle for scholars in both China and the West. For instance, ZHANG Dainian 張岱年 admits that it is "the most unintelligible concept in Chinese philosophy" (ZHANG Dainian 1983, 133). Donald J. Munro calls it an "elusive term" (Munro 1988, 117).

The above observations lead us to think about two interrelated questions: What is the main content of *cheng*? Why is it so crucial and, at the same time, so obscure? To answer these questions, I will examine in this book the representative uses of *cheng* in the entire history of Chinese philosophy, and compare it with relevant conceptions in Western culture. As the first step of the project, I will sketch out the traits that differentiate *cheng* from other major concepts in Chinese philosophy, and then discuss issues regarding its translation in Western languages.

I. Two Traits

As a philosophical concept, *cheng* has two remarkable traits. They ensure *cheng*'s unique position in the whole conceptual system of Chinese philosophy and partially account for the intellectual power that it possesses. Meanwhile, these traits contribute to the theoretical complexity, causing directly the variety in its translations. The first trait of *cheng* is that it is common property of the three major philosophical schools, Confucianism, Daoism, and Buddhism. Despite the fact that the leading thinkers on *cheng* are mostly from the Confucian school, it has been commonly treated as an intellectual treasure by the other schools as well. A brief comparison with the other two concepts, "rightness" (*yi* 義) and "non-action" (*wuwei* 無爲), will highlight this trait.

"Rightness" is undoubtedly a distinctive concept of the Confucian school. Since introduced by Confucius into philosophical discourse, it has occupied an eminent position in all Confucian works. The philosophers from other schools, especially Daoism, often regard it ironically and even negatively. For example, Laozi 老子 says, "When the great Way declined, there were humaneness (*ren* 仁) and rightness. When intelligence and wisdom emerged, there was great artifice" (*Laozi*, 18). According to him, the emergence of "humaneness and rightness" resulted from the "decline" of the Way. In essence, they are nothing but expedient measures to manage a state without the Way as its regulating principle. However, the application of these measures accelerated the process of social deterioration, and even created a state in which the measures replaced the Way to be a regulating principle. His message is that "humaneness and rightness" do not contribute to the establishment of an ideal society, and their prevalence worsens, rather than cures, the social problem from which we humans have already suffered.

In contrast to "rightness," "non-action" is primarily a Daoist concept, which Laozi and Zhuangzi 莊子 intensively examined and applied. Since then, it has been a favored notion in Daoist circles. It is true that both Confucianism and Chinese Buddhism borrowed this term in their early development. For instance, Confucius once used it to signify the governance of the sage king Shun 舜: "Among those that 'ruled by non-action' surely Shun may be counted. For what action did he take? He merely placed himself gravely and reverently with his face due south; that was all" (*Lunyu*, 15.4). Also, in the early period of Chinese Buddhism (before 600 C.E.), it was often used to render the Buddhist term "Nirvana." This is exemplified in Mouzi's 牟子 *Disposing of Error* (*Lihuo Lun* 《理惑論》): the sage (meaning, the Buddha) is someone who "leads people to 'non-action'" (*Mouzi*, 4). Regarding this passage, TANG Yongtong 湯用彤 says, "'Non-action' is an ancient translation of 'Nirvana.' It actually comes from Laozi, meaning 'to follow nature (spontaneity)'" (Tang, 63). Nevertheless, "non-action" gradually vanished from both Confucian and Buddhist texts. The mainstream Confucians since Mencius either avoided using it, or refused to apply it in tune with the Daoists. Similarly, due to the increasing translation and transliteration from the original language, Sanskrit or Pali, Chinese Buddhists realized that Daoist "non-action" could not fully and appropriately convey the meaning of "Nirvana"; its presence in the Chinese version of the Buddhist sutras was confusing, even misleading. Consequently, this ancient translation was abandoned.

The story of *cheng* differs from those of "rightness" and "non-action." In Daoism, it was employed to signify either the "reality" of a thing or things, or a force that causes desirable external changes. As for the Buddhist tradition, the privileging of *cheng* was reflected in their interest in *Centrality and Commonality*, a text in which *cheng* is a pivotal concept. As FENG Youlan 馮友蘭 (1895-1990) noted, from the Northern Song 宋 Dynasty (960-1126) to the Qing dynasty, the text continuously attracted commentators from the Buddhist school. Feng tells us,

> We know of the monk Zhi Yuan 智圓 (976-1022), for example, that he gave himself the title of 'Master of *Centrality and Commonality*' (*zhongyongzi* 中庸子) and wrote a work called *Biography of Master of Centrality and Commonality* (*Zhongyongzi Zhuan* 《中庸子傳》). Likewise, the monk Qi Song 契嵩 (1007-72) wrote an *Explanation to Centrality and Commonality* (*zhongyong jie* 《中庸解》). (Feng 1953, 424)

The respectful treatment from the three schools evidences that *cheng* contains certain elements appealing to all of them, and features not only Confucianism, but also the Chinese philosophy as a whole.

A further comparison with "rightness" and "non-action" shows the second trait of *cheng*: It has a history of evolution. In general, it is difficult to write an intellectual history for "rightness" or "non-action," although they have been used throughout a time-period even longer than that of *cheng*. The reason is that, in the final analysis, their connotations are maintained as originally coined by Confucius or by Laozi and Zhuangzi, rather than evolving continuously. In spite of their frequent occurrences in later texts, people can rarely find any remarkable changes in their contents. In other words, the later Confucians and Daoists were mainly stuck with the meanings that their masters addressed long ago. They diligently applied the concepts in the same way to explain social and natural issues, but seldom added anything substantial to enrich the concepts.

In contrast, *cheng* as seen today is not conceptualized by a single thinker in a single text, but gradually formed throughout history. As a living and dynamic concept, it has a variety of definitions, instead of a single universally accepted one. This trait, in fact, is closely associated with the first trait. It is mainly because of the continuous pouring of new intellectual elements from the three schools that the idea of *cheng* acquired a number of diverse meanings as its components and had been in a process of construction for a rather long period. With regard to the contributions of Daoism and Buddhism to its final formation, we need to listen to three prominent modern scholars.

Traditionally, most Chinese thinkers held that *Centrality and Commonality* was a central text in the conceptual history of *cheng*, and the standard interpretation of the text and the concept itself lay in ZHU Xi's *Commentary on Centrality and Commonality* (*Zhongyong Zhangju* 《中庸章句》). They even further asserted that *cheng* was a typical Confucian concept, and *Centrality and Commonality* was one of the most representative Confucian classics (partially because of its extensive discussion of the concept). QIAN Mu 錢穆 cast a doubt on this position: "The author of *Centrality and Commonality* was influenced by Zhuangzi and Laozi. He attempted to fuse the doctrines of both Confucianism and Daoism to open a new intellectual realm" (Qian, 18-20). People can reasonably infer from his statement that as the pivotal concept of the text, *cheng* may carry certain Daoist elements.

Wing-tsit Chan 陳榮捷 further pointed out the interactions of the three schools in the history of the interpretation of the text. According to him, even before this classic work drew an attention from the Neo-Confucians in the Song Dynasty, its subtle doctrines already had a strong appeal to both Daoists and Buddhists. Chan even argued that the text "formed a bridge between Daoism and Buddhism and the Confucian school, and in this way prepared for the influence of Buddhism and Daoism on Confucianism, thus ushering in the Neo-Confucian movement" (Chan, 95).

In the same vein, XIONG Shili 熊十力 explicitly indicated the affinity between *cheng* and the Buddhist term, the "principle of truth" (*zhenli* 真理). In his *Commentary*, ZHU Xi followed CHENG Yi to define *cheng* as the "principle of reality" (实理). Despite the fact that this term appeared neither in *Centrality and Commonality*, nor in any Pre-Qin classics, it became an authoritative definition since the Yuan 元 Dynasty (1279-1368). It was Xiong's argument that

> The principle of truth is the name of substance (*benti* 本體). The Buddhists would like to call "genuine-thusness" (*zhenru* 真如) a "principle of truth." In contrast, both Yi Chuan 伊川 (CHENG Yi) and Master Zhu (ZHU Xi) preferred to use the expression "principle of reality." It is also a name of substance. (Xiong 1962, 88)

He even assumed that people might understand more about Zhu's term if they had a clear idea about the "principle of truth." This demonstrated a further permeation of Buddhism into Zhu's interpretation of *cheng*.

II. The Variety in Translation

The two traits—the diversity of philosophical sources and the continuity of historical evolution complicate *cheng*, making its translation a difficult task. *Cheng* was first rendered in English as "sincerity" by James Legge in 1893 (Legge, 413). However, scholars gradually became aware that *cheng* also had other meanings that could not be fully conveyed by the English term "sincerity." In order to interpret it more comprehensively and accurately, other English terms were introduced: "perfection" (Wieger 1917; Werner 1927), "truth" (Bruce 1923; Zenker 1927), "realness" (Hughes 1942), "integrity" (Graham 1958), and "creativity" (Ames and Hall 2000). The scholars who were still stuck on "sincerity" had to add more explanations. Benjamin Schwartz wrote,

> If the *Great Learning* turns attention back to the inner life of the heart, the *Mean* [*Centrality and Commonality*] seems to provide a strong ontological foundation for the possibility of the achievement of inner self-realization. Thus the word often translated as "sincerity" is here both an ethical and an ontological category. (Schwartz 1985, 405)

To avoid the trouble caused by the various translations, Joseph Needham suggested, "The word is so untranslatable and at the same time so important that it probably ought to be retained in mere transliteration, like *dao* 道 and *li* 禮. This we do" (Needham, 468).

Nevertheless, as we all know that a translation, after all, is simply an interpretation. The translation may carry only one meaning, while the original may contain many other meanings besides the one given by the translation. As far as *cheng* is concerned, I believe that divergent interpretations often emerge because different interpretive efforts have focused on different texts from different sources or historical periods. In other words, it is the variety among the texts that mainly accounts for the divergence of interpretations.

Munro's works are good examples to justify the above thesis. He interpreted *cheng* in 1969 as "single-minded devotion to the good.... [I]n other words, *cheng* referred to the unwavering attempt to realize the specific social virtues.... *Cheng* was then read into nature" (Munro 1969, 33). In terms of this elucidation, *cheng* is originally an ethical-moral concept, and later, through a process of being "read into" nature, gains cosmological and metaphysical significance. In 1988, Munro offered another interpretation: "My translation of *cheng* as 'integrity' rather than 'sincerity' comes from the term's sense as a completeness that contains all natural attributes, none of which is fraudulent or missing" (Munro 1988, 120). In this new context, *cheng* seems to be a concept close to "Oneness" or "absolute Idea" in the Hegelian sense, signifying a unity of attributes. Checking the contexts of Munro's two interpretations, people may find that they respectively come with his study of the *Mencius* and *Centrality and Commonality,* and of the Song Neo-Confucians, chiefly ZHU Xi. The discrepancy of Munro's translations should be properly explained by the difference between the *Mencius* and *Centrality and Commonality*, and the works of ZHU Xi.

FENG Youlan observed a troubling fact regarding the relation between original Chinese classics and their foreign translations. "There have been many translations of the *Laozi* and the *Analects.* Each translator has considered the translations of others unsatisfactory. But no matter how well a translation is done, it is bound to be poorer than the original." For a full reflection of the classics in their original forms, he assumed a need to combine "all the translations already made and many others not yet made" (Feng 1960, 14). Despite the fact that this suggestion mainly refers to an entire text, it may be also applicable to *cheng* as a single idea. Roughly, we can divide all the above translations of *cheng* into three groups: (1) sincerity ("sincerity"); (2) reality ("truth," "realness"); (3) the integration of sincerity and reality ("perfection," "integrity," and "creativity"). As will be shown in the next chapter that discusses the prehistory and framework of *cheng*, "sincerity" and "reality" are the two basic meanings of *cheng*, and their unity characterizes *cheng* in Confucianism. Hence, the conclusion is that all these translations are appropriate in the sense that each of them has correctly identified, at least, one meaning of *cheng*. Meanwhile, none of them is comprehensive enough to cover independently the whole range of the idea of *cheng*. This may be the reason why Feng proposed the "combination" and Needham preferred to retain *cheng* in "mere transliteration." I think that their suggestions are appropriate, and even wise.

Readers may have already sensed the richness of *cheng* from the foregoing statemet. In fact, as a result of the historical evolution and the involvement of diverse philosophical schools, it is no longer a concept in regular sense, but a conceptual unity with multiple, yet inter-related layers and dimensions. For the sake of clarity in demonstrating the entire process to its final formation, I would like to note some of the differing terms by which I discuss *cheng*. First, the Chinese romanization "*cheng*" denotes *cheng* as a technical term. Examples are "*cheng* in the *Book of Poetry* (*shijing* 《詩經》), "*cheng* in Chinese Buddhism," and "*cheng* in contemporary China." Secondly, the "concept of *cheng*" specifies *cheng* as a philosophical concept, such as the "concept of *cheng* in Mencius," or the "concept of *cheng* in ZHU Xi." Thirdly, the "idea of *cheng*" represents *cheng* as an integral unity that evolves in the history of Chinese philosophy and consists of various interrelated meanings and dimensions. It may read like, "ZHOU Dunyi's contribution to the idea of *cheng*," or "ZHU Xi's exploration of 'principle' adds new content to the idea of *cheng*." Finally, I use a slash (/) between the romanized Chinese *cheng* and a particular term to connote either a fixed usage accepted in certain intellectual traditions or an equation between *cheng* and a content that the term designates. For instance, "*cheng*/transformation" means *cheng* as understood, interpreted, and applied in the tradition of transformation; and "*cheng*/no irregularity" indicates that, in the present context, *cheng* is interchangeable with "no irregularity."

Chapter I

Background and Framework

Cheng as a philosophical concept has a prehistory in Chinese ancient classics before the *Mencius*. It witnesses diverse intellectual elements woven together to form the concept as well as the appearance of its basic meanings of "sincerity" and "reality" that center in all its later uses. By integrating these two meanings, Confucian philosophers propose a distinctive use of *cheng* for human life (ethical *cheng*). It functions as a primordial pattern from which *cheng* stretches out to Nature as a ground for consistency, regularity, and predictability in natural phenomena (cosmic *cheng*). Finally, based on the parallelism between ethical and cosmic *cheng*, Chinese thinkers further philosophize *cheng* as a general principle governing and regulating both human life and natural phenomena (universal *cheng*). In this chapter, I will trace the evolution from the word *cheng* to the concept *cheng*, and discuss the key role that the terms *shi* 實 and *xin* 信 play in the process. In addition, I will highlight the essence of Confucian *cheng* by comparing it with the Western term "sincerity," and examine the logic for *cheng*'s development from an ethical concept to a universal one. Also, I will outline two interpretive modes concerning *cheng's* influence on humans and Nature: "transformation" (*hua* 化) and "change" (*bian* 變). Employed by thinkers from various schools, they actually represent two traditions running throughout the entire history of *cheng*.

I. 1. The Prehistory

As seen in both Chinese and Western cultures, the history of a word does not necessarily lead to the formation of a concept denoted by the word, although the concept may, in part, retain the basic meaning of the word. In essence, the formation of a concept is mainly caused by intellectual tendencies in a certain age, and may be regarded as an answer to the questions raised in that period. To understand the full meaning of a concept, we need to investigate not only the history of the word, but also the questions surrounding it. It is possible that the specific meaning of a philosophical concept may first lie in a term or terms that are initially different. In this sense, the real predecessor of the concept may not be the word itself, but the relevant synonym or synonyms. Let me expound this point by referring to some German scholarship.

Hans-Georg Gadamer, when dealing with Wilhelm Dilthey's (1833-1911) key term "Erlebnis" (the lived experience), distinguished its history as a word from its history as a concept. He noted, "Erlebnis is a second form from the verb 'erleben' (to live), which is older and often appears in the age of Goethe." "Erleben" primarily means "to be still alive when something happens." Thus the word suggests the immediacy with which something real is grasped. Meanwhile, it has a variation of noun form, "das Erlebte" (the experienced), which means the permanent content of what was experienced. Gadamer held that, "[b]oth meanings obviously lie behind the coinage of Erlebnis: both the immediacy, which precedes all interpretation, reworking, and communication, and merely offers a starting point for interpretation—material to be shaped—and its discovered yield, its lasting result" (Gadamer, 61).

As for the history of a word, unlike the verb "erleben," the noun "Erlebnis" became common only in the 1870's. Its first appearance, seemingly, was in one of Hegel's letters. In describing a journey, Hegel used a phrase "my whole Erlebnis." However, as Gadamer indicated, "[o]ne should note that this is a letter, in which one does not hesitate to use unusual expressions, especially colloquial ones, if no more customary word can be found" (Gadamer, 60). The point is that the word "Erlebnis" in Hegel hasn't gained a capacity as a philosophical concept yet, although it appeared in a form identical to the latter.

It is Dilthey who first used Erlebnis as a concept in his *Das Erlebnis und Die Dichtung* (*Lived Experience and Poetry*). It "clearly contains two elements, the pantheistic and positive, the experience (Erlebnis) and still more its result (Ergibnis)" (Gadamer, 64). His Erlebnis is a pantheistic concept, because it sustains a micro-macro relationship with life as a whole, being "the smallest part of the entirety of life," "the smallest unity" in the flow of life, and "the cell of the historical world" (Dilthey, 118). On the other hand, it is a positive concept, because it is "the basic unity of meaning," and the real object from which historical investigation can derive a clear and distinct knowledge about the essence of life itself.

A careful study of the intellectual tendency in Dilthey's age shows that the first meaning coincides with the common theme of Romanticism that prevailed in Germany since the end of the eighteenth century, while the second reflects Dilthey's effort to apply the idea of epistemology of nineteenth century to establish a solid foundation for human sciences. In other words, his Erlebnis has two intellectual sources: the German Romanticism and the epistemology of nineteenth century. To clarify its history, people need not only to study the word itself, but also, and more importantly, to explore the relevant concepts even if they may appear in other names or forms. Gadamer writes, "It is true that we do not yet find the word Erlebnis in Schleiermacher, and apparently not even the verb 'erleben.' But there is no lack of synonyms that cover the range of meaning of Erlebnis, and the pantheistic background is always clearly in evidence" (Gadamer, 63-4).

Gadamer's view on Erlebnis suggests a useful method of looking for synonym or synonyms in studying the history of idea. By means of his method, I will first examine the word *cheng*, and then the relevant synonyms, aiming to reveal the intellectual path through which the concept *cheng* emerged.

I. 1. 1. The Word "Cheng"

The Scholars of Chinese Studies generally agree that the most authentic texts before the Warring States era (403-221 B.C.E.) include five books: *New Text of the Book of History* (*Jinwen Shangshu* 《今文尚書》), the *Book of Poetry*, Confucius' *Analects* (*Lunyu* 《論語》), *Zuo's Commentary on the Spring and Autumn Annals* (*Zuozhuan* 《左傳》), and the *Conversations of the States* (*Guoyu* 《國語》). The word *cheng* occasionally appears in them primarily as modifier (adjective or adverb).

The *Book of Poetry* reads, "The earl of Shen 申 faithfully (*xin* 信) prepared to leave, the King gave him a farewell dinner in [the place of] Mei 郿. The earl of Shen went to the south, and sincerely (*cheng* 誠) arrived in [the place of] Xie 謝" (*Shijing*, 213). Here *cheng* denotes a psychological state with which the earl of Shen conducted his action of departure. In contrast, the *Analects* provides a different use of *cheng*: "The Master said, 'Only if the right sort of people had charge of a country for a hundred years would it become really possible to stop cruelty and do away with slaughter.' How true (*cheng* 誠) the saying is" (*Lunyu*, 13.11). *Cheng* in Confucius' context mainly refers to a quality in the saying that is praiseworthy.

More significant is the noun-usage that occurs rarely. In the *Conversations of the States*, Shensheng 申生, the legal heir of the throne in the state of Jin 晉, was buried in an improper form after his death in a court conspiracy. Later, Duke Hui 惠 who benefited from the incident decided to re-bury Shensheng. By then, the coffin carrying the corpse sent forth a terrible odor. The populace who were still loyal to Shensheng sang that, "[Duke Hui would] rectify a mistake, but there is no auspicious response. Who is the person [who conducts the re-burial]? Why is there such an odor? The rectification wins no audience [from the deceased], [because] there is no *cheng* in the confidence [of Duke Hui]" (*Guoyu,* 316). Here *cheng* seems to mean a sincere and non-utilitarian concern in the necessity of the reburial. Its absence accounts for Duke Hui's failure in gaining trust and forgiveness from both Shensheng and the populace.

Another relevant noun-usage lies in *Zuo's Commentary*. "In the past the family Gao Yang 高陽 contributed eight talented people... [They all possessed] equilibrium, intelligence, broadness, profundity, acuteness, faithfulness, generosity, and *cheng*." KONG Yingda 孔穎達 (574-678), the exegete of *Zuo's Commentary* in the Tang dynasty (618-896), describes the *cheng* this way: "keeping one's mind pure and upright, and conducting one's action with firmness and genuineness" (*Zuozhuang*, 636-7). Similar to the case of the *Analects*, *cheng* in this passage means a quality or attribute in one's personality in virtue of which one is praised and admired by other people.

One could identify a subtle but important difference by comparing carefully the above four cases. *Cheng* in the *Book of Poetry* and the *Conversations of States* mainly designates a psychological state with which people implement their words or deeds, and due to which these words and deeds earn other people's trust. Thinking along this line, XU Shen 許慎 (about 58-147 C.E.), the editor of the first Chinese dictionary, *Explanation of Script and Elucidation of Characters* (*Shuowen Jiezi* 《說文解字》) writes, "*cheng* means *xin* 信 (trustfulness / trustworthiness / faithfulness). It belongs to the category of speech" (Xu, 52). In terms of his definition, *cheng* is manifest in people's everyday conversation and it, as a word, is interchangeable with "*xin*." Meanwhile, *cheng* in the *Analects* and *Zuo's Commentary* primarily denotes a praiseworthy and admirable quality or attribute in a statement or a person. KONG Yingda signifies this meaning with another definition, "*cheng* means *shi* 實 (realness/reality)" (*Zuozhuan*, 637). It characterizes people or things as themselves and differentiates them from other beings.

Now we are in an interesting, but a little awkward situation. The word *cheng* in the five texts seems to refer to two things, namely admirable inner state (*xin*) and praiseworthy quality (*shi*). In the meantime, the frequency of its occurrence, especially that of its noun-usage, is quite low and its meanings are not always clear, thus it is difficult to examine the prehistory of the concept *cheng* by studying the word *cheng* directly. Here we can employ Gadamer's method of looking for "synonyms," which I mentioned before, to escape the predicament. *Cheng* is alternatively defined as *xin* and *shi* by XU Shen and KONG Yingda, and these two words appear in an abundant number of passages in the five texts, signifying unequivocally what the concept *cheng* means later in the Warring States period. Thus, to clarify the prehistory of the concept *cheng*, we need to shift our focus from the word *cheng* to these two terms and, accordingly, regard them as the precursors of the concept.

I. 1. 2. Two Precursors: Xin *and* Shi

Xin is used in three ways in the five texts. First, it is close to the English word "trust" or "trustfulness," referring to a belief in other people's conducts (words or deeds) or in a certain objective existence. The typical use may sound like that, "I *xin* (trust in) this person and what he says," or "you should *xin* (trust in) the sequence of the four seasons and the regularity in the movement of heavenly body." Secondly, like the English word "trustworthiness," it denotes an attribute possessed by a person that we can identify by observing his/her conducts. Because of its existence, the person may earn a trust from us. Thirdly, it is similar to the English word "faithfulness," meaning a belief in one's own conduct, or to be more exact, in the correspondence between what one really feels and what he/she expresses through his/her own words and deeds. It differs from the first use in that, now, the object in which one trusts is no longer something outside, but within one's own mind and heart. I would like to quote some passages from the five texts to expound the three uses and their connection.

For the emergence of the concept *cheng*, the last two uses are more significant. *Zuo's Commentary* provides an example regarding "trustworthiness." There BO Zhouli 伯州犁, a minister of the state Chu 楚, persuaded his ruler by saying that

> The multitude of states are assembled here, and isn't it inappropriate to show them that we are untrustworthy (buxin 不信)? The states expect trustworthiness (xin 信) from Chu, and on that account, they come to show their submissions. If we don't demonstrate our trustworthiness, we are just throwing away that by which we gain the submission of the states. (*Zuozhuan*, 1133)

It is apparent that in this context "trustworthiness" and its adjective form "trustworthy" denote an attribute that Bo expects his ruler to demonstrate through his proper manner, attitude, and activity. It is Bo's belief that the external signs of "trustworthiness" will impress the multitude of states to conclude that the Chu ruler deserves their trust. In other words, only when the states see the evidence of the ruler's "trustworthiness" with their own eyes, can they truly submit themselves.

Another record in the same text further shows the importance of "trustworthiness" for a state and its people. The marquis of the state Jin 晉 laid siege to the city of Yuan 原 and having ordered the soldiers to be provided with three days worth of provisions, said that if within three days Yuan didn't surrender, he would give up the siege. On the third day, spies came out to inform him that Yuan was going to surrender in a couple of days. The officers of the army entreated the marquis to wait; but he responded: "Trustworthiness is the precious jewel of a state; it is what the people depend on. If I get Yuan and lose my trustworthiness, what can people depend on? My loss would be greater than my gain" (*Zuozhuan*, 435). He then withdrew the troops. According to the marquis, "trustworthiness" is an assurance on which people, including soldiers, can count and a treasure much more valuable than a single city. A lost city can be captured again, but if "trustworthiness" is lost, his state is doomed to perish.

Since "trustworthiness" is such a crucial element for a state and its ruler, a question logically arises: what ensures its existence? Put differently, what is the root from which "trustworthiness" grows? The first candidate to answer the question is the third use of "*xin*," namely "faithfulness." *Zuo's Commentary* contains an outstanding example in this regard. In order to solidify the friendship between the two courts, the sons of the Zhou 周 and the Zheng 鄭 rulers were sent to each other's state as guests. However, in spite of this exchange, the two courts fell into enmity a short time later. On this issue, a gentleman commented:

> If there is no good faith in one's heart (*buxin you zhong* 不信由中), guests are of no use.... When intelligence and faithfulness (*mingxin* 明信) are present, whatever grows by the streams in the valleys, by the ponds, or in the pools, whether they are gatherings of duck-weed, white southern wood, or pone-weed, in baskets round and square, and cooked in pans and pots with the water from standing pools and road hollows, may be devoted to the spirits, and set forth for kings and dukes. (*Zuozhuan*, 27)

Traditionally, many Chinese scholars regarded the "gentleman" as Confucius himself. Whatever the facts are, the passage conveys an important message: "faithfulness" means "good faith in one's own heart;" it is the opposite of "self-deception" in which one actually disbelieves what he is saying and doing. With "self-deception," all gestures, no matter how friendly they appear at the beginning, will turn out to be meaningless. On the contrary, with "faithfulness," all the presents— no matter where they come from or in which way they are prepared—will look beautiful to rulers and spirits. They will be accepted with genuine pleasure, and win favors in return.

Logically, the three uses (trust, trustworthiness, and faithfulness) constitute three interrelated links in a chain that represents the full connotation of "*xin*" and reveals the path to the acquisition of trust. Let me start my elucidation with the first link: trust.

The simple fact that we humans live a community life forces everyone to think about his or her relationship with other people, as well as one's own position and role in the community. We have to ask ourselves frequently: how can we trust in or get trust from other people? In analysis, this can be further divided into two subquestions: how can we enable others to trust us, and why should we have trust in another person? For the sake of convenience, the following analysis will focus on the first one.

Usually, this is the answer: in order to get trust from others, I need to be trustworthy first. Concretely, there must be a correspondence between our words and deeds. We should not talk about helping someone and then break our promise for a relatively unconvincing reason. Moreover, there must be a consistency in our words or deeds. We should not teach one person to be filial in the morning, but argue with another in the night that filiality is not a virtue at all. The two terms, *correspondence* and *consistency*, collectively represent an ideal mode of conduct, as well as the content of the second link—trustworthiness. (Henceforth I will use the single term "consistency" to denote the mode itself).

However, the question continues: how can we assure the presence of this mode in our conduct? Put differently, what is the guarantee for our consistent conduct? This ushers in the third link "faithfulness." As the previously cited case implies, it refers to a psychological state in which I am true to myself and act just as my heart tells me. After all, we can hardly expect others' trust in our conduct if even we ourselves doubt on its trustworthiness. Thus, the conclusion is that faithfulness is the necessary condition for the presence of consistency and therefore the final assurance for the acquisition of trust. Obviously, this "faithfulness" is close to the first meaning of the word *cheng*, referring to a good inner state that assures us of acting consistently. In what follows, I employ the English term "sincerity" to specify this particular use.

Shi is another precursor of the concept *cheng*. In XU Shen's definition, "*Shi* means abundance (*fu* 富). Its graphic form belongs to the categories of 'house' and 'shell.' The shell refers to shell-money" (Xu, 150). Thus, *shi* is generally used to denote all kinds of wealth. As *Zuo's Commentary* records, "A descendant of [the officer] Jin Yun 縉雲 was devoid of ability and virtue. He indulged in eating and drinking, craved for money and property… and accumulated a store of wealth (*shi*)" (*Zuozhuan*, 640). Also, *shi* is used as a general term for all kinds of products, goods, and articles. An example of this use is in the same text, "The creatures (*shi*) found in the mountains, forests, streams, and marshes, the materials for ordinary articles of use, the business of underlings, and the charges of inferior officers: with all these the ruler has nothing to do" (*Zuozhuan*, 43). Next, *shi* means fruit of a plant or the result. In the *Analects,* the Master sighed for the death of YAN Yuan 顏淵, his best student, "There are shoots whose lot it is to spring up but never to flower; others whose lot it is to flower but never bear fruit (*shi*)" (*Lunyu*, 9.21).

Furthermore, in opposition to emptiness/void (*xu* 虛), *shi* denotes a state of fullness. The follwing passages exemplify this use. In the *Conversations of States*, FAN Li 范蠡, the legendary minister of the state of Yue 越 persuaded his ruler, "[We need to] cultivate wastelands to fill (*shi*) our stores with grain and goods, and to make our people rich" (*Guoyu*, 640). Also, *Zuo's Commentary* records, "The earl of Liang 梁 increased the number of his walled cities, and had no people to fill (*shi*) them. One went by the name of Xin li 新裡 was taken by the state of Qin 秦" (*Zuozhuan*, 379).

Finally, *shi* means "true" or "truth," being an antonym of "false" or "fallacy" (*wei* 僞). *Zuo's Commentary* tells a story about a collaborative campaign launched by the armies of the states of Lu 魯 and Qi 齊 against the state of Cheng 郕. Consequently, Cheng only gave in to the army of Qi. Enraged by this, a minister of Lu suggested the Duke of Lu to attack the Qi army. The Duke rejected his advice, and said, "No. I am the one who is truly (*shi*) not virtuous. Of what wrong doing is the army of Qi guilty? The fault is all mine" (*Zuozhuan*, 173).

These uses of *shi*—"real" or "realness," "full" or "fullness," and "true" or "truth"— share a common meaning. They all refer to something existing and real, something standing as the opposite of dream, imagination, emptiness, and falsity. A person who possesses *shi* is someone whose words are true and full of content and whose actions are consistent and predictable. Similarly, a warehouse that possesses *shi* is a space full of the goods that it is supposed to provide. Put differently, both the person and the warehouse have a quality that matches their names, a quality that can be termed as "reality." This use corresponds to the second meaning of the word *cheng*, a praiseworthy quality or attribute that a true person or good thing possesses.

In the period of the Warring States, *shi* was introduced into philosophical contexts. XU You 許由, a hermit in the *Zhuangzi*, refused the empire ceded by the sage king Yao 堯, saying that "You govern the world and the world is already well governed. Now if I take your place, will I be doing it for a name? But name is only the guest of reality (*shi*)—will I be doing it so I can play the part of guest?" (*Zhuangzi*, 24). Likewise, the *Mencius* says of the well-field system that,

> In the Xia 夏 Dynasty, each family was given fifty *mu* 畝 of land, and the *gong* 貢 method of taxation was used. In the Yin 殷, each family was given seventy *mu* and the *zhu* 助 method was used. In the Zhou 周, each family was given a hundred *mu* and the *che* 徹 method was used. But the reality (*shi*) of them is the same, namely a taxation of one in ten. (*Mengzi*, 3A3)

There is no doubt that, in both cases, *shi* is used as a technical term, meaning the nature or reality of a thing or things.

I. 2. The Western "Sincerity" and the Confucian "*Cheng*"

The concept of *cheng* appears with high frequency from the time of Mencius (around fourth century B.C.E.). It is a response to two key questions raised during that time: What is the ultimate source from which a person or state can achieve and maintain a goal in the long term? What differentiates the essential attribute of a thing from its other attributes? In principle, the key to both questions lies in the two components of the concept *cheng*, which are the two precursors already examined. Roughly speaking, "sincerity" (*xin*) is the anwer to the first question, while "reality" (*shi*) is that to the second. A person or thing can be properly named as someone or something with *cheng* so long as either "sincerity" or "reality" is present.

ZHU Xi argued for the legitimacy of treating *cheng* as "sincerity": "*Cheng* is 'principle of reality [1];' it also means 'sincerity' (*chengque* 誠慤)." According to him, the interpretation of *cheng* has experienced a remarkable change over time. The thinkers since the Han Dynasty (202 B.C.E.-220 C.E.) had mainly read *cheng* as "sincerity." CHENG Yi changed this trend by interpreting it primarily as "principle of reality." "However," Zhu contended, "in *Centrality and Commonality, cheng* is used as both 'principle of reality' and 'sincerity' in different contexts. It is incorrect to read *cheng* solely as 'principle of reality,' but not as 'sincerity' as well" (Zhu 1986, 102). As for treating *cheng* as a synonym for "reality," there are also many textual evidences. For example, in a long period from the *Outer Chapters of the Zhuangzi* (*Zhuangzi Waipian* 《莊子外篇》) to GUO Xiang 郭象 (?-312 C.E.), *cheng* was often applied to denote the essential attribute or reality of a thing, or things. This is particularly true in the texts of Daoists and Confucians with some Daoist background. In fact, "*cheng* and sincerity" (*chengxin* 誠信) and "*cheng* and reality" (*chengshi* 誠實) have been popularly used in both pre-modern and modern China as two fixed word-compounds, in which *cheng* and sincerity, or *cheng* and reality, are actually interchangeable.

Nevertheless, in mainstream Confucianism, *cheng* has a distinctive use: it is not a synonym for either sincerity or reality, but the unity of the two. In form, it is similar to "sincerity," meaning "to be true to oneself." In content, "true" refers to a true feeling possessed universally by humans, while "self" refers to a nature or reality common to all humans. This use is a crucial contribution that Confucianism made to the history of *cheng*. It also accounts for a fact that many scholars in the past and present have treated *cheng* as a typical Confucian concept, and fused Confucian *cheng* with the idea of *cheng* as such. To make the point about the unity clearer, I would like to compare Confucian *cheng* with the Western concept of sincerity.

I. 2. 1. Sincerity and Truth

The word "sincerity," according to Lionel Trilling, enters the English language in the first third of the sixteenth century. It originated from

---

[1] I will explain this concept in the fourth chapter.

the Latin word "sincerus," meaning first "clean," "sound," or "pure." People can speak of sincere wine, not in the modern fashion of describing the taste of wine by attributing to it some moral quality, but simply to mean that it has not been adulterated or sophiscated. Similarly, they can speak of sincere doctrine, religion, or Gospel, meaning that it has not be tampered with, or falsified, or corrupted. In the same vein, sincerity can also be used to describe persons. "It is largely metaphorical—a man's life is sincere in the sense of being sound, or pure, or whole; or consistent in its virtuousness" (Trilling, 12-3).

However, the word soon came to mean the absence of dissimulation, feigning, or pretence, denoting mainly "congruence between avowal and actual feeling" (Trilling, 2). People believe that the criterion of sincerity and the calculation of the degree of congruence is not how excellent a person's work is, but how true people are to themselves. The truer you are to yourself, the higher the degree of congruence you attain. Hence, "to be true to oneself," an inner oriented action to unify the person as intentional agent with the person's original, natural "self," becomes final ground for the presence and evaluation of sincerity. Since a person, being true to his/herself, is likely to be sincere when dealing with others, people often equate "to be true to oneself" to the congruence.

It is a widely accepted idea that sincerity will bring about positive or favorable consequences. A passage in Shakespeare's *Hamlet* exemplifies this conviction. Polonius, a slippery minister in the Danish court, advised his son Laertes who was leaving for Paris that "This above all: to thine own self be true, and it doth follow, as the night the day, thou canst not then be false to any man." On this passage Trilling comments,

> Our impulse to make its sense consistent with our general view of Polonius is defeated by the way the lines sound, by their lucid moral lyricism. This persuades us that Polonius has had a moment of self-transcendence, of grace and truth. He has conceived of sincerity as an essential condition of virtue and has discovered how it is to be attained. (Trilling, 3)

According to Trilling's interpretation, "to thine own self be true" will assure a person to be truthful to others. As a loving father, Polonius expected that Laertes' sincerity would win him the trust from other people, and therefore prompt them to act in his favor. To emphasize the significance of the relation between sincerity and its consequence, Polonius used a phrase "this above all" to remind his son that it was the most important thing for his well-being in Paris.

From the foregoing discussion, we can see the full meaning of "sincerity" as that. Sincerity originates from a need to earn trust from other people. It means firstly the congruence between avowal and actual feeling; the condition by which a man maintains his "sincerity" is "to be true to himself;" and sincerity will assure positive consequences resulting from other people's trust. A comparison with the three meanings of the Chinese word "*xin*" (trustfulness, trustworthiness, and faithfulness) and their logical relationship shows a clear similarity between the two terms. In fact, this is the linguistic root by which Legge translated *cheng* as sincerity.

In philosophy, sincerity as a concept seems to have its root in Aristotle's "*aletheutikos.*" Actually, J. A. K. Thomson, one of the translators of *Nichomachean Ethics,* simply renders it as "sincerity," or "truthfulness" (Thomson, 165-7). Aristotle groups people into three types: "boastful man," "truthful (sincere) man," and "mock-modest." The *truthful* man is a person who hits the mean—-the middle position, and says just enough. In contrast, a person who is not at the mean position (and in either extreme) is *untruthful.* The boastful man goes too far and says too much, while the mock-modest doesn't go or say enough. About the truthful man Aristotle writes,

> We are not speaking of the man who keeps faith in his agreements, i.e. in the things that pertain to justice or injustice (for this would belong to another virtue), but the man who in the matters in which nothing of this sort is at stake is true both in word and in the life because his character is such. [This type of person is worthy of praise,] for the man who loves truth, and is truthful where nothing is at stake, will still more be truthful where something is at stake; he will avoid falsehood as something base, seeing that he avoided it even for its own sake. (Aristotle 1941, 999)

Here "truthfulness" is listed as secondary to truth; and truth to the people then primarily means "certain axiomatic truths, adamantine, unbreakable, from which it is possible by severe logic to deduce certain absolutely infallible conclusions" (Berlin 1999, 2). Aristotle's view on the relation between "truthfulness" and truth implies an important point: truthfulness and its equivalents, "honesty," "integrity," and "sincerity" are valuable not for their own sake, but for, and only for, their loyal service for truth. Later, this point was further developed to be a notion, which prevailed especially in the medieval ages, that "truthfulness" or "sincerity" has no independent value; it may either serve for "truth" or for "falsity."

In medieval Europe, people with Christian beliefs upheld three theological virtues based on their association with truth and their function in dispositioning people to move toward truth: faith, hope, and charity. Using "faith" as an example, Peter Geach, a modern scholar, says that

> Faith that is known to God alone still has to be faith in something true: faith is the virtue by which a man can discern his genuine last end, from which he is disoriented by Original Sin, and can return to the true compass-bearing when temptations swerve him from it. And faith is only by the gift of God, who is Truth, who cannot set his seal upon a lie. (Geach, 160)

Similarly, other values, including the four ancient cardinal virtues: prudence, justice, temperance, and courage could be judged as virtues or vices only through their relation with the truth of God, and their service or disservice for the truth. Geach explains this notion by referring to the case of courage. "This is one particular aspects of a general truth about courage: there can be no virtue in courage, in the facing of sudden danger or the endurance of affliction, if the cause for which this is done is worthless or positively vicious" (Geach, 160).

This also applies to sincerity. For example in a religious community whose members share the same concept of truth, the more sincere a person is, the more he is praised and admired by his fellow members. However, when two communities with different views on truth encounter one another, and when their diagreement seem incompatible, the same "sincerity" may cause trouble. The general notion then was that truth was one, and was the one preached by my church and held by me. It was always right to be a martyr to truth, but only to truth; and adversaries who sincerely cherished their own truth were both "dangerous" and "pitiful." For a true Christian knight, the deeper the sincerity of such heretics or unbeliever—Muslims, Jews, or atheists and the like—the more dangerous they were, and the more likely they would lead souls to perdition, hence the more ruthlessly should they be eliminated. Because heresy was surely a poison more dangerous to the health of society than even hypocrisy or dissimulation, which at least did not openly attack the true doctrine. Nevertheless, the knight, after killing his brave enemy, would not spit upon his corpse, but rather, felt *pity* for his death because so much courage, so much ability, so much devotion had been expended on a cause so palpably absurd or dangerous. As a result of the conflict of truths, "sincerity" turned to be a neutral, even negative value.

As Berlin observes, "sincerity becomes a virtue in itself" only after the prevalence of Romanticism that Rousseau (1712-78) and German Romantics advocated since the mid-eighteenth century (Berlin 1997, 554). The key for the change lays in two interrelated elements: the promotion of the concept of "self" and the new interpretation of "truth." This new trend had its root in a psychological fact. We all experience at certain moments that we are yielding to some "lower" impulse, acting from a motive that we dislike, or doing something that we detest at the very moment of doing. We may reflect that we are untrue or disloyal to ourselves; and this feeling certainly leaves us in a state of frustration or depression, even in a mood of self-contempt. For instance, a warrior fostered in a Buddhist context must be deeply depressed and self-blaming after killing an enemy soldier, although the warrior knows clearly that the killing is justifiable in terms of self-defense, or even as the only right thing one could do in the particular situation. Actually, the depression and self-blame is independent from the warrior's knowledge of any factual or religious truth. Emphasizing this kind of experience, Romantics contended that the most important thing was to preserve the well-being and integrity of "self," and to act in accordance with the calling of one's "self," heart or soul.

It should be noticed that this "self" is an *individualistic* concept, not referring to an essential attribute common to all humans, but to an individuality or uniqueness possessed by a particular person and

distinguishing this Peter from that John. Rousseau's *Confessions* provides the best example in this regard.

> I have resolved on an enterprise which has no precedent, and which, once complete, will have no imitator. My purpose is to display to my kin a portrait in everything true to nature, and the man I portray will be myself. Simply myself. I know my own heart and understand my fellow man. But I am made unlike anyone I have ever met; I will even venture to say that I am like no one in the whole world. I may be no better, but at least, I am different. (Rousseau, 17)

Rousseau believes that he is fully true to himself, so that his portrait must exactly resemble his own "self." For him, this "self" is an entity with the highest value, which characterizes him as a person "different" from, say, Voltaire or Diderot, and to which he must be loyal or truthful, even at the cost of his property, reputation, health, or life itself.

Along with the promotion of individualistic "self," Rousseau and his Romantic friends reinterpreted the concept of "truth." As Berlin writes, "There run through their writings a common notion, held with varying degrees of consciousness and depth, that truth is not an objective structure, independent of those who seeks it, the hidden treasure waiting to be found, but is itself in all its guises created by the seeker" (Berlin 2000, 17). In fact, it primarily means a faithful or truthful attitude toward oneself and to others; it depends on a person's motive, intention, or will, and has nothing to do with the person's knowledge of objective facts or religious doctrine.

Trilling explains the relation of this new concept of truth and sincerity with the following example. "In French literature sincerity consists in telling the truth about oneself to oneself and to others; by truth is meant a recognition of such of one's own traits or actions as are morally or socially discreditable and, in conventional course, concealed" (Trilling, 58). With this conception of truth in mind, Rousseau proudly claimed, at the last trumpet, he would present his *Confessions* before his Sovereign Judge, asking all the other people who groaned at his depravities, and blushed for his misdeed. "But let each one of them reveal his heart at the foot of thy throne with equal sincerity, and may any man who dares to say, 'I was a better man than he'?" (Rousseau, 17).

Here we should particularly attend to his phrase "equal sincerity." On the one hand, this sincerity means to be true to one's (individual) self; on the other hand, it should be "equally" held by everyone. Accordingly, the truer people are to themselves, the more sincere they should be regarded; and the more sincere they are, the closer they are to the ideal image of humankind. The conclusion is that "sincerity," which signifies a person's loyalty to one's own self, should be taken as a general criterion to evaluate and judge persons and their conducts. Rousseau is confident that God's judgment will be in his favor, not because he is more praiseworthy than others in terms of social norms, but because he dares to face his own self, and to reveal it as it is. In a broad sense, according to the criterion of sincerity, the crucial thing is not what a person has done (consequence), but how the person does it— with or without wholeheartedness (intention); not what a person believes (content), but how the beliefs are carried out—with or without true dedication (willing). Due to the prevalence of the Romantic trend, as Berlin indicates, "'integrity' and 'sincerity' become admirable independently of the [traditional] truth or validity of the beliefs or principles involved" (Berlin 1997, 553). Paradoxically, in my point of view, this value of sincerity starts with elevating the *individualistic* "self," but ends being a *universal* criterion for evaluation and judgment, especially in the domains of ethics and aesthetics.

The tension of individuality and universality associated with sincerity may cause two kinds of social consequences, depending on what psychological structure a sincere person possesses. Negatively, people may stress the side of individuality, and thereby intensify their efforts to realize or even to universalize their own "self" by various social activities. Berlin mentions that, "If it goes too far, if someone is a Hitler, then we do not think that his sincerity is necessarily a saving quality" (Berlin 1999, 141). As for this fact, the medieval warning is still legitimate: people can sincerely do something against the well-being of humankind as a whole; and, in that case, the more sincere they are, the more dangerous to humans.

In contrast, if the emphasis is put on the side of universality, a feeling of "respect" between two parties, who differ in their understanding of social issues, might ideally replace the medieval feeling of "pity." It is the rationale that, no matter what you believe in, correct or incorrect in my view, you still have my respect and admiration so long as your attitude toward your beliefs is itself honest, and you have truly devoted to your beliefs. Here the point is not that I accept the *content* of your beliefs, but that I respect your *attitude* towards truth. The content differentiates you from me, while the attitude underscores the commonality of us. As history already proved that the confrontation among major cultures and religions would finally attain a point at which no party could continue to impose its beliefs on another party by force, a point at which continuous conflicts in beliefs would lead to nowhere but total peril of the parties concerned. As a great contribution to humankind as a whole, Romantic conception of sincerity sets a common ground for the dialogue among all culturally divided parties, as well as for their tolerance and compromise to each other. It is a philosophical foundation upon which a genuine religious or cultural diversity can stand: various parties discuss peacefully with each other for the interest of the entire humankind, while continuing to hold their own views of truth.

I. 2. 2. The Universality of Cheng

Evolving from the traditions of "*xin*" (trustfulness, trustworthiness, faithfulness) and "*shi*" (reality), *cheng* contains what the Western "sincerity" denotes—"to be true to oneself," and, at the same time, differs from it in two ways. First, what is conceived to be "true" and "self" means differently in *cheng* from those entailed in "sincerity." Second, compared with "sincerity," the theoretical scope of *cheng* is much larger, and its conceptual structure is more complicated. I will limit my discussion to the first point in this section, aiming to underscore the distinctiveness of *cheng* in mainstream Confucianism.

In a long passage pertaining to the fulfillment of an exemplary person (*junzi* 君子)'s official duty, *Mencius* writes that,

> If a man in a subordinate position fails to win the confidence of his superiors, he cannot hope to govern the people. There is a way for him to win the confidence of his superiors. If his friends do not trust him, he will not win the confidence of his superiors. There is a way for him to win the trust of his friends. If in serving his parents he fails to please them, he will not win the trust of his friends. There is a way for him to please his par-

> ents (*yueqing*, 悅親). If he examines himself and finds that he is not true to himself (*cheng*), he will not please his parents. There is a way to make him true to himself (*chengshen* 誠身). If he does not understand goodness (*mingshan* 明善), he cannot make him true to himself. (*Mengzi*, 4A12)

Mencius' argument involves six phases: "govern the people," "win the confidence of superiors," "win the trust of friends," "please the parents," "to be true to oneself," and "understand goodness." It presents a chain reasoning from the far to the near, from large scales to smaller ones, and from a person's external actions to the inner heart. In this process, each succeeding phase functions as a necessary condition for the realization of the preceding one, and each success signifies the person's new achievement in realizing social ideals. Although the completion of the entire six phases is expected mainly for social elite, the chain is also relevant to those who will never assume any office. After all, even the most ordinary people still need to know how to communicate properly with their parents and friends. Regarding the topic of *cheng*, what interests us the most is the relation among the last three: "please the parents," "to be true to oneself," and "understand goodness."

According to Mencius, "to be true to oneself" is motivated by the need to "please the parents." This connection implies an important, but often-neglected, point: *cheng* originates from family life, and its first beneficiaries are one's parents. Unlike other human relationships, such as those between friend and friend, superior and inferior, teacher and students, the relationship between parents and their children is principally a natural, rather than a societal one. Normally, seeking to "please parents" doesn't come with any utilitarian or pragmatic concerns; it is an intuitive action as natural as needing to eat and drink. Meanwhile, to "please parents" is also a perennial need, which will last as long as one lives. The need pushes people to search for its satisfaction, and the naturalness accounts for the intensity and durability that feature the search. Mencius recommends "to be true to oneself" as the most reliable way for satisfying the need, because it will ensure that people are consistent when dealing with their parents, and that they are always good to them.

At the same time, Mencius stresses that "to be true to oneself" is conditioned by "understanding goodness." Following the interpretation of KANG Youwei 康有爲 (1858-1927), I would hold that this "goodness" means human's "good nature" (*shanxing* 善性) endowed by Heaven (Kang, 137); it is simply another name for "self" to which one should be true. Concretely, it consists of the "four hearts:" "the heart of compassion" (*ceyin zhi xin* 惻隱之心), "the heart of shame" (*xiuwu zhi xin* 羞惡之心), "the heart of respect" (*cirang zhi xin* 辭讓之心), and "the heart of right and wrong" (*shifei zhi xin* 是非之心) (*Mengzi*, 6A6). In contrast to the individualistic "self" of Romanticism, this nature or "self" is a *universalistic* concept that characterizes humankind as a particular species, differentiating them from animals. Thus, "understanding goodness" actually refers to a clear acknowledgment of this nature and its worthiness, which will encourage people to treasure their nature or to be loyal to their "self." In accordance, "to be true to oneself" should be properly read as "to abide by the nature" or "to be loyal to the self."

The universality of *cheng* shows also in another element: "true" or truth. Similar to the Romantics, the Confucian "true" means primarily a "true feeling" or an honest attitude toward one's self, rather than a true cognition or knowledge of religious doctrine or objective fact. However, at the same time, it contains a meaning absent in Rousseau and other Romantics. In Confucian lexicon, as Thomas Metzger phrases it, there are two kinds of feeling: the "selfish feeling" and the "unselfish" or "empathetic feeling" (Metzger, 31). The first is close to "desire" in Western language, denoting a longing for what simply benefits an agent, an impulse to pursue some sensual pleasure. It comes with some personal or individualistic qualities, and may cause a conflict with other people who also have their own "selfish feeling." The second refers to a sentiment that enables a person to act for the entire humankind. It is not unique to this or that person, but possessed by all humans; it will never cause any conflict among people, because it protects the interest common to all humans. One example of the second feeling is being "sensitive to the suffering of others" (*bu renren zhi xin* 不忍人之心), which Mencius illustrates with the following tale:

> Suppose a man were, all of a sudden, to see a young child on the verge of falling into a well. He would certainly be moved to compassion, not because he wanted to get in the good grace of

> the parents, nor because he wished to win the praise of his fellow villagers or friends, nor yet because he disliked the cry of the child. (*Mengzi*, 2A6)

Mencius believes that this unselfish feeling was a person's "true feeling," a quality coming with birth. It is not something out of human nature/self, or something for human nature/self. Instead, it is a necessary and central part of the nature/self, and an indispensable pillar for his thesis that "human nature is good."

In terms of this analysis, "to be true to oneself" or "*cheng*" actually means to face one's universal nature with a universal true feeling. Apparently, it already consists of "sincerity" and "reality" as its two aspects. As XIONG Shili says,

> The term *cheng* simultaneously highlights both 'truth' (*zhen* 真) and 'goodness' (*shan* 善). People may just talk about goodness, while truth is already implied. Therefore, an absolute truth is never short of goodness. By the same token, an absolute pure goodness is never short of 'truth.' How can truth and goodness be separated? (Xiong 1976, 49)

Unlike "sincerity" in the medieval ages, this *cheng* is an independent value, whose validity has no relation to factual or religious "truth." Meanwhile, in contrast to Romanticist "sincerity," *cheng* contains no individualistic element, and it is, as ZHOU Dunyi 周敦頤 (1017-1073) phrases it, "pure and perfectly good" (Zhou, 31). The idea that "someone may sincerely do something bad," which medieval people worried about, will never occur to *cheng*, because the universality in both "true" and "self" already ensures that it is a value beneficial to people anytime and anywhere. It is true that there is a circular argument, which only works by assuming the universality of "good nature." People may point out that there actually exist those who are born violent and cruel. However, as for Mencius, this so-called fact will not deny the correctness of his basic thesis at all. We can ignore these cases as exceptional when characterizing human nature just as we needn't particularly attend to anomalies when studying the general physiological features of humankind.

I. 3. Extension and Influence

Cheng as described above is an ethical concept acquired from and applied to human life. Now there come two inter-related questions. First, how is it read into Nature, or what is the rationale by which an ethical concept is interpreted to be a cosmic one? Second, how does *cheng* exert its influence on humans and Nature, or what is the way by which Chinese thinkers explain the influence and its consequence? These are the topics I am going to discuss in this section.

I. 3. 1. The Extension to Nature

"Reading" ethical *cheng* into Nature is done through analogy—a method of elucidating some observed facts by referring to a familiar idea or theory. Analogy, which must be preceded by the observation and its result, is essentially an explanation of what was observed. In the present case, the idea or theory is ethical *cheng*, and the fact is regularity in natural phenomena. Let's first look at the fact.

Confucius claims, "Heaven does not speak; yet the four seasons run their courses thereby; the hundred creatures, each after its kind, are born thereby" (*Lunyu,* 17.19). According to the Master, the silent Heaven is an inner cause of external consistency—regular motions of heavenly bodies and the predictable changes of the four seasons. In addition, regularity is also shown in another type of natural phenomenon. CHEN Chun 陳淳 (1153-1217), an astute student of ZHU Xi, observes, "Let's consider the case of fruits and plants. The sweet one will be sweet forever; the bitter one will be bitter forever; the green one will be green forever; the white one will be white forever" (CHEN Chun, 127). The essential attributes of certain fruits and plants do not change because of the assumed presence of "Heaven," so that people can surely predict what they will harvest when they start to plant.

However, what is "Heaven" and why can it cause natural regularity? In Western civilization, people often invoke God: because of God's imposition of laws on the universe, regularity appears in natural phenomena. Jean-Paul Sartre expresses this notion with a rather exaggerated tone from Zeus:

> See those planets wheeling on their appointed ways, never swerving, never clashing. It was I who ordained their courses, according the law of justice. Hear the music of the spheres, that vast, mineral hymn of praise, sounding and resounding to the limits of the firmament. It is my work that living things increase and multiply, each according to his kind. I have ordained that man shall always beget man, and dog give birth to dog. It is my work that the tides with their innumerable tongues creep up to lap the sand and draw back at the appointed hour. I make the plants grow, and my breath fans round the earth the yellow clouds of pollen. (Sartre, 155)

This notion of God is totally foreign to the overwhelming majority of thinkers in pre-modern China. The *Analects* records, "Zi Lu 子路 asked about serving the spiritual beings. Confucius said, 'If we are not yet about to serve humans, how can we serve spiritual beings?' 'I venture to ask about death.' Confucius said, 'If we do not know about life, how can we know about death?'" (*Lunyu*, 11.11) Another passage from the same text reads, "FAN Chi 樊遲 asked about wisdom. Confucius said, 'Devote yourself earnestly to the duties to humans, and respect spiritual beings but keep them at a distance. This may be called wisdom" (*Lunyu*, 6. 20). Confucius' sayings exemplify a long tradition of religious skepticism, even atheism, in Chinese elite culture, because of which thinkers often either deny or refuse to think about the existence of an anthropomorphic God capable of knowing, feeling, and willing to act. Hence, they do not seek for an omniscient Being in Nature, who, like human beings, possesses *cheng* and intentionally arranges natural phenomena with consistency. Actually, the "silence" of Heaven that Confucius mentioned in the foregoing passage simply reflects this doubt and concern.

The analogy from ethical *cheng* to the inner cause of natural regularity occurs at this point. It satisfies a theoretical need for the Chinese thinker—It points out the inner cause of natural consistency, while avoiding the introduction of a transcendental deity such as God. The analogy runs like this: Since human "consistency" comes from their inner state of *cheng*, and since a comparable consistency exists also in natural phenomena, there must be a parallel between the way Nature functions and the way ethical *cheng* does in humans. WANG Fuzhi 王夫之 (1619-1692) argues,

> What assures Heaven of being Heaven is invisible. However, we know the no duplicity of the Heaven's (meaning, cosmic) *cheng* from its breadth and depth, height and brightness, its subtlety and everlastingness, and its unfathomable way to produce things. What assures absolute *cheng* of being itself is not easy to be identified by humans. However, we know its ceaselessness from what is manifest in front of us: the breadth and depth, the height and brightness, and subtlety and everlastingness. (WANG Fuzhi/2, 167)

Following *Centrality and Commonality*, Wang first applies the term *cheng*, which originates from human life, to denote the way of Nature. Secondly, he contends that we have full confidence in its existence, because the similar consistency, with which we are familiar in humans, can be unmistakably identified in natural phenomena. Thirdly, he claims that the way of Heaven displays two qualifying attributes: "no duplicity" and "ceaselessness," which characterize also the reality of the sage in humans. The first attribute determines that all things must be themselves—a dog cannot change to be a cat, and a summer cannot be directly followed by winter; while the second connotes that the "no duplicity" in Nature will last forever. His argument shows a process in which *cheng* expands, step by step, from humans to Nature, evolving to be "cosmic *cheng*." The two kinds of *cheng* are common at one point that they are both the final reason for external consistency. At the beginning, this commonality might be simply a theoretical assumption, but soon it was taken as self-evident. In premodern China, none of the major thinkers thought to question its validity, let alone deny its existence.

The parallelism between ethical *cheng* and cosmic *cheng* lays a foundation on which the universal *cheng*—a general principle responsible for all kinds of consistency, correspondence, regularity, and predictability in both humans and Nature— is conceived. This idea, in turn, validates a number of notions prevalent in China, including that of the "unity of Heaven and humans" (*tianren heyi* 天人合一).

Roughly speaking, this notion appears in three forms. The first is the "exchange between Heaven and humans" (*tianren jiaotong* 天人交通), or the "correspondence between Heaven and humans" (*tianren ganying* 天人感應). It claims that Heaven and humans respond to and influence on each other, and therefore, humans should adjust their behaviors in accordance with the message that Heaven sends through natural phenomena, such as a good harvest or a calamity. The second is the "identity of the virtues in Heaven and humans" (*tianren hede* 天人合德). It tells that, since the virtues found in humans are the same as those in Heaven, hence the cultivation and preservation of human virtues is the most direct and reliable way to emulate the model that Heaven presents. The third is the "integration of Heaven and humans" (*tianren weiyi* 天人爲一). It teaches that both Heaven and humans belong to the same flux of the universe, which flows constantly and consistently. Death and life are simply two aspects of universal transformation. Humans should enjoy the years Heaven gives them when they are alive, and calmly accept the fact of having to leave this world when they are dying (ZHANG Heng 張亨, 1992). The three forms all presuppose that there is a common property between Heaven and humans, and a capstone connecting the two sides together. In actuality, what the universal *cheng* occupies is just this position. It integrates Heaven and humans into a unity, ensuring Heaven's enforcement of human morality and humans' moral influence on Heaven.

With *cheng*'s extension to Nature and its universalization to be a general principle, its impact on human life is also tremendously strengthened. Now "to be true to oneself," "to be sincere in one's conduct," or "to cultivate and retain one's *cheng*/nature" are no longer simply a matter concerning people's choices, but rather a moral imperative, a mandate from Heaven by which people must abide. This partially explains why, in later times, there occurr so many investigations on the significance of *cheng* for the stability and prosperity of human society, and so many proclamations of its reliability in guiding and regulating human conducts.

I. 3. 2. The Forms of Influence

It seems to be a myth for many Western readers that almost all thinkers in pre-modern China cherish an unshakable conviction in the power of *cheng*. The *Great Learning* (*Daxue* 《大學》) reads, "What is true (*cheng*) within will be manifest without." (*Daxue*, 6). This "without" includes one's physical appearance, other people's behavior, general social circumstance, and in some extreme cases, even natural processes. In more concrete terms, the influence makes a series of waves from near to far. People who possess *cheng* will first influence their family members, the members in their neighborhoods, and then people in a larger community to which they belong. The influence may continue to move on to a state, and to the world as a whole. The ideal is to create a harmonious society in which everyone keeps *cheng* constantly, and always conducts their words and deeds with *cheng*.

In pre-modern Chinese philosophy, this influence is often interpreted as with two distinctive forms, which I respectively name as "transformation (*hua* 化)" and "change (*bian* 變)." These are two popular terms in Chinese culture and philosophy. In general, transformation refers to an immanent alteration in which no external force intervenes, whereas change refers to an imposed alteration caused by external force. For instance, due to the interaction of *yin* 陰 and *yang* 陽 within a plant, the plant actualizes its potency through a regular course of "origination (*yuan* 元)," "flourishing (*heng* 亨)," "advantage (*li* 利)," and "firmness (*zhen* 貞)," and accordingly alters itself in both inner structure and outer appearance. In contrast, as the result of a violent storm and heavy rain, rivers break their banks, and destroy people's houses and rice fields. The former is the case of transformation, while the latter is that of change.

Applied to human affairs, they represent two modes regarding the alteration of people and society. In the tradition of transformation, *cheng* is primarily viewed as a pure moral force that inspires and awakens the same attribute or force hidden in other people, attracting them to work with the initiator for a desirable goal. This tradition presupposes that, due to the good nature endowed by Heaven, people are morally perfectible and naturally inclined to follow an ideal model of morality if they can find one. In this sense, they are potentially transformable. Being such a model, the sage has no need to intentionally apply any governmental measures or artificial methods to reward and punish people, to "push" and "propel" them toward a social ideal. Instead, the sage's only business is to cultivate and maintain the absolute *cheng* which will naturally "attract" and "draw" people close. The sage's goal—a great harmony among people and between humans and Nature—is realized in a process in which people voluntarily and actively emulate the sage. As ZHU Xi summarizes, "the point is not to use 'principle of reality' (*cheng*) for certain purpose, but that if there is 'principle of reality' people must be moved" (Zhu 1986, 1330). This tradition runs through all the works of mainstream Confucians, including Mencius, the author of *Centrality and Commonality*, LI Ao, and all the philosophers in the Neo-Confucian movement.

Nevertheless, some thinkers derived a pragmatic or instrumental conclusion from the foregoing theory. The self-cultivation of *cheng* will naturally bring out an external consistency in people's conducts. That means a consistent issuing and implementation of regulation and law for a ruler, and a consistent acceptance of and submission to them for the ordinary people. In this sense, *cheng* and self-cultivation is actually a way of governance, a statecraft that may be more efficient and reliable than sheer reward and punishment. Essentially, this pragmatic approach is a variation of "transformation," which does not attract people to better themselves for the universal harmony in the world, but rather to "guide" them toward a goal that is specifically designed for a well-ordered state. Generally speaking, this is the way by which many thinkers of political philosophy in the Qin-Han period interpret the function of *cheng*. It is also a legacy inherited by many political leaders, such as JIANG Jieshi, in contemporary China.

In the tradition of "change," however, *cheng* is mainly viewed as a material force residing in the heart of a sage or immortal, which may radiate out, affecting people's conducts and feelings. From the perspective of the affected parties, this *cheng* signifies an invisible force to which they have to submit. The notion of *cheng*/change, which is typically associated with religious Daoism, brings a mystical implication to the idea of *cheng*. Later, this implication is widely accepted in Chinese folk society, and even comes to be an important part of the collective consciousness of Chinese people. A phrase that is often heard and read in China even today, "When there is *cheng*, a lucky omen will come (*cheng ze ling* 誠則靈)," exemplifies its popularity. It means that, as what happens to the sage and immortal, an ordinary person's *cheng* can also affect the mind of other people and the decisions of ghosts and spirits for doing something in the person's favor.

Conclusion

There are at least three reasons responsible for the complexity of the idea of *cheng*. First, its relation with the two precursors, "*xin*" and "*shi*," is not always clear. Consequently, it is often difficult to identify its core meaning that originates from people's community life and absorbs the intellectual elements that "*xin*" and "*shi*" denote. Secondly, as a dynamic idea that evolved throughout a long historical period, *cheng* is continuously enriched by various notions or concepts affiliated to multiple philosophical and religious schools. These contributions expanded the connotation of *cheng*, and, at the same time, blurred its core meaning. As a result, people's efforts to seek for a comprehensive understanding of *cheng* are often misled by its secondary and derivative meanings. Finally, *cheng* has been described as a force effecting either in the form of "transformation" or in that of "change." In the former, its influence is often exaggerated, while in the latter, it even looks, more or less, mystical. Despite all these difficulties, however, its core meaning is still identifiable. It consists of what the English terms "sincerity" and "reality" designate. In general, the term *cheng* can be properly applied to a person or a thing so long as either "sincerity" or "reality" or the unity of the two is present.

Chapter II

The Emergence

Toward the fourth century B.C.E. the development of Chinese thought entered a rather productive phase. Different schools of thought were shaped, and various compelling and penetrating questions were raised and discussed. In the ferment of intellectual debates, arguments, and confrontations, *cheng* as a philosophical idea emerged. This signals that Chinese thinking in general has reached a new depth and breadth. Now, in addition to continuing its traditional investigation on a series of virtues—humaneness, rightness, propriety, wisdom, faithfulness, and courage—it began to explore the common "root" from which they grew; and in addition to furthering its pursuit of efficient political measures for governance, it began to seek for the final ground that underlies all proper measures. Also, Chinese thinking became more speculative: what concerned it was no longer limited to the consistency, regularity, and predictability in human conducts and natural phenomena, but also the reasons that brings about these traits; not only the moral imperative applicable to human society, but also the ultimate principle that governs and regulates both humans and Nature; not only the attribute of a certain species, but also the universal reality common to all beings. The texts particularly contributory to the emergence of *cheng* at that time were five books: the *Mencius* 《孟子》, the *Xunzi* 《荀子》, the *Zhuangzi* 《莊子》, the *Great Learning* (*daxue* 《大學》), and the *Centrality and Commonality*. Together they defined the basic philosophical uses of *cheng*, opened multiple dimensions for its applications, and laid down a foundation for its further development.

II. 1. The *Mencius*

Mencius is the first major thinker who used *cheng* as a philosophical concept. As a part of his conceptual system, *cheng* is closely related to the other key terms that he uses, especially "Heaven" and "human," "reciprocity" (*shu* 恕), "extension" (*tui* 推), and "good knowledge and good ability" (*liangzhi liangneng* 良知良能). To comprehend its full meaning, we need to take these terms into account within the context of his system. Generally speaking, Mencius' main contribution to the history of *cheng* is twofold. First, he clearly construes it as a conceptual unity with two components: an inner state endowed by Heaven and an inner-oriented moral action to safeguard the state. Secondly, he ushers in the tradition of "transformation" by expounding the relation between *cheng* and its influence on various scales of society: family, state, and the world as a whole. These two points enable him to tie human nature with the way of Heaven, to underline the necessity of self-cultivation for the realization of social harmony, and to form a primordial pattern that prepares the further evolution of *cheng* to be both a cosmological and metaphysical concept.

II. 1. 1. Family and the World

As stated in the first chapter, Mencius believes that *cheng* originates from family life; its first beneficiaries are people's parents. At the same time, he regards *cheng* as the ultimate assurance for a person's social success. With a process sequentially phased by "win the trust of friends," "win the confidence of superiors," and "govern the people," he explains how a person's *cheng* expands its influence, step by step, from a family to all of society.

In the *Mencius*, the influence of *cheng* goes through two paths: one happens naturally, while another involves people's intentional efforts. In the first case, people with *cheng* will treat their parents well simply for the sake that they are their parents. Despite the fact that they have no thought of profit or cost, still less of promoting their social status, their natural conducts actually influence their friends and superiors. Mencius is confident that the natural occurrence of influence is beyond any doubt, since humans all possess good nature, tend to commend and praise good conducts, and promote a person who is consistent and trustworthy. As he says, "There has never been a man with absolute *cheng* who fails to move others. On the other hand, one who is not true (*cheng*) to himself can never hope to move others" (*Mengzi*, 4A12).

In the meantime, Mencius also encourages the exemplary person (*junzi* 君子) to engage intentionally and actively in social and community affairs. For him, the family-fostered *cheng* has a societal dimension. With a long-time training in family life, people's attitude associated with *cheng* may be internalized as a persistent psychological state. If being constantly sustained, the state will enable them to enlarge the scope of *cheng*'s beneficiaries from their parents to all people in the society. Unlike the case of serving one's own parents, this is an intentional effort related directly to the exemplary person's vision of and aspiration to the society. An analysis on the two terms in the *Mencius*, "reciprocity" and "extension," will help to clarify this issue.

The term "reciprocity ," which Confucius first introduced into Chinese intellectual discourse, signifies in both positive and negative forms a moral imperative close to the Christian Golden Rule. Its positive form reads, "As for humanness—you yourself desire rank and standing; then help others to get rank and standing. You want to turn your own merits to account; then help others to turn theirs to account." And its negative one reads, "When you go abroad, behave as if you were receiving a great guest. Employ the people as if you were assisting at a great sacrifice. Do not do to others what you do not want them do to you" (*Lunyu*, 12, 2). In correspondence with Confucius, Mencius further argues, "All the ten thousand things are there in me. There is no greater joy for me than to find, on self-examination, that I am in (the state of) *cheng* (*fanshen er cheng* 反身而誠). Try your best to exercise reciprocity, and this is the shortest way to humaneness" (*Mengzi*, 7A4). It is his position that the principles regarding social life, which Heaven bestowed on us, will always be there if we keep our heart in the state of *cheng*. They enable us to distinguish intuitively the good from the bad, the desirable from the deplorable, and constitute a ground on which we exercise "reciprocity:" to help people if we want to be helped, or not to harm them if we don't want to be harmed.

Another term regarding the intentional influence is "extension" or "to extend." When talking with a king about the best government, Mencius suggests, "Treat with respect the elders in your family, and then extend that respect to include the elders in other families. Treat with tenderness the young in your family, and then extend that tenderness to include the young in other families. And you can roll the world in your palm" (*Mengzi,* 1A7). Here "extension" means to extend virtues, such as *cheng,* that you acquired from family life to the outside world to treat other people with the same *cheng* as you did to your parents. In Mencius's view, this is the easiest measure to harmonize people around, and the "shortest" way to make humaneness prevail in the entire world.

In essence, the way "reciprocity" and "extension" works is similar to "natural influence" at one point. They do not refer to an action to "reform," "reshape," or "remold" people's character or nature, but rather to an effort to advance people to look for their own *cheng* and externalize it for the interest of themselves and their society. This kind of influence represents a typical form of "transformation" that I described in the last chapter.

From the end of the Warring States era (475-322 B.C.E.) to the beginning of the Han dynasty, Mencius' idea about *cheng*'s influence has been echoed in many prominent Confucian texts. The famous "eight-items" (the investigation of things, the extension of knowledge, the rectification of heart, the sincerity of will [*chengyi*], the cultivation of person, the regulation of family, the order of state, and the peace of the world) in the *Great Learning* maps out the phases from *cheng* to the final realization of an exemplary person's social ideal. Similarly, *Commentary on the Book of Changes* (*Wenyan* 《文言》) states the same idea with two well-known passages. An exemplary person "does away with what is false and preserves his *cheng.* He improves his era and doesn't boast about it. His character is influential and transforms people" (*Yijing* 《易經》, 63). Also, "By working on his words, so that they rest firmly on *cheng,* the gentleman [exemplary person] makes his work enduring" (*Yijing,* 64). The first stresses the necessity of preserving *cheng* for the transformation of people, while the second encourages writers to concentrate on *cheng* when conceiving and writing their works, because this is the way to ensure that the works will have longlasting influence on future generations. The statements from the *Great Learning* and the *Commentary* show that the idea of transformation as a major form of *cheng's* influence has been widely accepted by mainstream Confucians in that era.

II. 1. 2. Heaven and Humans

As the conclusion to his chain reasoning from "governing the people" to "understanding goodness," Mencius claims, "Hence *cheng* is the way of Heaven, and thinking to be true (*cheng*) is the way of humans" (*Mengzi*, 4A12). Scholars of Chinese philosophy have generally read this passage as evidence for Mencius' conviction of the unity of Heaven and human. Although it is not wrong principally, this reading neglects a point significant to the history of *cheng*. When making his statement, Mencius' first concern may not be the common essence of Heaven and human itself, but the relation between *cheng* as an inner state and *cheng* as a moral effort to preserve the state. I would like to explain this point by analyzing the terms of "Heaven" and "humans," and "the way of Heaven" and "the way of humans" in the above passage.

ZHAO Qi 趙岐(108-201), the first exegete of the *Mencius*, explains the passage as that "It is Heaven that grants humans a nature of *cheng* and goodness. And it is humans who think of practicing this *cheng* in order to comply with Heaven" (ZHAO Qi, ND. 7B). ZHENG Xuan 鄭玄 (127-200), the first exegete of *Centrality and Commonality*, comments on a similar passage in the text by saying that, "'*Cheng*' is a heavenly bestowed nature; while 'striving to be true (*cheng*)' means striving to be true (*cheng*) through learning" (ZHENG Xuan, 23).[2] In the same vein, ZHU Xi's commentary on the *Mencius* reads, "'*Cheng*' means the principle in me, which is completely true, without any falsity. It is the natural course (*benran* 本然) of the way of Heaven. 'Thinking to be true (*cheng*)' means [an effort] to ensure that the principle in me is completely true, without any falsity. This is the dutiful

[2] There is a slight difference between the above passages in the *Mencius* and in *Centrality and Commonality*. The first one reads, "Thinking to be *cheng* (*si cheng zhe* 思誠者) is the way of humans," while the second reads, "Striving to be *cheng* (*cheng zhi zhe* 誠之者) is the way of humans. Most leading scholars from the Han dynasty have agreed that this difference is basically negligible.

course (*dangran* 當然) of the way of human" (Zhu 1983, 282). Correspondently, his commentary on *Centrality and Commonality* reads, "'*Cheng* means truth, reality, and no irregularity. It is the natural course of the principle of Heaven. 'Striving to be true (*cheng*)' means [an effort] to turn what is not true, unreal, and irregular into true, real and regular. This is the dutiful course of human life" (Zhu 1983, 12).

According to the *Mencius* and *Centrality and Commonality*, as well as these commentators, "Heaven" in Mencius' passage refers to natural states or movements and their products, while "human" refers to conscious actions from humans and their consequences. *Cheng* belongs to the category of Heaven, signifying the human nature/reality that comes with every person innately. Humans possess *cheng* just as they are born with four limbs, and as the original color of sky is blue. After all, this is pre-determined, having nothing to do with their free choices. In contrast, "thinking to be true (*cheng*)" or "striving to be true (*cheng*)" belongs to the category of "human," referring to an intentional effort (self-cultivation) to adjust one's actions to match up with the state of *cheng*. In this sense, to preserve or not to preserve *cheng* is a matter of choice, associated with people's deliberation and decision-making. Humans can make such choices just as they can decide to keep or amputate their arms, protect or pollute the sky.

By likening the relation of "*cheng*" and "thinking to be *cheng*" to that of "Heaven" and "humans," Mencius stresses simultaneously two points. First, *cheng* as an inner state is naturally pure and good, which represents human nature/reality. Second, as a species brought into being by Heaven, humans are dutifully to pursue a life that doesn't depart from, but comply with their nature. For persisting in living this kind of life, they must always be engaged in self-cultivation to keep away all thinkings and actions contradictory to *cheng*. In fact, Mencius makes a clear distinction between *cheng* and "thinking to be *cheng*," the inner state and the self-cultivation. However, due to the internal connection of the two, and the necessity of self-cultivation for the preservation of *cheng*, he and his successors often loosely apply the same term *cheng* to both of them.

II. 1. 3. Knowledge and Action

The road that humans take to integrate with Heaven is winding, and full of obstacles. Potentially, every person is perfectible since we all possess a nature/reality identical to the Heavenly way. In actuality, however, humans are doomed to be born into an imperfect environment that is often short of good moral education and adequate economic supplies. This often forces us to be engaged in a struggle with all kinds of temptations and base desires, and to vacillate between preservation and abandonment of *cheng*. The conflict between the potentiality and actuality traps us in an existential dilemma. On the one hand, we know clearly that *cheng* is something worthy to follow; while, on the other hand, we often act in a way just contrary to its guidance. This presents a fundamental contradiction between knowledge and action, a problem that has troubled Chinese philosophers as well as their Western counterparts for a long time. To identify the universality of the problem and the trait of Mencian solution, in what follows, I will compare relevant ideas from Western and Confucian thinkers.

In the West, St. Augustine claims that evil, immorality, wretchedness, and violence are wrong, and punishable by the law of God. However, "I had known it, and acted as though, I know it not—winked at it, and forgot it" (St. Augustine, 175-6). Herein he locates a fundamental contradiction or conflict between our knowing and action: knowing what is good does not necessarily translate into doing what is good, although the former may be helpful to the latter to certain extent. In many cases, people commit bad acts when they are clearly aware that what they are doing is wrong.

To resolve the contradiction, St. Augustine traces wrong actions to their root, which he names as the "carnal will" (or mind). "My [carnal] will was the enemy master of, and thence had made a chain for me and bound me. Because of a perverse will was lust made; and lust indulged in became custom; and custom not resisted became necessary. By which links, as it were, joined together (whence I termed it as a 'chain'), did a hard bondage hold me enthralled" (St Augustine, 170). Because of the carnal will, humans are inescapably selfish and bad; they cannot love anyone beyond themselves, and thus they produce all the miseries of the world.

St. Augustine believes that humans also possess "spiritual will" as the contender with the carnal one. Nevertheless, it never triumphs over the latter unless God helps. Only when God chooses humans, which they cannot do on their own, can humans escape their carnal will, and therefore able to refrain from doing bad actions. "There are two kinds of minds in us—one is good, the other evil. They themselves verily are evil when they hold these evil opinions; and they shall become good when they hold the truth, and shall consent unto the truth, that thy apostle may say unto them, 'Ye were sometimes darkness, by now are ye light in the Lord'" (St. Augustine, 180). In brief, as to St. Augustine, humans can only depend on the intervention of God to eliminate "carnal will," and therewith to resolve the contradiction between knowing and acting.

Having noticed the same contradiction, Immanuel Kant, in contrast to St. Augustine, focuses on the side of knowing for its resolution. According to Kant, humans possess an "ordinary practical reason," an intuitive ability "to distinguish, in all cases that present themselves, what is good or evil, right or wrong." It is the "first principle" of moral knowledge, a principle common to "every human, even the most ordinary." Thus, "There is no need of science or philosophy for knowing what man has to do in order to be honest and good, and indeed to be wise and virtuous" (Kant, 71-2).

Because of its presence, Kant further argues that "practical judgment" has a great advantage over "theoretical judgment." As for the latter, when ordinary reason ventures to depart from laws of experience and the perceptions of senses, it falls into sheer unintelligibility and self-contradiction, or at least into a chaos of uncertainty, obscurity, and vacillation. On the practical side, however, what occurs is simply the opposite when the ordinary mind excludes all sensuous motives. Now "it can…have as good hope of hitting the mark as any that a philosopher can promise himself" (Kant, 72). This being so, as Kant inquires,

> Might it not then be more advisable in moral questions to abide by the judgment of ordinary reason and, at the most, to bring in philosophy only in order to set forth the system of morals more fully and intelligibly and to present its rules in a form more

> convenient for use—but not in order to lead ordinary human intelligence away from its happy simplicity in respect of action and to set it by means of philosophy on a new path of enquiry and instruction? (Kant, 72)

To this question Kant offers a negative answer: "Innocence is a splendid thing, only it has the misfortune not to keep well and to be easily misled" (Kant, 72). From the human needs and inclinations, which stand as a powerful counterweight to the command of reason, there arises a disposition that he terms as "natural dialectic." It is "to quibble with these strict laws of duty, to throw doubt on their validity or at least on their purity and strictness, and to make them, where possible, more adapted to our wishes and inclinations; that is, to pervert their very foundations and destroy their whole dignity—a result which in the end even ordinary human reason is unable to approve" (Kant, 73). Kant concludes that "ordinary practical reason" is not reliable for serving as the foundation of moral judgments, because it always entangles with the interference of "natural dialectic," which we humans, in principle, cannot completely get rid of. So, the correct path is to conduct "a full critique of our reason" to establish the "categorical imperative" as the guidance of all moral actions.

Kant's "ordinary practical reason" has a Chinese counterpart—"good knowledge and good ability" in Mencius. Mencius defines "good ability" as "the ability possessed by humans without their having acquired it by learning," and "good knowledge" as "the knowledge possessed by them without deliberation" (*Mengzi*, 7A15). WANG Yangming 王陽明 (1472-1528), a Neo-Confucian philosopher in the Ming 明 dynasty (1368-1644), makes the most elaborate explanation of this Mencian idea.

> The sense of right and wrong requires no deliberation to know, nor does it depend on learning to function. This is why it is called 'good knowledge.' It is my nature endowed by Heaven, the original substance of my mind, naturally intelligent, shinning, clear, and understanding. Whenever a thought or a wish arises, my mind's faculty of good knowledge itself is always conscious of it. Whether it is good or evil, my mind's faculty of good knowing itself also knows it. It has nothing to do with others. (WANG Yangming, 191)

However, departing from Kant at this point, he claims that "good knowledge" is reliable in any time, any circumstances; it cannot be clouded or distorted by "natural dialects" in any form. As for the two sides in the contradiction between knowing and acting, in his lexicon, "knowing" refers to "good knowledge," which belongs to the category of Heaven; while "acting" belongs to that of "human," which involves a variety of mundane concerns and calculations. Since the former is always correct, people can only blame the latter for the occurrence of immoral conducts, as well as the presence of the contradiction itself.

For Wang, the solution lies in the constant self-cultivation or "making one's will [in the state of] *cheng* (*chengyi* 誠意)," as phrased by the *Great Learning*. This is an inner-oriented action to preserve *cheng*, an uninterrupted moral effort to distance people from the "self-deception" (*ziqi* 自欺) that denies the warning from the "good knowledge." It aims at attuning people's actions to the rhythm of their "good knowledge," and, ideally, will habituate people's good acting, enabling them to respond spontaneously in a way consistent with "good knowledge" when facing moral choices.

Wang, with his doctrine of the "unity of knowledge and action" (*zhi xing heyi* 知行合一) points out an ideal state to which constant self-cultivation leads.

> The *Great Learning* points to true knowledge [meaning, "good knowledge"] and action for people to see, saying that they are 'like loving beautiful colors and hating bad odors.' Seeing beautiful colors appertains to knowledge, while loving beautiful colors appertains to action. However, as soon as one sees that beautiful color, he has already loved it. It is not that he sees it first and then makes up his mind to love it. (WANG Yangming, 6)

His statement reveals two traits of the unity: naturalness and simultaneity. It tells us that, when the unity is established, "seeing" (knowledge) and "loving" (action) both become natural responses to the beautiful color, and both occur at the same time. To clarify the route to the ideal state and the validity of constant self-cultivation, I would add another example from our daily life.

Think of this case: driving on a highway and intending to change to the left lane, you, all of a sudden, realize that another car just behind you has already occupied the lane. Without any deliberation or reasoning, you spontaneously shift back to the original lane. This correct action is not a natural gift, but a result of long-time driving practice. It is essentially consistent with what a sound reasoning tells you, although the latter doesn't actually function as instructor at that moment. The ethical lesson derived from this case is that, a long-time training under the guidance of "good knowledge" can internalize a psychological state that enables people to act as natural and correct as "good knowledge" instructs. At this point, knowing and acting become the same, or as Wang termed, they are united together.

For Wang and for Mencius as well, this unity is principally reachable. As proved by Confucius' reference to himself, "At seventy, I could follow my heart's desires without transgressing the line" (*Lunyu*, 2.4). In this case, to follow his "desires" means to act naturally and spontaneously, while not to transgress the "line" means to restrain one's action within the boundary of morality. They occur simultaneously, without consulting each other, but parallel to each other. This is the final goal of constant self-cultivation and the Confucian solution to the contradiction of knowing and acting.

II. 2. The *Xunzi*

Xunzi is the second major Confucian thinker expounding extensively about *cheng* in the Warring States era. Similar to Mencius, he treats *cheng* as a common foundation underlying both Heaven and humans. Meanwhile, due to his distinctive understanding of both human nature and Heaven, his *cheng* differs significantly from that of Mencius. Xunzi asserts that human nature is "bad" because it is inclined to "seek for gain" (*Xunzi*, 434), therefore an exemplary person with *cheng* needs not only serve as a teacher to "transform" people, but also an executive to implement governmental measures to "change" them. "Transformation" alone is not sufficient for the establishment of a harmonious society; it must work side by side with "change." Also, differing from *Mencius*, "Heaven" in Xunzi is no longer a relatively vague concept regarding primarily what accounts for the existence of a myriad of things, but a naturalistic one, denoting unmistakably the blue sky, or Mother Nature. Taking ethical *cheng* as a pattern, he coins some new phrases, like "*cheng* in Heaven," to signify the source of the consistency, regularity, and predictability in natural phenomena. Because of this effort, *cheng* crosses over its original boundary of human life to be also a concept with cosmological significance. These two points specify Xunzi's main contribution to the evolution of the idea of *cheng*.

II. 2. 1. Ethical Cheng

Following Confucius, Xunzi divides people as exemplary person and ordinary mass. According to him, "exemplary person" is not a concept of blood or family lineage, but that of moral merit; to be or not to be an exemplary person is not something pre-determined, but a matter open to one's own choice. Moreover, the key for becoming an exemplary person lies in the cultivation of *cheng*—"for the nourishment of an exemplary person's mind, there is nothing better than *cheng*; he needs to watch for nothing, but his *cheng*" (*Xunzi*, 46). At the same time, the term "exemplary person" signifies not only an honorary title, but also a social responsibility that its holder must fulfill. Xunzi describes the flow from an exemplary person's self-cultivation to his final success in guiding the ordinary mass to an orderly society by saying that,

> What the exemplary person should preserve is simply humaneness, while what he should implement is simply rightness. Preserving humaneness sincerely (*cheng*), [what is in his mind] will be manifest; being manifest, it will be divine; being divine, it will be able to transform the mass. Implementing rightness sincerely, [his rule] will be disciplined; being disciplined, it will be clear and definite; being clear and definite, it will be able to change the mass. (*Xunzi*, 46)

To reach the final goal, the exemplary person needs both "transformation" and "change." The transformation means that one should first establish oneself as a moral model by sincerely preserving the humaneness within, and thereby inspires the mass to correct their mistakes. In contrast, the change requires one to set clear and definite order and rule by sincerely implementing rightness without, and thereby deters the mass from wrong doings. Unlike the "transformation-only" governance that Mencius prefers, Xunzi's approach consists of two wings, which assist each other for his social ideal to fly. Xunzi derives this theory from his observation that "Human nature is bad; his goodness is the result of conscious activity" (*Xunzi*, 434). So, to understand Xunzi's view about the necessity of "change," we have to clarify first his concept of "human nature."

It is interesting that Xunzi and Mencius start with opposing points on human nature, but end at the same conclusion that education, self-cultivation, and preservation of *cheng* is the key for personal success and social harmony. In my view, this is because the same term "human nature" connotes differently for the two philosophers. Emphasizing the uniqueness of humankind as a particular species, Mencius defines their nature as what differentiates them from beasts. Therewith he explains his thesis that "human nature is good" this way: "As far as what is genuinely in their nature is concerned, humans are capable of becoming good. That is what I mean by good" (*Mengzi*, 5A6). On the contrary, Xunzi defines "human nature" as some attributes common to both humankind and beasts. "Humans' inborn nature is to seek for gain.... Therefore to follow humans' nature and their feeling will inevitably result in strife and rapacity, combined with rebellion and disorder, and end in violence" (*Xunzi*, 434). Looking at human nature from Xunzi's point of view, we can certainly understand why both "transformation" and "change" are indispensable for an exemplary person to realize the social ideal.

The disagreement on "human nature" also causes the two philosophers to diverge on the issue of "transformation" itself. Being optimistic to people's perfectibility, Mencius mainly regards "transformation" as an intrinsic principle, by means of which a perfect moral model ignites the good qualities incipient in people's heart, attracting them to work voluntarily for the social harmony. In contrast, worrying that the bad nature will lead people to conflicts, Xunzi conceives "transformation" basically as an instrumental principle (education and teaching) with which the exemplary person channels the desire of the mass to a right direction.

As for the co-operation of "transformation" and "change," Xunzi suggests, "Humans must be first transformed by the instruction of teacher and guided by ritual principles and only then will they be able to observe the dictates of courtesy and humility, obey the forms and rules of society, and end in order" (*Xunzi*, 434-5). Here the "instruction" of the teacher represents the major form of "transformation," while "ritual principle" refers to social norms and regulations. One of them assures the mass of having a sense of "courtesy and humility," another forces them to abide by the "forms and rules." Together they will direct them to "end in order," or to live an orderly social life. Xunzi summarizes the co-operation of "instruction" and "ritual principle," and "transformation" and "change" by saying that

> Ritual is the means by which to rectify yourself; the teacher is the means by which ritual is rectified. If you are without ritual, how can you rectify yourself? If you have no teacher, how can you understand the fitness of ritual? If you unerringly do as ritual prescribes, it means that your emotions have found rest in ritual. If you speak as your teacher speaks, it means that your understanding has become like that of your teacher. If your emotions find rest in ritual and your understanding is like that of your teacher, then you have become a sage. (*Xunzi*, 33-34)

In brief, to establish an orderly society, according to Xunzi, the exemplary person must carry out a twofold method: transformation and change. The first side involves "teacher," "instruction," and the sense of "courtesy and humility," while the second "ritual," "discipline," and "guidance." Ultimately, they both come from the same source— the exemplary person's *cheng*. As will be shown in the next chapter, Xunzi's ideas of "change" and instrumental "transformation" greatly influenced a number of thinkers in the Qin-Han period, including HAN Fei 韓非 (d. 233 B.C.E.), one of his students.

II. 2. 2. Cosmic Cheng

By introducing *cheng* that originates from human life into Nature, Xunzi forms a notion of "cosmic *cheng*." It denotes the ultimate reason for the consistency, regularity, and predictability in natural phenomena, such as the consistent motions of heavenly bodies, the regular changes of the four seasons, the constant flowing of rivers from the high to the low, and the predictable life cycle of plants.

Continuing his long passage that I quoted in the beginning of the last section, Xunzi characterizes cosmic *cheng* as that,

> While Heaven has never spoken out, people revere its highness. While earth has never spoken out, people revere its thickness. While the four seasons have never spoken out, people expect their sequence. This is because all these regularities (*youchang* 有常) culminate in [the states of] *cheng*. (*Xunzi*, 46)

The logic that links these two passages together is the analogy between this cosmic *cheng* and the ethical *cheng*. Xunzi's reasoning seems to be that, from the consistent conduct of those who are *cheng* (ethical *cheng*), people around them recognize their trustworthiness, and like to listen to and work with them. Furthermore, with the persistence of their consistency, and with increasing numbers of people participating in their plan, their influence reaches farther. In parallel, Heaven/earth exhibits its consistency through regular changes and movements in natural phenomena, and thereby produces and reproduces a myriad of things. This convinces people to act in conformity with its trustworthy rhythm—for instance, to always sow in spring and harvest in autumn. It is from the natural consistency and its consequence that people infer, by analogizing with what happens in humans, that there exists also *cheng* (cosmic *cheng*) in Heaven/earth.

However, there is a substantial difference between ethical *cheng* and its cosmic counterpart. Humans, the carrier of ethical *cheng*, are conscious agents, capable of acting intentionally to preserve their *cheng*, and therewith, making their conducts consistent. But it is difficult for Xunzi to say the same thing about Heaven/earth since he, like most Chinese thinkers, simply denies the concept of creator as an anthropomorphic deity. Thus, instead of treating cosmic *cheng* as an initiator behind or underneath natural consistency, he cautiously says, "all these regularities culminate in their *cheng*." His message is that cosmic *cheng* is not something transcending over or staying out of natural consistency, but rather the culmination or perfection of the consistency itself.

Essentially, cosmic *cheng* signifies a specific pattern with which all natural phenomena, if they are regular, consistent, and predictable, must be in conformity. "This cosmic pattern," as Derk Bodde points out, "is self-contained and self-operating. It unfolds itself because of its own inner necessity and not because it is ordained by any external volitional power" (Bodde, 68). Borrowing a term from A. N. Whitehead, we may name this view of Nature as "immanent," in contrast with that of "imposition," which some leading philosophers and scientists in the West have taught from the seventeenth to the twentieth century (Whitehead, 142). Through this natural consistency, Xunzi establishes the cosmic *cheng* as the counterpart of ethical *cheng*, and thereby sets up a parallelism between them.

But a question still remains. The ethical *cheng* contains concrete contents, such as the inner state and the action to preserve that state, but what is the content of cosmic *cheng*? This is a legitimate question whose answer may lead Chinese thinking to explore what Western science did in modern times. However, Xunzi remains silent on this point, providing no reply, even showing no attempt to reply. A simple, but essentially correct explanation about his shunning the question is that he has no particular interest in the topic. As Needham observes, he "exemplifies perfectly" the Confucian tradition toward Nature. On the one hand, he is rationalistic and opposes to any superstitious or supernatural forms of religion. On the other hand, his concentration upon human life is so intense that it even negates the significance of investigation of non-human content as such (Needham, 12, 28). A passage that Xunzi writes directly against Daoists shows both sides.

> Is it better to exalt Heaven and think of it, or to nourish its creatures and regulate them? Is it better to obey Heaven and sing hymns to it, or to grasp the mandate of Heaven and make use of it? Is it better to long for the seasons and wait for them, or to respond to the seasons and exploit them? Is it better to wait for things to increase of themselves, or to apply your talents and transform them? Is it better to think of things but regard them as outside of you, or to control things and not let them slip your grasp? Is it better to long for the source from which things are born, or to possess the means to bring them to completion? (*Xunzi*, 317)

With these rhetorical questions, Xunzi exhibits clearly his humanistic stance toward Heaven. First of all, he reads Heaven as a naturalistic existence, close to "blue sky" or "mother Nature" in the modern sense. Next, he positions Heaven in the system of human world, judging the value of all knowledge of Nature in terms of its relation to human activities, and looking everywhere for the social and moral significance that the knowledge may imply. For this reason, an investigation on the content of cosmic *cheng* itself seems to deviate from the interest in knowing what the world is and what directly benefits human life, because what actually affects humans and their world is natural consistency, not something in Nature that possibly causes the consistency.

In fact, the concept of cosmic *cheng* is meaningful to Xunzi only in the following two senses. First, it satisfies human curiosity about the consistency in natural phenomena by assuming *cheng* as its ground. Second, and more importantly, it signifies a principle in Nature that parallels to that in humans. With a concern about the unity of Heaven and humans in mind, Xunzi claims, "While Heaven and earth are great enough, they could not transform a myriad of things if they wouldn't possess *cheng*. While the sages are wise enough, they could not transform a myriad of people if they wouldn't possess *cheng*" (*Xunzi*, 46). The alleged parallelism of the two realms convinces him that *cheng* is the foundation on which the unity is based, and a universal principle functioning in both Nature and humans.

By assuming *cheng* as the common principle behind the consistency in the two realms, Xunzi further elevates it to be a universal concept (universal *cheng*). This universality, in turn, strengthens the imperative force of *cheng* in human life. Xunzi reminds people of the power of *cheng* by saying that, "While the relation between father and son is intimate enough, it will become distant if it doesn't contain *cheng*. While a ruler is venerable enough, he will be humiliated if he doesn't have *cheng*. *Cheng* is what an exemplary person should keep up, and that on which political and administrative affairs are based" (*Xunzi*, 48). After taking a long journey through Nature and transcendental realm, Xunzi brings *cheng* back to human society with all the reverence and aura it gained from the journey. Now *cheng* turns to be a quality with heavenly significance, an imperative by which people should abide dutifully. It is the foundation of all human relationships, a proper course for personal conducts and social organizations, and a final assurance for the unity between human and Heaven.

II. 2. 3. General Principle and Natural Law

Like almost all major Chinese thinkers in the pre-Modern times, Xunzi believes that there exists a general principle in the universe, which unites humans with their environment, and serves as a standard to judge and evaluate things in Nature and humans. In addition to *cheng*, he also assigns another term "*li*" 禮 (ritual) for its identification.

> Through ritual Heaven and earth join in harmony, the sun and moon shine, the four seasons proceed in order, the stars and constellations march, the rivers flow, and all things flourish; humans' likes and dislikes are regulated and their joys and hates made appropriate. Those below are obedient, those above are enlightened; all things change but do not become disordered; only he who turns his back upon ritual will be destroyed. Is ritual not wonderful indeed? (*Xunzi*, 355-6)

"Ritual" is similar to *cheng*, at least, in two ways. First, they both originate from human world, and latter are "read into" Nature. Secondly, they are both regarded as general principles after the journey of being read into Nature, and thereby acquiring an imperative force to regulate human conducts. Obviously, there is a similar circle of reasoning in both cases, which begins and ends at the same point—human society. This justifies a point I mentioned before: Nature, as well as its immanent pattern (cosmic *cheng*), is important to Xunzi only when it is related to human affairs and helpful for thinkers to enforce strict, but practicable ethical norms.

Now I would like to examine briefly two concepts, "natural law" and "law of Nature" in Western civilization, aiming to reveal another reason for Xunzi's failure to investigate the content of cosmic *cheng*. Paul Foriers and Cham Perelman indicate that "natural law" came from an awareness that certain phenomena in Nature answer to laws. This knowledge logically led philosophers in ancient Greece to generalize that "all phenomena answer to laws and that notably societies, peoples, and relations among individuals would answer to a pre-established integral order which needed only to be sought and discovered" (Foriers and Perelman, 14). Furthermore, the philosophers even supposed that there was a single principle governing everything, including human beings placed at the center of the universe and societies which have the same characteristics as the other elements in the external world. For example, Heraclitus defined wisdom as consisting of "a single thing, to know the thought which governs all things everywhere" (Foriers and Perelman, 14). From these ideas came the notion of "natural law," a principle responsible for the pre-established order of all natural and social phenomena.

In the Roman Empire, "natural law" was mainly used in social contexts. Cicero asserted, "True law is right reason which conforms to nature." Later, thinkers summarized that natural law differed from "positive law" (which is represented by legal codes) in four distinctive ways: (1) its origin goes back to the beginning of humankind; (2) its domain is common to all, not limited to human beings; (3) it has the worth of being a measure and standard for everything, including legal codes; (4) it has the rigor of being immutable in its most parts (see Foriers and Perelman, 18).

The notion of "law of Nature" grew from the same root as "natural law," but later, departed from it as a result of investigation on the interrelations in the physical world. In the seventeenth century, the Spanish theologian Suarez made a sharp distinction between the world of morality and that of non-human Nature. He maintained that the idea of law applied only to the former, and natural necessity can be called a law only in a sense of metaphor. In Descartes (1596-1650), the notion was further advanced. His *Principia Philosophiae* (1644) concluded that it had discussed "what must follow from the mutual impact of bodies according to mechanical laws, confirmed by certain and everyday experiments." Taking the same approach, Spinoza (1632-1677) distinguished the laws "depending on the necessity of Nature" from the laws resulting from human decree. In addition, he agreed with Suarez that the application of the term "laws" to physical things was simply based on a metaphor (Needham, 541). As a matter of fact, modern science has developed from the notion of "law of Nature," rather than "natural law."

By comparing Xunzi's general principle with "natural law" and "law of Nature" in the West, we can recognize that his *cheng* and "ritual" falls in the category of "natural law," especially its original mode formulated in ancient Greece. In contrast, what the "content of cosmic *cheng*" refers to is actually "law of Nature." For its thorough investigation, people first need to differentiate the law of Nature from that of humans. This requires a logic of scientific investigation, a systematic procedure of experiments, and perhaps, a notion of law as an "imposition" from a transcendent source, such as God in Christianity. Nevertheless, all of these were absent in Xunzi's time. After all, he could not accomplish the task simply by using "analogy," one of the few methods with which he was familiar.

II. 3. The *Zhuangzi*

Since GUO Xiang, one of the earliest commentators of the *Zhuangzi*, scholars have grouped the text into three divisions: seven "Inner Chapters" (*neipian* 《內篇》), fifteen "Outer Chapters" (*waipian* 《外篇》) and eleven "Miscellaneous Chapters" (*zapian* 《雜篇》). According to Liu Xiaogan's classification, the "Inner Chapters" are written by Zhuangzi himself in the mid-Warring States period, whereas the "Outer" and "Miscellaneous" are from others in the last years of the same period (Liu Xiaogan, 48). Similar to the *Analects*, *cheng* appears in the "Inner Chapters" mainly in the form of modifier, meaning, "true" and "real," or "truly" and "really" (*Zhuangzi*, 216-7). Nevertheless, things changed surprisingly in the "Miscellaneous Chapters." There it is applied as a philosophical concept in three ways. First, as in both the *Mencius* and the *Xunzi*, it refers to an inner state in humans' heart that needs to be cultivated constantly, although the goal of cultivation shifts from the construction of a harmonious society to the preservation of individual life. Secondly, like what is in the *Xunzi*, it is regarded as the source of "change," although it no longer designates a ground on which exemplary persons implement governmental measures for an orderly society, but a material force to alter the behaviors of other people. Thirdly, it is used as a name to signify the reality of a thing or things that characterizes one thing as itself.

II. 3. 1. "Cultivation of Cheng*" and "Preservation of Life"*

The chapter "*Gengsang Chu* 庚桑楚" records a truth-seeker's inquiry of Laozi about the principle of life-preservation. With a series of rhetorical questions, Laozi answers, "Can you embrace the One (meaning the Way)? Can you keep from losing it? Do you know where to stop; do you know where to leave off? Do you know how to discard it in others and instead look for it in yourself? Can you be a little baby?" And then, taking baby as an example, he further explaines what the principle of life-preservation is. The baby howls all day, yet its throat never gets hoarse—harmony at its height! The baby makes fists all day, yet its finger never gets cramped—virtue is what it holds to. The baby stares all day without blinking its eyes—it has no preferences in the world of externals. Based on his observation of a baby, Laozi concludes that

> To move without knowing where you are going, to sit at home without knowing what you are doing, traipsing and trailing about with other things, riding along with them on the same wave—this is the basic rule of life-preservation, this and nothing more. (*Zhuangzi*, 785)

The image of a baby embodies the principle of life-preservation: because it possesses *cheng*, it is able to respond to external events in a natural way, and therefore avoid dangers from a turbulent world. To further articulate the desirability of *cheng*, Laozi points out the consequence caused by actions without *cheng*. "If you don't perceive *cheng* within yourself (*chengji* 誠己) and yet try to move forth, each movement will miss the mark. If outside concerns enter and are not expelled, each movement will only add failure to failure" (*Zhuangzi*, 794).

A similar use of *cheng* is also in another chapter, "*XU Wugui* 徐無鬼." To a Marquis' inquiry about his plan to lay down weapons for preserving people's lives, XU Wugui, a hermit, replies that laying down the weapons is actually to sow the seeds for more weapon-wielding. Instead, he suggests that

> If you must do something, cultivate *cheng* in your chest and use it to respond without opposition to the true form of Heaven and earth. Then the people will have won their reprieve from death. Why will you need to appeal to this "laying down of weapons"? (*Zhuangzi*, 827)

The message from the hermit is that "laying down weapons" is still a conscious action, an action not coming from *cheng*. Actually, it may encourage other states to act in opposition to what the Marquis expected: to launch a war against his state, and therefore force him to recruit more soldiers with more weapons. Thus, the best method is to listen to the guidance from *cheng* carefully, and to respond to what occurs naturally.

Cheng in both chapters refers to a state of heart, which connotes naturalness or spontaneity. People need to "perceive" and "cultivate" the state so as to "ride along with things on the same wave" and to "respond without opposition to the true form of Heaven and earth." In their arguments, Laozi and Xu, the hermit, both assumed a commonality between *cheng* in humans and the nature of Heaven and earth. For them, cultivating *cheng* means to keep people's heart in conformity with Heaven and earth, and responding with the guidance of *cheng* means to move in tune with the rhythm of Heaven and earth. It is the most reliable way to preserve life—the life of each individual and the lives of all people.

II. 3. 2. Transformation and Change

The chapter "Old Fisherman" records a conversation between the alleged Confucius and an old fisherman, another hermit. In spite of his possession of superb moral virtues, Confucius failed repeatedly in his social and political endeavors. Dispiritedly, he asked the old fisherman about the right course to realize his ideal. The fisherman's answer was that "If you were diligent in improving yourself, careful to hold fast to the real (*zhen* 真), and would hand over external things to other people, you could avoid these entanglements." "What do you mean by the real?" Confucius inquired. The fisherman replied,

> By the "real" I mean purity (*jing* 精) and *cheng* in their highest degree. He who lacks purity and *cheng* cannot move others.

> Therefore he who forces himself to lament, though he may sound sad, will awaken no grief. He who forces himself to be angry, though he may sound fierce, will arouse no awe. And he who forces himself to be affectionate, though he may smile, will create no air of harmony. True sadness need not make sound to awaken grief; true anger need not show itself to arouse awe; true affection need not smile to create harmony. When a man has the Truth within himself, his spirit may move among external things. That is why the Truth is prized. (*Zhuangzi*, 1032)

The old fisherman differentiated two ways of gaining others' emotional responses to illustrate his point. One was to sound sad intentionally to make other people also sad. The other was to immerse wholeheartedly in one's own sadness, paying no attention to others' response. Paradoxically, the latter is much more effective than the former in awakening other people's grief. To account for this fact, as the old fisherman implied, we have to appeal to empathy, a natural feeling arising from other people's hearts. Sadness with *cheng* that shows naturally in a person's facial and bodily expressions stimulates others to imagine a similar situation with which they themselves may be also entangled. This transfers the grief to those around the person. In the final analysis, the others are actually immersed in their own sadness, although this is caused by the sadness of another. This case tells us that, because of the existence of *cheng*, the sadness of one person can ignite the same feeling in other people. Obviously, the mode of influence here is in line with the "transformation."

In the meantime, *cheng* is also used by Zhuangzi to denote the source of "change," another type of influence. LIE Yukou 列御寇, a mythical figure in the chapter "LIE Yukou," was on his way to the state Qi 齊. But at five of the ten soup stalls at which he stopped to eat, he was served ahead of everybody else. He was scared by this and turned around to come home. To a friend's question why people's hospitality was so scary, he replied that

> If you cannot dispel *cheng* inside you, it oozes out of the body and forms a radiance that, once outside, overpowers men's minds and makes them careless of how they treat their own superiors and old people.... The soup sellers have nothing but their broth to peddle and their margin of gain can't be very large. If people with such skimpy profit and so little power still

> treat me like this, then what would it be like with the ruler of Qi, the lord of a state of ten thousand chariots?...he would want to shift his affairs onto me and make me work out some solution—that was what scared me. (*Zhuangzi*, 1037)

This passage interests us for two reasons. First, it seems to be the first record about *cheng* as a material force in the history of Chinese philosophy. This *cheng* may be roughly compared to a nuclear center overflowing with energy. The energy oozes out of LIE Yukou's body as a powerful radiance to prevail over other people's minds, making them alter their conduct. Secondly, the radiance of *cheng* is a natural process that involves no subjective consciousness or intention. Being a hermit, LIE Yukou enjoyed his individual freedom and cared only about his own life-preservation. He had never thought of attaining some social or ethical goals with his *cheng*, and never even realized how powerful it was until his trip to the state of Qi. These two points distinguish the "change" of Zhuangzi from that of Xunzi. In Xunzi, a ruler or teacher with *cheng* sincerely and intentionally implements the regulations or promotes doctrines that they value, whereas *cheng* in the context of Zhuangzi seems to be a mystical force. It changes people through a natural course, which is out of the control of even its possessor. As will be seen in the next chapter, this use later becomes very popular in the circle of religious Daoism.

*III. 3. 3. "*Cheng *of Heaven and Earth" and "*Cheng *of the Great Man"*

The third use of *cheng* in Zhuangzi is also contained in the chapter "*XU Wugui*," meaning something equivalent to "*shi*" (reality) that we examined before. To concretize its content, I would like to focus my discussion on two phrases, "*cheng* of Heaven and earth" (*tiandi zhi cheng* 天地之誠) and "*cheng* of the great man" (*daren zhi cheng* 大人之誠). In the chapter, Ziqi 子綦, a sage-like person, says about his life style as that

> When my son and I go wandering, we wander through Heaven and earth. He and I seek our delight in Heaven and our food from the earth. He and I do not engage in any undertakings, do

> not engage in any plots, and do not engage in any peculiarities. He and I ride on the *cheng* of Heaven and earth and do not allow things to set us at odds with it. He and I stroll and saunter in unity, but never do we try to do what is appropriate to the occasion. (*Zhuangzi*, 858)

"*Cheng* of Heaven and earth" has a conceptual affinity to the "realness of Heaven and earth" (*tiandi zhi zheng* 天地之正), a phrase from "Xiao Yaoyou 逍遙游" (Free and Easy Wandering) in the *Inner Chapters*.[3] Hence, a study of the latter may throw a light on the meaning of the former. "Free and Easy Wandering" refers to the same LIE Yukou by saying that,

> Liezi could ride the wind and go soaring around with cool and breezy skill, but after fifteen days he came back to earth.... He escaped the trouble of walking, but he still had to depend on something to get around. If he had only mounted on the realness of Heaven and earth, ridden the changes of the six breaths, and thus wandered through the boundless, then what would he have to depend on? (*Zhuangzi*, 17)

About this passage GUO Xiang writes, "'Heaven and earth' is the general name for all things. The things are the substance of Heaven and earth while 'nature' (*ziran* 自然) is their realness. 'Nature' means to exist spontaneously without any action.... Therefore 'mounted on the realness of Heaven and earth' simply means following the nature of all things" (*Zhuangzi*, 17). From his interpretation we derive that the terms "nature," "realness," and *cheng* are all interchangeable with each other, and the realness or *cheng* of Heaven and earth means actually the essential attributes of all things in Nature. With the case of Ziji, Zhuangzi teaches his readers that all things possess a unique realness or *cheng*, which humans need to identify and follow with, rather than oppose. Ziji is wise because he knows that, for instance, rivers possess their own *cheng*, which can either carry on or turn over

---

[3] Many specialists of the *Zhuangzi* agree that the chapter "XU Wugui" has a close affinity to the *Inner Chapters*. For examples, ZHANG Hengshou argues, "When examining its content carefully, we find that it contains a number of historical materials and theoretical discussions as valuable as those in [the inner chapters] 'Free and Easy Wandering' and "Discussion on Making All things Equal" (*Qi wu lun* 齊物論) (ZHANG Henshou 1989).

a boat. Hence, to avoid a disastrous consequence, he will not put too much heavy cargo on the boat. This is the reason why he is able to preserve his life in any circumstance.

The similar use of *cheng* exists also in Zhuangzi's another phrase, "*cheng* of the great man." The context in which the phrase occurs reads that,

> The sea does not refuse the rivers that come flowing eastward into it—it is the perfection of greatness. The sage embraces all Heaven and earth, and his bounty extends to the whole world, yet no one knows who he is or what family he belongs to.... This is what is called the great man.... Nothing possesses a larger measure of greatness than Heaven and earth, yet when have they ever gone in search of greatness? He who understands what it means to possess greatness does not seek, does not lose, does not reject, and does not change himself for the sake of things. He returns to himself and finds the inexhaustible; he follows antiquity and discovers the imperishable—this is *cheng* of the great man. (*Zhuangzi*, 852)

The "greatness" is the connotation of "*cheng* of the great man." It is a quality that enables the sea to accept the flowing of rivers, and the sages to embrace in their minds all things. This quality always comes with those who are great, "inexhaustible" and "imperishable." Because of its presence, these people are entitled "great," enjoying life constantly within the flux of the universe.

Zhuangzi's two phrases, "*cheng* of Heaven and earth" and "*cheng* of great man" exemplify a productive pattern for conceiving new concepts. By the same model, Chinese thinkers in later times devised a great number of terms, which all point to the nature or reality of a thing, or things, such as *cheng* of mountains, *cheng* of crops, and even *cheng* of dogs.

II. 4. *Centrality and Commonality*

Centrality and Commonality may be divided into four parts in accordance with its intellectual content. The first part (ch.1), as ZHU Xi says, is the "quintessence" (*tiyao* 體要) of the entire text (Zhu, 1983, 18). It explicitly defines five concepts, "human nature," "Way," "education" (*jiao* 教), "centrality" (*zhong* 中), and "harmony" (*he* 和).

Jointly they constitute a philosophical framework regarding the relationship of Heaven and humans. The second part (chs. 2-11) quotes a number of passages from Confucius to explain the term "centrality" and "commonality" and people's various attitudes toward them. The third part (chs. 12-19), in a miscellaneous manner, quotes Confucius' words to elucidate the universality of the Way. The fourth, and the most important part (chs. 20-33), discusses *cheng* and its relation to "human nature" and "the way of Heaven." The text brings almost all the uses of *cheng* that we have examined hitherto into a coherent system, providing us with a brief, but comprehensive statement about *cheng*. For this reason, it has been regarded as the most important text in the history of *cheng*, even "perhaps the most philosophical in the whole body of ancient Confucian literature" (Chan, 96).

However, despite the text's lofty position in Chinese culture, dispute about its authorship has never ceased. SIMA Qian 司馬遷 (?135B.C.E. -?), the author of *Shiji* 《史記》 (*the Records of Grand Historian*), first mentioned that it was Zisi 子思, the grandson of Confucius, who "composed *Commonality and Centrality*." This opinion was widely accepted by mainstream scholars, including the classicists ZHENG Xuan and KONG Yingda, and the philosophers LI Ao and ZHU Xi. OUYANG Xiu 歐陽修 (1007-1072) might be the first major scholar who questioned its legitimacy. His voice was echoed by other Song scholars, such as YE Shi 葉適 (1150-1223) and WANG Bo 王柏 (1197-1274). Later in the Qing dynasty, more scholars, including YUAN Mei 袁枚 (1716-1798) and CUI Shu 崔述 (1740-1816) joined this group of skeptics. Based on careful examination of its intellectual and textual contents, they pointed to the contradictions and inconsistencies that arose when Zisi was treated as the author. In modern times, most scholars, including FENG Youlan and QIAN Mu, have sided with the skeptical group. They generally agreed that more than one person was involved in the composition of the text, and its final formation might be dated to roughly the third century B.C.E.. This is the view with which I agree.

In parallel to the traditional view is a time-honored position that the text primarily reflected the idea of Zisi-Mencius school—the mainstream Confucianism of the time. The obvious evidence was that Mencius' long passage about *cheng* (*Mengzi*, 4A12), which I quoted before, was almost completely reiterated in *Centrality and Commonality*. I accept this position with a significant reservation. It seems to me that, as far as the formation of the system of *cheng* in the text is concerned, Xunzi's contribution may be much greater than what people have often thought. The strong evidence lies in the similarity between the statement regarding ethical, cosmic, universal *cheng*, and their relationship in *Centrality and Commonality* and that in Xunzi's long passage examined before. To avoid unnecessary misunderstandings, of course, I would like to add that *Centrality and Commonality* greatly enriches and refines the points that Xunzi holds.

II. 4. 1. Cheng *and Other Virtues*

In *Centrality and Commonality*, *cheng* is not only a cardinal virtue like prudence, justice, temperance, and courage in the ancient Greece, but also a central conception that holds up all the other virtues together, and lays a ground for them to be regarded as virtues. To specify this "centrality," I would like to contrast it with the term "good" that Aristotle elucidates in his *Nicomachean Ethics*. According to Aristotle, human beings have a specific nature; and that nature is such that they have certain aims and goals, and by nature they move toward a specific *telos*. The "good" refers to this "telos," which stands as a core concept in the virtue system, or as an "overriding conception" of virtues. About the content of "good" and its relation with other virtues, MacIntyre explains,

> Aristotle has cogent argument against identifying good with money, with honor or with pleasure. He gives to it the name of *eudaimonia*—as so often there is a difficulty in translation: blessedness, happiness, prosperity. It is the state of being well and doing well in being well, of a man's being well-favored himself and in relation to the divine.... The virtues are precisely those qualities the possession of which will enable an individual to achieve *eudaimonia* and the lack of which will frustrate his movement toward the *telos*. (MacIntyre, 148)

We can roughly define the relation between virtues and good as that of means and end: the exercise of virtues is a means to the end of achieving the good for human beings, although, as MacIntyre warns, that description may be a little "ambiguous."

In contrast, *cheng* as a central concept associates with other virtues in a different way. *Centrality and Commonality* reads,

> There are five universal paths (*dadao* 達道), and the way by which they are practiced is three. The five are those governing the relationships between ruler and minister, between father and son, between husband and wife, between older and younger brothers, and of intercourse between friends. These five are universal paths in the world. Wisdom (*zhi* 智), compassion (*ren* 仁), and courage (*yong* 勇), these three are the universal virtues (*dade* 達德). The way by which they are practiced is one. (*Zhongyong*, 28-9)

In terms of the logic of the text, the three "universal virtues" are the assurance for the proper practice of the five "universal paths," and, in turn, the "one" is the assurance for the presence of the three. Using the metaphor that Chinese thinkers favored, people may name the one as the "root" from which grows up the three branches as well as the five fruits. With the same approach, the text continues to claim that

> There are nine standards (*jiujing* 九經) by which to administer empire, states, and families. They are: cultivating one's own character, honoring the worthy, being affectionate to relatives, being respectful towards the great ministers, identifying oneself with the welfare of the whole body of officers, treating the common people as one's own children, attracting all classes of artisans, showing tenderness to foreigners, and extending kindly and awesome influence on the feudal lords." (*Zhongyong*, 30)

After a detailed elucidation of the necessity for implementing the nine standards, the text summarizes, "There are nine standards by which to govern the empire, its states, and the family, but the way by which they are followed is one" (*Zhongyong*, 30). Unlike the passage about the "universal paths" and "universal virtues," which address every person in a society, this passage mainly appeals to the rulers, demanding them to fulfill their duty of harmonizing the entire world by faithfully applying the nine "standards." Nevertheless, that the same "one" occurs also here indicates that it is the sole ground for the proper conducts of all people, including the rulers themselves, and for the proper course of any social activities and administrations.

Chinese thinkers since the Song dynasty all agree that this "one" refers to nothing but *cheng* (Cheng and Cheng, 1156-7; Zhu 1983, 29-30). It is related to the other virtues in a way unfamiliar to both Geach and Aristotle. As mentioned in the last chapter, for Geach's interpretation of virtues, Christian "truth" is such a crucial notion that a brave action should not be properly named as "courage" if it doesn't serve "truth." Meanwhile, Aristotle views "courage" as the means for the end of human "good;" it is the final attainment of the end or *telos* that proves the legitimacy and desirability of "courage." However, to the author of *Centrality and Commonality*, since "courage" and *cheng* are in a relationship comparable to that of branch and root, if there is *cheng*, there must also be "courage." People are not pursuing *cheng* by practicing their "courage, but rather concentrating on the cultivation of *cheng* to bring their "courage" into being. This is the reason why the *Great Learning* proposes, "From the son of Heaven to the common people, all must regard cultivation of the personal character as the root. There is never a case when the root is in disorder and yet the branches are in order" (*Daxue*, 4).

In the Song dynasty, ZHU Xi introduced a new pair of concepts, namely body or substance (*ti* 體) and functions (*yong* 用) to expound the relationship between *cheng* and other virtues. A passage from his *Conversations* reads, "Question: Zhou (Dunyi) said, '*cheng* is the root of the five cardinal virtues.' Does this mean that *cheng* is the real principle that functions in these five ways? Answer: Yes" (Zhu 1986, 2393). Let me illustrate this relationship with a case of "flame." A flame as a substance has a number of functions in reference to various contexts. People may use it for light to read at night, to start a fire for warming in the cold, and to frighten beasts away for a safe sleep in the woods. The point is similar to the model of root and branch: if there is flame (*cheng*), there must be its various uses (virtues). So, for pursuing virtues, there is nothing more helpful than cultivating *cheng* in our heart.

II. 4. 2. The Sage

One of the major contributions of *Centrality and Commonality* to Chinese philosophy is that it enriches and systemizes the concept of sage. I would like to show this by surveying briefly the history of the concept. In the *Analects*, the term occurred eight times, four as "*sheng*" 聖 (sage), four as "*shengren*" 聖人 (sagely person) (Taylor, 40). It mainly referred to an ideal ruler, such as the sage king, Yao or Shun, who is capable of enacting humaneness to transform the whole world to peace and order (*Lunyu*, 6.8). The *Analects* records,

> A great official asked Zigong 子貢, a student of Confucius, "Is the Master a sage? How is it that he has so many skills?" Zigong said, "Certainly Heaven has intended him to become a sage, and also he has many skills." When Confucius heard this, he said, "Does the great official know me? When I was young, I was in humble circumstances, and therefore, I acquired many skills to do simply things of humble folk. Does an exemplary person need to have so many slills? He doesn't." (*Lunyu*, 9.6)

This paragraph shows three opinions concerning the sagehood of Confucius. The great official assumes that Confucius is a sage since he has so many skills. His saying implies that "having many skills" may characterize a person as a "sage." In contrast, Zigong differentiates the sagehood from "having many skills" and, as an admirer of the Master, he adds that Confucius possesses not only the quality of a sage, but also many skills. It is Zigong's point that sagehood and skills are two different categories. A sage doesn't necessarily have many skills and, by the same token, "having many skills" doesn't necessarily make a person sage. The more important is Confucius' assessment of himself. He first changes the topic about sagehood to that of an exemplary person, and then argues in Zigong's line of thinking that his possession of many skills has nothing to do with his quality of being an exemplary person, since the latter needn't possess many skills. It is noteworthy that Confucius doesn't view himself as a sage; what he expects is simply to be regarded by others as an exemplary person.

The same use of the term is found in the *Mencius,* although Mencius gives much attention to the moral virtues that the sage exemplifies. A passage from him reads,

> The compass and the carpenter's square are the culmination of squares and circles; the sage is the culmination of humanity. If one wishes to be a ruler, he must fulfill the duties proper to a ruler; if one wishes to be a subject, he must fulfill the duties

> proper to a subject. In both cases all one has to do is to model oneself on [the sage kings of] Yao and Shun (*Mengzi*, 4A2).

In addition, Mencius proposed a new idea that the sage and ordinary people are the same in nature, and therefore, all people are able to become sages so long as they persistently cultivate their own heart-mind. It is his argument that

> Now things of the same kind are all alike. Why should we have doubts when it comes to human? The sage and I are of the same kind.... All palates have the same preference in taste; all ears in sound; all eyes in beauty. Should heart prove to be nothing in common? What is common to all hearts? It is reason (*li* 理) and rightness. The sage is simply the man first to discover this common element in my heart. (*Mengzi*, 6A7)

Actually, this argument for the commonality between the sage and ordinary people is a crucial part in his theory of the good nature of humans.

While treating the sage still as an ideal ruler, Xunzi further presents the sage as a perfect character to whom the ordinary people need to emulate and submit. "Heaven is the acme of loftiness, earth is the acme of depth, the boundless is the acme of breadth, and the sage is the acme of the Way (of humans)" (*Xunzi*, 357). Besides the contribution to a society, according to Xunzi, the sage also plays an indispensable role for the universe.

> Heaven can give birth to creatures but it cannot order them; earth can bear man up but it cannot govern them. All creatures of the universe, all who belong to the species of man, must await the sage before they can attain their proper places. (*Xunzi*, 366)

This saying sounds a little mystical: since the sage is not an anthropomorphic deity as God in Judaic-Christian tradition, but a human being who undertakes actions only in society, how can the sage affect all creatures in the universe? A possible explanation is that, as for Xunzi, the universe is an organic unity in which the three "acmes"—Heaven, earth, and the sage all have major domains for their performance, and, at the same time, the consequence caused by the action in one domain will influence what is going on in the others. In the same sense, the sage's construction of orderly society is not only a social event, but also contributes to the harmony in the entire universe.

The three ideas—the sage is an ideal ruler (Confucius); the nature of a sage is the same as that of ordinary people (Mencius); the sage is indispensable for a good human society, and for a harmonious universe as well (Xunzi)—are all contained in *Centrality and Commonality*. Meanwhile, the text starts to associate the sage with the "absolute *cheng*" (*zhichenng* 至誠) (*Zhongyong*, 21). Similar to Bodhisattva in Mahayana Buddhism, Jesus Christ in Christianity, or Mohammed in Islam, the sage stands as a spiritual linkage connecting Heaven with humans. The sage is a human being, living among ordinary people and sharing with them all kinds of earthly feelings—happiness, anger, sorrow, and pleasure. Meanwhile, as a perfect person, the sage's mind fully reflects the reality of Heaven, and the sage's actions naturally conform to the wave, movement, and rhythm of the universe. Therefore, the sage is able to "hit upon what is right without effort, apprehend without thinking, and be naturally and easily in harmony with the Way" (*Zhongyong*, 31).

In a manner reminding us of Xunzi, *Centrality and Commonality* draws a detailed picture about the sage's influence on humans and Heaven. It is a "gradual" influence, starting with cultivation of one's own nature, and ending at the harmony with the universe.

> Only he who is possessed of absolute *cheng* can fully develop (*jin* 盡) his nature. If he can fully develop his nature, he can then fully develop the nature of others. If he can fully develop the nature of others, he can then fully develop the nature of things. If he can fully develop the nature of things, he can then assist (*zan* 贊) the transforming and nourishing process of Heaven and earth. If he can assist the transforming and nourishing process of Heaven and earth, he can thus form a trinity with Heaven and earth. (*Zhongyong*, 32)

This passage depicts five steps through which sages exert their influence: developing their own nature, developing others' nature, developing the nature of things, assisting the transforming and nourishing process of Heaven and earth, and forming a trinity with Heaven and earth. Obviously, it presupposes that there is a nature or reality common to all beings, the sages and ordinary people, Heaven and earth. For completing all the steps, the sages need only to attend to the cultivation of their own heart to let their heavenly endowned nature develop fully. This establishes the sage as a moral model, an example that other people can emulate to fully develop their own nature. Next, thanks to the full development of their nature, people will let a myriad of things develop their nature.

A key term regarding the development of the nature of things is "*shi*" 時 (time, or proper time). As mentioned by Mencius, there is "the time (busy season) in the fields," "the time to hatch and axe wood," and "the time for chickens, pigs, and dogs to breed." A wise ruler who properly issues his orders in terms of the "time" will ensure that people have "more grain than they can eat," "more timber than they can use," and "more meat than they can consume" (*Mencius*, 1A3). Actually, "time" is a concept of Nature that no sage could or would change. Ultimately, the sage's role is simply to encourage people to act in terms of it and to prevent any humans from interrupting and violating the seasonal development of things. By this way, the sage assures the full development of the nature of things.

A controversy on the meaning of "*zan*" occurs among scholars when the last two steps come forth: what does the term "*zan*" mean? And how does the sage "*zan*" the transforming and nourishing process? CHENG Yi held that "*zan*" meant "to participate in" (*canzan* 參贊), referring to the sage's participation in the movements of the universe and acting in tune with its rhythm (Cheng and Cheng, 133). Disagreeing with him, ZHU Xi, based on his observation of the different functions of Heaven and the sage, asserts that "*zan*" means "to assist" (*zanzhu* 贊助). "Heaven can give birth to plants, but it is humans who plough and sow; water can moist things, but it is humans who do irrigation; .... What does this mean if it is not 'assist?'.... So Master CHENG Yi is wrong!" (Zhu 1986, 1570).

Modern thinkers mainly read "*zan*" in three ways. QIAN Mu and FENG Youlan explain it as "to know the transforming and nourishing process" of Nature (Qian, 2. 239; Feng, 3. 119). In my view, this reading transforms a problem of action into a problem of knowledge; it seems not to be in line with the basic concern of *Centrality and Commonality*. TU Wei-Ming interprets "*zan*" as an "ontological assertion that there is a possibility of human participation in the cosmic creativity" (Tu, 78). In the same vein, Thomas Metzger says that the text means that the sage possesses a "vast, material transformative power" (Metzger, 121). They both assign to the sage a role of co-creator of the universe, a role played often by anthropomorphic deity. This may not be consistent with the tradition of religious skepticism in Chinese philosophy. The third explanation echos ZHU Xi's interpretation to limit the sage's action of "*zan*" to the human world. It argues that the sage's achievement ultimately helps Heaven and earth to fulfill their task, since the human world is also a part of the universe. This is the position with which I concur.

After the Warring States period, the concept of sage was further evolved along two lines: mystification and moralization. The advancement of Confucius' position exemplifies the first case. Before the Han times, Confucius was respected primarily as a great "teacher" who transmitted the culture of Zhou 周 dynasty (11 century-256 B.C.E.) through his teaching and editing of ancient classics. However, since DONG Zhongshu 董仲舒, he was often viewed as a sage, even a sage-king. Dong contended that Confucius, shortly before his death, received from Heaven a mandate to correct the fault of the decadent Zhou dynasty and to establish the institutions of a new king and new dynasty. Confucius then made use of the *Spring and Autumn* to accomplish this mission (Dong, 157).

Next, Confucius was further conceived as a supernatural figure in various texts of "prognostication and apocrypha" (*chenwei* 讖緯). An Apocryphal text around first century B.C.E. says that

> On Confucius' breast there was a writing that said: 'the act of instituting a new dynasty has been decided and the rule of the world has been transformed.'... Sages are not born for nothing; they must surely institute something, in order to reveal the mind of Heaven. Thus, Confucius, as a wooden-tongue bell, institutes laws for the world. (Feng 1953, 129)

Equipped with an idea from *Centrality and Commonality* that the sage is "as great as a spirit" because he is able to "foreknow" if a nation or a family is about to flourish or perish (*Zhongyong*, 33), another text stated with an even more mystical tone.

> The sage-king knew that when a period of highest property has been reached, it is followed by decay; when heat attains its apogee, it is followed by cold; when joy reached its height, it is fol-

> lowed by grief.... The purpose of instituting rites and creating music is thereby to reform the popular manner, promote auspicious customs, cause the rains and dews to come at proper time, and enable people to obtain blessings from sovereign Heaven. (Feng 1953, 127)

Contrary to the mystification, the Neo-Confucians in the Song-Ming period (around 10- 16 centuries) strove to moralize the sage. WANG Yangming pointed out, "The reason why the sage has become sage is that his mind has become completely identical with the principle of Heaven (*tianli* 天理) and is no longer mixed with any impurity of selfish human desire (*renyu* 人欲)" With the same consideration, he criticized a long-existing error among thinkers—seeking for sagehood only in knowledge and ability.

> They regard the sage as knowing all and being able to do all, and they feel they have to have all the knowledge and ability of the world before they can succeed. Consequently they do not direct their efforts toward the principle of Heaven but merely cripple their spirit and exhaust their energy in scrutinizing books, investigating the names and varieties of things, and imitating the forms and traces [of the acts of the ancients]. As their knowledge becomes more extensive, their selfish desire become more numerous, and as their abilities become greater and greater, the principle of Heaven becomes increasingly obscured from them. (WANG Yangming, 119)

Wang believes that the "sage" is not a concept of intelligence or ability, but that of morality or virtue. Since the potency of being the sage exists in the heart of all people, anyone "even an ordinary person, if he is willing to learn so as to enable his mind to become completely identical with the principle of Heaven can also become a sage" (WANG Yangming, 119).

The two tendencies of mystification and moralization both find their successors in Chinese history. Inheriting the first one, religious Daoists moved to paint the sage as an immortal figure who, with supernatural powers, can change human affairs and even the course of natural events. In the meantime, all the major Confucian thinkers since the Song-Ming period tended to view the sage as the embodiment of a perfect moral ideal. By arguing for the accessibility of sagehood to everyone in the world, they encouraged people to undertake moral cultivation so as to unite with the principle of Heaven.

II. 4. 3. The System and Images

The narrative order of the fourth part of *Centrality and Commonality* epitomizes the historical process in which *cheng* evolved from human life to the transcendental realm. In this section, I will first discuss the system of *cheng* in the text by referring to the correspondence of the narrative and the historical. Then, I will examine two terms in the text, "ceaselessness" and "no duplicity," that tell people what *cheng* is, or even more exact, what it "looks" like.

As is seen before, the use of *cheng* in the twentieth chapter of the text is still limited to the human world, designating the common foundation of the "five universal paths," the "three universal virtues," and the "nine standards" (ethical *cheng*). However, without any warning, a theoretical leap occurs: "*Cheng* as such (*chengzhe* 誠者) is the way of Heaven, and striving to be *cheng* (*chengzhizhe* 誠之者) is the way of humans." With the two terms in this passage, "*cheng* as such" refers to the reality of Heaven, while "striving to be *cheng*" to the moral effort to live in accordance with "*cheng* as such," and to retain the human nature that Heaven imparts. Also, they are personalized respectively as the sage and the worthy. Because of its association with the reality of Heaven and the sage, *cheng* acquires a universal significance (universal *cheng*).

However, the real point of the text is not to solidify the distinction between the sage and the worthy, but rather to underscore the possibility for their unification. "When enlightenment (*ming* 明)results from *cheng*, it is to be ascribed to nature; when *cheng* results from englightenment, it is to be ascribed to education" Both CHENG Yi and ZHU Xi, among others, hold that the first sentence explains how the sages enlighten other people by their *cheng*, while the second explains how the worthy attains *cheng* by education (Cheng and Cheng, 1158; Zhu 1983, 32). In light of this interpretation, the unification can occur from two directions: from *cheng* to enlightenment (the sage), and from enlightenment (education) to *cheng* (the worthy). The text shows its confidence on the unification with another sentence:

"Given *cheng*, there must be enlightenment, and given enlightenment, there must be *cheng*" (*Zhongyong*, 32).

The next three chapters shift back to the sages to depict their influence. As stated in the last section, the sages form a trinity with Heaven and earth by developing their own nature or *cheng*. Here the text further specifies the process in which they complete transformation of people.

> As there is *cheng*, there will be its expression. As it is expressed, it will become conspicuous. As it become conspicuous, it will become clear. As it becomes clear, it will move others. As it moves others it will change them. As it changes them, it will transform them. Only the absolute *cheng* in the world (the sage) can transform others." (*Zhongyong*, 33)

After defining the sage as the humanly embodiment of *cheng*, the text, in the twenty-fifth chapter, begins to illustrate its universality by referring alternately to humans and Nature. "*Cheng* means self-completion, and the Way means self-directing." According to ZHU Xi, the first sentence is about *cheng* in Nature, defined as the ground for self-completion of things, while the second is about *cheng* in humans, conceived as the path which humans walk along by themselves (ZHU Xi 1983, 33). The point is that *cheng* as a universal principle simultaneously affects both things and humans, letting them complete their developments or fulfill their social duties. The alternate description is phrased more obviously in the following passage. "*Cheng* is the beginning and end of things. Without *cheng* there would be nothing. Therefore the exemplary person values (the effort of) pursuing *cheng* (*cheng zhi wei gui* 誠之爲貴)" (*Zhongyong*, 34).

I would like to further articulate on the cosmic *cheng* about which the first sentence talks. It is CHENG Yi's comment that,

> *Cheng* simply means 'reality.' If there is really such principle (*cheng*), there must be this thing; if there is really such thing, there must be such function.... a dustpan that cannot winnow away the chaff is not a dustpan; a dipper that cannot ladle out wine and soup is not a dipper. Seeding rice here, people can harvest rice; seeding wheat here, people can harvest wheat. Failing to seed, but expecting to harvest, people even cannot gain barnyard grass, not to mention rice and wheat. (Cheng and Cheng, 1160)

Here *cheng* denotes the reality of a thing or things, whose existence ensures that the thing or things can be properly named as such. The presence of "winnow away the chaff" as a function shows that a dustpan still keeps its reality/*cheng*. Similarly, when the function of "ladle out wine and soup" ceases to exist, the dipper loses its reality /*cheng*. By the same token, without seeding real rice (the rice with its reality /*cheng*) in spring, there will be no harvest in the autumn. Also, the reality/*cheng* of rice differs from that of wheat, so this harvest must be a harvest of rice, not wheat or something else. In correspondence, we humans also have our own reality/*cheng*, which Mencius defines as "good nature" or the "four hearts." Losing it, a human would not be human anymore. The exemplary persons value *cheng*, attending to be sincere to their universal mind/nature/reality/*cheng*, because they want to retain their nature.

As an attribute, "*cheng* is the most simple and the easiest," (Cheng and Cheng, 1158), because we can easily sense it in things around. Meanwhile, it is also the most important, because it is the common ground for assuring a myriad of things as themselves. As a concept, it is the highest abstract that signifies the common reality of all things, and, at the same time, characterizes each thing as being itself.

To give people a clear idea of what *cheng* is, or what *cheng* looks like, *Centrality and Commonality* describes it with two metaphorical terms, "ceaselessness" and "no duplicity." Regarding the first one it says that,

> Absolute *cheng* is ceaseless. Being ceaseless, it is lasting. Being lasting, it is evident. Being evident, it is infinite. Being infinite, it is extensive and deep. Being extensive and deep, it is high and brilliant. It is because it is extensive and deep that it contains all things. It is because it is high and brilliant that it overshadows all things. (*Zhongyong*, 34)

The term "ceaseless" presents an image that people can perceive when, for example, observing the flowing of rivers, the motion of heavenly bodies, or the vicissitude of the seasons. The message is that, as exhibited by these constant movements, *cheng* exists in all things, and penetrates through all the steps in which they develop. It is always there; its influence continues without any interval.

In the same vein, the text talks about "no duplicity" that, "The way of Heaven and earth may be completely described in one sentence: They possess no duplicity and so they produce things in an unfathomable way" (*Zhongyong*, 34). Here "The way of Heaven and earth" is another name for *cheng*. By referring to the metaphor of "no duplicity," the text alludes to an impression we have when comparing a mountain today with the same one a decade ago, or a fruit we pick up today with the fruit from the same tree one year ago. The mountain is still the same mountain, and peach does not change into apple. The same mountain will accommodate the same kinds of animals and birds, and the same tree will bear the same fruit. This pictures, in another way, the essence of *cheng*.

With an eloquent and colorful passage, the text explains why and how *cheng* of Heaven and earth continuously (ceaseless) and consistently (no duplicity) produces and reproduces things year-by-year, generation-by-generation.

> The Heaven now before us is only this bright, shining spot; but when viewed in its unlimited extent, the sun, moon, stars, and constellations are suspended in it and all things are covered by it. The earth before us is but a handful of soil; but in its breadth and depth, it sustains mountains like *Hua* 華 and *Yue* 岳 without feeling their weight, contains the rivers and seas without letting them leaking away, and sustains all things. The mountain before us is only a fistful of straw; but in all the vastness of its size, grass and trees grow upon it, birds and beasts dwell on it, and store of precious things (minerals) are discovered in it. The river before us is but a spoonful of water, but in all its unfathomable depth, the monsters, dragons, fishes, and turtles are produced in them, and wealth becomes abundant because of it. (*Zhongyong*, 35)

The pictorial terms—"bright, shining spot," "a handful of soil," "a fistful of straw," and "a spoonful of liquid" respectively refer to *cheng* of Heaven, earth, mountains, and rivers. The message is the same as what we have already learned—that *cheng* is simple, but fundamental; it is invisitble, but powerful; it is neither behind or above things, but in them and responsible for their existence.

It is noteworthy that the text also describes the sage with the similar metaphors. One example reads,

> The *Book of Songs* says, "the mandate of Heaven, how beautiful and everlasting (*buyi* 不已)!" This is to say, this is what makes Heaven to be Heaven. Again, it says, "How shining is it, the purity of (the sage) King Wen's 文 virtue!" This is to say, this is what makes King Wen what he is. Purity likewise is everlasting. (*Zhongyong*, 35)

The term "everlasting," which is interchangeable with "ceaseless," is applied to both Heaven and the sage. This evidences again that, according to the text, the sage is the embodiment of universal *cheng*, and an arch-stone that integrates ethical *cheng* and cosmic *cheng*.

II. 5. The Contemporary Scholarship

In recent years, Roger T. Ames nd David L. Hall have undertaken an expansive project to free the research of pre-Modern Chinese philosophy in the West from the limitations set by the traditional translations. In terms of their analysis, there are two things responsible for the limitation. First, the "tendentious motives of Christian missionaries" resulted in a number of "theologically freighted terms that have entered the Chinese/English dictionaries that serve as primary resource for our understanding of Chinese culture." Secondly, and the more serious, it is "associated with the employment of the default vocabulary of both demotic and philosophical discourse in the West" (Ames and Hall, 5-6). Ames and Hall maintain that "Our Western languages are substance-oriented and are, therefore, most relevant to the descriptions and interpretations of a world defined by discreteness, objectivity, and permanence. Such languages are ill-disposed to describe and interpret a world, such as that of the Chinese, that is primarily characterized by continuity, process, and becoming" (Ames and Hall, 6). As a part of their project, they retranslated *Centrality and Commonality* with a "language of process" or "language of focus and field," "in order to illuminate [its] context and argument" (Ames and Hall, 7).

As a response to this inspiration and challenge, *Dao: a Journal of Comparative Philosophy* issued a symposium with eight scholarly essays. Here I would like to join their discussion to show my position on the term "creativity," which Ames and Hall rendered for *cheng*.

II. 5. 1. New Position

Whitehead, from whom Ames and Hall borrowed the term "creativity," writes that,

> In all philosophical theory there is an ultimate which is actual by virtue of its accidents.... In the philosophy of organism this ultimate is termed 'creativity'.... In monistic philosophies... [t]his ultimate is God, who is equivalently termed 'The Absolute.' In such monistic schemes, the ultimate is illegitimately allowed a final 'eminent' reality, beyond that ascribed to any of its accidents. In this general position the philosophy of organism seems to approximate more to some strains of Indian, or Chinese, thought than to Western Asiatic, or European, thought. (Whitehead 1978, 10-11)

Along with his line of thinking, Ames and Hall defines "creativity" by contrasting it to "power:"

> "Creativity" is a notion that can be characterized only in terms of self-actualization. Unlike power relationships that require that tensions among component elements be resolved in favor of one of the components, in relations defined by creativity there is no otherness, no separation or distancing, nothing to be overcome. (Ames and Hall, 12)

According to them, "power" refers to an external causation or effective causality in which God as the Omnipotent Other stands over as a maker, causing the world into being, and imposing laws on the world. In contrast, "creativity" refers to an internal relationship, in which the immanent creative principle or natural tendency of everything renews itself in its transactional relationship with other creative processes. Power is the production of intended effects; creativity, on the other hand, is the spontaneous production of novelty, irreducible through causal analysis. Power is exercised with respect to and over others; creativity is always reflexive and is exercised over and with respect to "self" (Ames and Hall, 13).

In Chinese philosophy, according to Ames and Hall, the term *cheng* denotes what "creativity" conveys. Their position is clearly in line with the idea of, at least, two distinguished contemporary scholars. Wing-tsit Chan insists that *cheng* "is not just a state of mind, but an active force that is always transforming things and completing things, and drawing man and Heaven together in the same current" (Chan 1963, 96). Phrasing the same idea more bluntly, TU Wei-ming claims that *cheng* "... can be conceived as a form of creativity... it is that which brings about the transforming and nourishing process of heaven and earth" (Tu, 81-2).

With the similar approach, Ames and Hall first try to justify their new translation by associating it with the traditional ones, "integrity" and "sincerity."

> In a world of changing events, "integrity" suggests an active process of bringing circumstances together in a meaningful way to achieve the coherence that meaningfulness implies. As such, "integrity" suggests a creative process. "Sincerity" connotes the subjective form of feeling with which that creative process proceeds. That is, it suggests the mode or emotional tone that promotes successful integration.... Thus "sincerity" as "the absence of duplicity," "integrity" as "wholeness," and "creativity" as the process leading to the achievement of such wholeness, can within different contexts all be viable translations. (Ames and Hall, 61)

Meanwhile, the authors of the aforementioned statements argue that, compared with the other two translations, the sense that "creativity" carries is the "most central" to *Centrality and Commonality*, because it "brings attention to the centrality of cosmic creativity" as its main theme (Ames and Hall, 61-2).

It seems to me that Ames' and Hall's position is composed of three points. First, "creativity" is not the only proper translated name for *cheng*, but rather clustering with "integrity " and "sincerity" to designate the entirety of *cheng*. It underlies the main theme of *Centrality and Commonality*, although this doesn't mean that the other two names are improper and therefore should be abandoned. Secondly, the new name is mainly employed to underline the cosmic significance of *cheng*, indicating that *cheng* is the ultimate ground for the existence of a myriad of things and that the existence and interaction of things are spontaneous, involving no external power or imposed law. Thirdly, the new name is coined primarily for *cheng* in *Centrality and Commonality*. This seems to imply that it is improper to extend its use to all Chinese texts in which *cheng* appear as a philosophical concept. These three points complement and condition each other to constitute the two authors' position on the new translated name, to which I certainly consent.

II. 5. 2. Further Exploration

The topic of this study, the history of the idea of *cheng*, allows me to move beyond *Centrality and Commonality* itself to examine two issues related to "creativity." The first refers to the scope of its validity when applied to interpret *cheng*, and the second to the reason assuring its coherent use for both Nature and humans. In a sense, this is a supplementary statement to what I have discussed in the present chapter.

Mou Zongsan distinguished two concepts regarding the existence of a thing or things: the "principle of formation" (*xinggou zhili* 形構之理) and the "principle of actualization" (*shixian zhili* 實現之理) (Mou, 88-9).[4] In his view, the first explains why a thing has its particular trait, or why a thing is called its particular name. This principle "is only responsible for description and explanation, not for creation and actualization" (Mou, 93). Xunzi's concept of nature (*xing* 性) exemplifies this principle: "That which is as it is from the time of birth (*sheng* 生) is called the nature of man. That which is harmonious from birth, which is capable of perceiving through the senses and of responding to stimulus spontaneously and without effort, is also called the nature" (*Xunzi*, 412). By his definition, human "nature" is a quality that comes with the birth of a human being; it doesn't create its life, although it signifies its substance. In contrast, the "principle of actualization" involves a force to bring all things into being. The example is the "Grand Ultimate" in the Neo-Confucian movement. Actually, the first principle is close to Aristotle's concept of category, while the second to that of God in Judaic-Christianity or the "sufficient reason" in Leibniz. The first refers to the realities of

---

[4] The English translation is his.

multiple categories of things, being used to account for the difference among them, while the second to a single Being or Oneness that gives things both their reality and existence. The first is static and explanatory, while the second is dynamic and creative.

There is no doubt that, as Ames and Hall points out, the basic connotation of *cheng* in *Centrality and Commonality* is "creativity," which is in line with Mou's "principle of actualization." However, this doesn't mean that *cheng* has never been employed as "principle of formation" in other texts, and that "creativity" as a translated name can sufficiently cover the full range of the meaning of *cheng*. For example, as seen in the *Zhuangzi*, the "*cheng* of great man" is obviously a concept of category, denoting the reality of a group of people whose quality allows them to be named as "great man." In the next chapter, we will meet more cases in which *cheng* is used just in this way. In my translation of *cheng* as sincerity/reality, the "reality" refers to both the force that creates all things in the universe and the essential attribute that features things as themselves. It is a "principle of actualization" and a "principle of formation" as well.

Chinese thinkers believe that *cheng* as a universal principle is the sole source for the creation in both Nature and humans. However, there exists a theoretical gap that needs to be filled for the coherent application of *cheng*/creativity to the two realms. As stated before, Mencius mainly reads *cheng* as an ethical concept, referring to a unity with two aspects of reality (human nature) and sincerity (self-cultivation), and a basis on which the sage kings extend their virtues to implement a "humane government" (*renzheng* 仁政). Nevertheless, a philosophical problem emerges along with *cheng*'s expansion to Nature. In terms of Ames' and Hall's distinction of "maker" and "creator," as well as Mou's analysis of "principle of formation" and "principle of actualization," Mencius' "sage king" is definitely a "maker" with will, intention, and purpose; he or his *cheng* is "powerful" enough to "actualize" his goals in a society. Embodying simultaneously both "power" and "actualization," the sage king serves for humans just as God does for cosmos. Hence, there comes the possible incoherence: on the one hand, *cheng* of the sage king is a "maker" with "power;" on the other hand, *cheng* in cosmos functions as a "creator" with "creativity." Now people may wonder how Chinese thinkers avoided or resolved this problem. In my observation, this question has escaped the attention of many scholars on *cheng*.

Centrality and Commonality inherits both Mencius' idea of *cheng* on the sage king and Xunzi's expansion of *cheng* to Nature, but, at the same time, avoids the incoherence by appealing to the notion of "transformation." Contrary to the governance of "changing" people by persistently imposing laws and penal codes on them, as the Legalists advocate, the sage in the text "transforms" people by developing his *cheng*/nature so as to stimulate them to actualize their own. From this point of view, the sage king does not "make" a new type of people, but rather brings about a friendly circumstance and atmosphere in which people can freely and voluntarily develop themselves. In this sense, the sage king is not an "external causation" over and beyond human community, but a member of the community, and an initiator to the interaction of transformation within the community. On the other hand, as *Centrality and Commonality* and other texts from mainstream Confucianism assert, "transformation" is also a typical mode by which cosmic *cheng* affects a myriad of things. ZHOU Dunyi summarizes *cheng's* coherent influence in the two realms by saying that,

> Heaven produces the ten thousand things through *yang* and brings them to completion through *yin*. To produce is humaneness, and to bring to completion is rightness. Therefore when the sage administers an empire, he cultivates all things with humaneness and sets all people right with rightness. As the Way of Heaven operates, all things are in harmony. As the virtue of the sage-ruler is cultivated, all people are transformed. (Zhou, 36)

By the notion of "transformation," *Centrality and Commonality* successfully establishes *cheng*/creativity as a "principle of actualization," which coherently operates in Nature and in the government of the sage king. At the same time, the text encourages rulers to emulate Nature and the sage king, following the pattern of transformation to materialize an immanent development for their states and people.

Conclusion

The idea of *cheng* emerged during the Warring States period. Appearing first was "ethical *cheng*;" it meant both a psychological state and an inner-oriented effort to preserve that state. The state causes the consistency in a person's words and deeds, enabling the person to earn trust from other people and even to have them transformed or changed. In scrutiny, "transformation" presupposes that *cheng* is an innate attribute common to all humans. This allows a person with *cheng* to stimulate other people to develop their *cheng* by establishing him/herself as a moral model. In contrast, the executives of "change" may either regard human nature as evil, or simply refuse to ponder upon it. Some of them hold that the possessor of *cheng* can influence people's behaviors by consistently implementing governmental or instrumental measures, while others believe that *cheng* in the heart-mind of the sage or immortal is a material force that will alter people's actions by radiating out to overcome their wills or intentions. Later, using ethical *cheng* as a primordial pattern, Chinese thinkers coined out its sister concept "cosmic *cheng*," and even invented the concept of "universal *cheng*" on the ground of the resemblance of them. Also, in addition to being continuously interpreted as the source of "actualization," *cheng* in that period still retains what "*shi*" denotes, namely the nature/reality of a thing or things. Together, all the meanings and notions I have listed above constitute a framework of the idea of *cheng*. In a rough sense, all the theoretical endeavors pertaining to *cheng* in later times can be simply viewed as its enrichment, concretization, and popularization.

Chapter III

Beyond "Transformation" and Back

From the Qin-Han period (about the 3rd to 2nd century B.C.E.) to the Tang dynasty (618-896), the idea of *cheng* continued its adventure in various forms. First of all, despite its frequent occurrence in a number of political philosophers, such as HAN Fei (about 280-233 B.C.E.), Lü Buwei 吕不韋 (?-235 B.C.E.) and the author of the *Guanzi* 《管子》, *cheng*'s content deviated from what the *Mencius* and *Centrality and Commonality* held to as an efficient method of governance, a praiseworthy mode of statecraft that all rulers should consciously employ. In correspondence, its goal was no longer a harmonious world where every person or even everything could fully develop its nature. Instead, the goal shifted towards an orderly society in which all people are pleased to accept their position or role assigned by the government. At the same time, the mystical tendency that came with the *Zhuangzi* was further strengthened. For instance, three major books in the Daoist circle—the *Wenzi* 《文子》, the *Huainanzi* 《淮南子》 and the *Liezi* 《列子》—all contained an idea that *cheng* is a material force residing in a person's heart, which may radiate out of the person's body, overpowering other people and even influencing the movements of natural phenomena. Finally, still other philosophers, including DONG Zhongshu, WANG Bi 王弼 (226-249), and GUO Xiang mainly used *cheng* to denote the reality of a thing or things. Depending on the context, the term may be interpreted as the reality of all things in the universe, that of a category of things, or that of an individual thing.

The introduction of Buddhism and its flourishing in the Sui-Tang 隋-唐 period (about 6th-9th century C.E.) brought to Chinese thinkers not only a great number of new ideas, but also a new perspective to understand the indigenous Chinese concepts. Paradoxically, this allowed them to read some traditional concepts in a way closer to the pre-Qin philosophers, rather than their successors since the Qin-Han times. For example, due to the inspiration of Taintai 天台 Buddhist interpretation of "nature," LI Ao restored the traditional Confucian connection between nature and the way of Heaven, as well as the universality of *cheng* that *Centrality and Commonality* discussed. His effort reinvigorated the spirit of mainstream Confucianism, and awakened people's interest in *Centrality and Commonality*, including its central concept—*cheng*. This also meant a rediscovery of the tradition of transformation that had been obscure since the Han dynasty.

III. 1. *Cheng* as a Method of Governance

For the thinkers in the tradition of transformation in the Warring States period, *cheng* is valuable for two reasons. First, as Mencius insists, *cheng* represents the nature of humans and therefore, its preservation signifies a person as a real human being. Secondly, the person with *cheng* will awaken or rekindle the same *cheng* in the heart of other people to have them working with him/her toward a harmonious society. Understandably, this second point has already implied a politically important conclusion that the application of *cheng* is the most efficient method of governance. With this thought in mind, a group of political philosophers, like the author of *Mr. Lü's Spring and Autumn Annals* (*Lüshi Chunqiu* 《吕氏春秋》), start to interpret the cultivation of *cheng* as a "method of government" (*zhishu* 治術). In them, the content of *cheng* is no longer, say, the "four hearts" seen in Mencius, but the "naturalness"—an ideal state of mind with which a ruler can establish a strong and wealthy state. In the meantime, another group of thinkers, represented by HAN Fei and the author of the *Guanzi*, read *cheng* primarily as a "governmental consistency" in a ruler's implementation of law and regulation, and in people's daily activities. They argue that *cheng* and its exercise is the shortest way for the establishment of a strong and wealthy state.

III. 1. 1. **Cheng** *as Naturalness*

Mr. Lü's Spring-Autumn Annals extensively discuss three interrelated topics concerning *cheng*: the content of *cheng* and its influence, the reason why it is influential, and the political conclusion derived from observing its influence. In what follows, I will present the author's position by analyzing three representative passages from the text. The first one refers to "baby," an image that we already knew from the *Zhuangzi*. It reads that,

> A three-month-old baby does not know to desire the carriage and the crown in front of it, or to fear the executing ax behind it. What it knows is the love of its mother. This is because of *cheng*. Therefore, when *cheng* is pure, one's feeling (*qing* 情) conforms to the feeling of others; when the nature (*jing* 精) is pure, one is connected with Heaven. When one connects with Heaven, he can move the nature of water, of fire, of wood, and of stone; how much more can he move those who have blood and breath? (*Lüshi Chunqiu*, 1225-6)

Here *cheng* is described as a state of mind or a natural feeling. Because of its existence, the baby cares about neither treasures nor danger, but only the love of its mother. This concentration necessarily moves its mother to act in its favor. For the same reason, *cheng* in our heart, if fully developed, will integrate us with other people and even with Heaven, moving all to act just as the mother responds to the baby. The author insists that this favorable response will occur so long as we rectify our heart to be as pure as that of a baby.

The second passage tells a sad story about a slave and his musician master. It further elucidates how the other people are moved by our *cheng*. One night, ZHONG Ziqi 鐘子期, a legendary musician, felt a deep sadness from hearing someone playing on the musical stone. He found the player and asked, "Why is your playing so sad?" The answer was that the man's father killed another man and was executed for his crime. As part of the punishment, his mother became a wine server and the man himself became a music server playing the musical stone, both in the Zhong household. The man hadn't seen his mother for three years until the previous night. He wanted to redeem her from slavery, but had no money, since he himself was also a slave. This was the reason why he was so sad.

After hearing his story, Zhong sighed and said, "How sad, how very sad! The heart is not the arm, the arm is not the stick, and the stick is not the stone. Yet since the sadness is in the heart, the wood and stone will respond to it." His comment refers to an extraordinary phenomenon that I call the "resonance of spirits." It means that, being purified to the utmost, a person's *cheng* can directly communicate with the natures of things and people. Consequently, a move or act in his or her mind will cause the same move or act from that of others. The "stick" and the "stone" sound sad because of their "resonance" with the man's sadness, and via them, the same sadness occurs also in Zhong's heart.

From the case of the sad man Zhong derives a conclusion about government: "Thus, *cheng* in an exemplary person's heart must be understood by others. When emotions rise up within him, others feel them. Why would he need to persuade forcefully?" (*Lüshi Chunqiu*, 507-8). In Zhong's view, *cheng* contains a potential of being felt by others, hence if a ruler concentrates on the purification of his *cheng*, thinking and acting with *cheng*, those in inferior positions will surely respond with the same thinking and action.

The next story from the same text further explores the political dimension of *cheng*. When MI Zijian 宓子賤, a contemporary of Confucius, was given charge of an area of Shanfu, he feared that his lord might listen to slanderers and interfere his administration of the place. Before taking his leave, he requested that the two officials close to the lord be allowed to go with him. When all the officials of Shanfu came in honor of him, Mi asked the two officials to write something. As they were writing, Mi kept pulling and shaking their elbows. Then he angrily accused them of their poor calligraphy, saying, "Your calligraphy is very bad. You, sir, should go home right away." After talking with the poor officials who were driven out of Shanfu, the lord immediately realized Mi's mind: "Master Mi is using this to reprove my unworthiness. There must have been many occasions on which I disrupted him and didn't allow him to put his *method* into practice." He thereupon dispatched his loved one to notify Mi: "Henceforth, Shanfu is not my possession. It belongs to you,

Sir. You may decide what is the most beneficial for Shanfu. Inform me every five-years of the essentials."

Three years later, WU Maqi 巫馬旗, a disciple of Confucius, went in a shabby cloth to observe what happened in Shanfu. Surprised at seeing that a nighttime fisherman threw back into the water what he just caught, he asked, "The aim of a fisherman is to catch fish. Now why do you throw back what you have caught?" The reply was, "Master Mi doesn't want people to take small fish. What I threw back was small fish." Wu went back and reported to Confucius. "Master Mi's virtue is perfect!" says Wu. "He made people behave so well even at night, as if there were a strict punishment at hand. May I ask how Master Mi is able to achieve this?" Confucius replied, "I once talked about this with him, and he said, 'When there is *cheng* inside, there must be its manifestation outside.' Master Mi must be practicing this method (*shu* 術) in Shanfu" (*Lüshi Chunqiu*, 507-8). With the same view, the text tells in another place that, "As for issues regarding persuasion and government, nothing equals *cheng*. Hearing grief in a person's words doesn't equal seeing him cry, nor does hearing anger in his words equal seeing him fight. If there is no *cheng* in the persuader and the ruler, their influence on other people will not be miraculous (*shen* 神)" (*Lüshi Chunqiu*, 1225-6).

According to GAO You, the first commentator of *Lü's Spring-Autumn Annals* in the Later Han dynasty, the book consists of the doctrines from at least two schools—with "[Confucian] morality as standard, and [Daoist] non-action as principle" (*Lüshi Chunqiu*, 4). This philosophical fusion leaves a clear trace on its notion of *cheng*. The author believes that a long-time moral cultivation or a long-time accumulation of certain feelings like joy, anger, or sorrow may form a "state" of *cheng* in people's heart, which will cause them to cry spontaneously when they grieve or fight fiercely when they become angry. By the same token, this state will assure rulers to act naturally and correctly when a governmental issue is at stake. With the assumption that an action from *cheng* in one's heart must be echoed by the same *cheng* in others, the author concludes that the most important thing for a ruler is to keep his heart in *cheng*. It is because that, compared with the deliberate and intentional "talking" or "persuading," a natural action initiated by *cheng* is actually more efficient in moving people. It seems this notion retains the Confucian idea of self-cultivation for preserving the inner state and, at the same time, replaces the Confucian content of that state (the "four hearts") with Daoist "naturalness."

III. 1. 2. **Cheng** ***as External Consistency***

Like other major thinkers, HAN Fei, a prominent legalist in the end of Warring States period, also relates *cheng* to "trust" and its acquisition. As for him, *cheng* is the key for a ruler to earn genuine trust from his people, and the best method that enables him to move them in the direction he desires. However, instead of reiterating what his Confucian and Daoist predecessors said, HAN Fei shifts to an approach close to the modern psychological behaviorism. He argues, given the fact that the inner side of other people is essentially inaccessible, they can be judged only by their external behaviors. In addition, what really matters for the establishment of an orderly society is not how people feel or think, but how they behave. Therefore the key is not to guess, assume, or speculate on people's inner life, but to draw a definite line, a workable administrative procedure to regulate their conducts. This idea is illustrated in the following passage:

> The sage established the standard; abided by it; and let all things settle themselves. On the basis of names he made his appointments, and where the name was not clear, he looked to the actual achievement to which it applied. According to how achievement and name tallied, he dispensed the reward and punishment that were deserved. When reward and punishment were certain (*cheng*) and convincing (*xin*), then subordinates would bare their true nature. (*Hanfeizi*, 122)

Here *cheng* means "certainty" and "predictability" in the sage's (or the wise ruler's) dispensation of rewards and punishments, in his unwavering insistence on civil and penal codes, and in his persevering implementation of rules, regulations, and laws. HAN Fei's *cheng* is the opposite of all kinds of irregularity, inconsistency, or unpredictability that are often caused by personal favor, bias, or opportunistic expedience. For the sake of clarity, I would like to specify this content as "governmental consistency." With its presence, according to HAN Fei, there will be neither ambiguity in a ruler's decision, nor confusion and perplexity in people's expectation of what their behavior will cause. In this sense, *cheng* is the source of a government's trustworthiness, as well as the most efficient measure for the construction of an orderly society.

HAN Fei's usage of *cheng* is not unique among political thinkers in the Qin-Han period. For example, it can be found also in the *Guanzi* (《管子》), a book dated around second century B.C.E., although its title assumes the authorship of GUAN Zhong 管仲, a legendary premier in the State Qi of the Spring-Autumn period. The author groups people of a society as four classes: merchants, artisans, peasants, and intellectuals, and accordingly examines the basis on which their labors are divided. As a conclusion, he advises his ruler: "Allow only true (*cheng*) merchant to earn his food from commerce. Allow only true artisan to earn his food from his craft. Allow only true peasant to earn his food from peasantry. And, allow only trustworthy (*xin*) intellectual to stand in the royal court" (*Guanzi*, 55).

According to the *Guanzi*, the labor-division should be undertaken on the basis of people's *cheng* and trustworthiness. The "true" merchants are those persons clearly aware of their business and capable of serving consistently the society with their successful commercial activities. Similarly, the "trustworthy" intellectuals are those persons equipped with good knowledge of government and who are able to promote consistently the welfare of and profit for the people. This *cheng* or trustworthiness underscores a consistency in people's knowledge of their field and in their ability to act. It is not necessarily associated with their moral characters or their willingness to conduct "self-cultivation," although a good ethical attitude may help them fulfill their social duties.

Another passage from the same text lists three methods for governance, among which is *cheng* and trustworthiness.

> Being notified, people will come; being dispatched, people will go; and people are willing to sacrifice themselves to what a ruler values; this is what the teaching causes.... Without any order, people still act; without any arrangement, people still go; without any urgency from the superior, people in inferior positions still contribute all they have; this is what the custom and habit cause. While the likes and dislikes just begin to form in a ruler's heart, people have already been transformed; before a punishment is implemented, people have already become scared; be-

> fore a reward is issued, people have already gotten encouraged. This is what *cheng* and trustworthiness cause. (*Guanzi*, 39)

It is noteworthy that *cheng* in this context is described as being directly responsible for the creation of a social atmosphere in which people internalize their ruler's regulations concerning punishment and reward, and therefore act intuitively in accordance with the ruler's willing or his "likes and dislikes." In fact, this description footnotes HAN Fei's use of *cheng*, demonstrating its efficiency and desirability in the ordering of a society.

III. 2. *Cheng* as the Source of Mystical Change

In the beginning of the Han dynasty, the Daoist sect known as "Yellow Emperor and Laozi School" (*Huang Lao xuepai* 黃老學派) became popular in China, affecting the governmental policy in politics, economy, and the general intellectual tendency. Among the most influential Daoist texts is the *Wenzi*, a book dated around the second century B.C.E.. This book, as its English translator Thomas Cleary indicates, "is one of the great sourcebooks of Daoism," which "covers the whole range of classical Daoist thought and practice" (*Wenzi*, 141). In spite of its nature as an elucidation of Laozi's doctrine, it presents a concept of *cheng* with two distinctive features: eclecticism and mysticism. The first feature shows the author's attempt to synthesize the ideas from mainstream Confucians, the author of *Lü's Spring and Autumn Annals*, and HAN Fei into a Daoist *cheng*. The second enhances the mystical conviction in the supernatural power of *cheng*, which originated from Zhuangzi. This mysticism later influences both the *Huainanzi* and the *Liezi*, two other major texts from the circle of religious Daoism, as well as the Chinese folk society.

III. 2. 1. Philosophical Eclecticism

In regard to *cheng*, the *Wenzi* starts with a notion found in both the *Zhuangzi* and *Centrality and Commonality*, namely the identity of the Way and the sage. It says that "the Way stores vitality (*jing* 精) within the sage's heart and lodges spirit (*shen* 神) in his mind," allowing him to act in the human world in the same manner as the Way to the entire universe. Naming the sage's state of mind as *cheng*, the text describes it with a number of subtle words: calm, unbounded, serene, light, joyful, harmonious, formless, tranquil, and soundless, etc. It claims that, because of a person's *cheng*, "Everyone in the land looks up to his virtue and emulates his ideal; everyone in different countries and with different customs observes them even at a distance" (*Wenzi*, 60).

Persisting in the parallelism between the Way and the sage, the *Wenzi* reads, "As Heaven reaches its height and earth reaches its depth, as sun and moon shine, as the stars twinkle, as *yin* and *yang* harmonize, there is no action in any of these. Make the way right, and things will spontaneously be natural" (*Wenzi*, 60). Similarly, "the sage," when dealing with issues in the human world, "minimizes his affairs, which are thus orderly. He seeks to have little and thus is sufficed; he is benevolent without trying, trusted without speaking. He gains without seeking, succeeds without striving" (*Wenzi*, 83). Different from the *Mencius*, the sage in the *Wenzi* seems not to be an ideal personality up to which everyone is potentially able to match, but a privilege reserved only for a certain great ruler. Meanwhile, similar to *Lü's Spring-Autumn Annals*, *cheng* in the *Wenzi* means primarily "naturalness" and "spontaneity" with which the sage governs his people.

To expound the sage's transformation of people, the *Wenzi* borrows from Mencius a typical Confucian term, "extension." It argues that, "The sage takes naturalness to heart, preserves ultimate reality, embraces the Way, and extends *cheng*, so the whole world follows him as echoes respond to sounds, as shadows imitate forms" (*Wenzi*, 83). Here, as expected, the sage's manner to extend his *cheng* is also identical to that of the Way. Thanks to its "naturalness" towards all beings in the universe, the Way assures their sustentations and developments, and therefore is called the "root of Heaven and earth." Likewise, the sage's extension of *cheng* allows people to achieve their own goals through a natural path, thus "what he works on is the root" of the human world (*Wenzi*, 83).

Wenzi's eclecticism reflects also in his position on the roles that *cheng* and statecrafts play for a society. Again, a comparison with Mencius will help to clarify my point. In the *Mencius*, *cheng* and statecrafts, virtue and punishment, rightness and profit seem often to stand opposite each other. Mencius contends that, since the key to "humane government" lies simply in a ruler's *cheng* or virtue, any emphasis on reward, punishment, profit, and the like is superfluous, misleading, and even counter-productive. In reply to King Hui of Liang's 梁 question, "You have come all this distance.... You must surely have some way of profiting my state?" Mencius says, "Your Majesty, what is the point of mentioning the word of 'profit?' All that matters is that there should be humaneness and rightness." He argues:

> If Your Majesty says, "How can I profit my state," and the Counselors say, "How can I profit my family?" and the gentlemen and commoners say, "How can I profit my person?" then those above and those below will be trying to profit at the expense of one another and the state will be imperiled." (*Mengzi*, 1A1)

This dialogue shows a contrast between the standing points of a "state" and the "world." Being concerned with the interest of his own state, the King understandably asks for an advice that "profits." Actually, this is the same standing point on which HAN Fei interprets *cheng* as "governmental consistency." On the contrary, Mencius regards himself as an advocate of "peace in the world" (*ping tianxia* 平天下), and views from the perspective of the interest of entire humankind rather than that of a single state or family. Therewith, as seen in the case of "universal nature and feeling" in the first chapter, his emphasis is on a commonality shared by all humans, a universality that can unite rather than separate people. He believes that the profit of one state may be translated as the loss of others, but the humaneness and rightness from one party will never hurt other parties.

One of the traits of the *Wenzi* lies in its effort to compromise the "world" with the "state," and *cheng* as inner state with *cheng* as governmental consistency. The author tries to retain the two sides and to promote a balanced exercise of them. A passage from it reads:

> What rewards the good and punishes the violent is regulation and law, and what makes them operable is purity and *cheng*. Although directives may be clear, they cannot be carried out alone, but must await purity and *cheng*. So if regulations and law

> are exercised over people, but people do not follow, it is because purity and *cheng* are not there." (*Wenzi*, 61)

On the one hand, Wenzi holds that the governmental measures—reward and punishment, regulation and law—all come from the sage, and are necessary for maintaining an orderly state; on the other hand, he views *cheng* (meaning "naturalness") as what ensures the efficient exercise of those measures. For him, *cheng* is something in a ruler's heart, while the measures are what he implements outside. Without the measures, *cheng* can only benefit the ruler himself, making him a solitary hermit, morally pure, but politically unsuccessful; while without *cheng*, the implement of the measures must be inconsistent, which will confuse people and bring the society into chaos. Using the metaphor of the bird again, as its two wings are complementary to each other for the successful flying of an orderly society. In brief, unlike Mencius, Wenzi doesn't treat *cheng* as the only source for the transformation; while different from HAN Fei, he doubts that the implementation of the measures will be always efficient if there is no assistance from *cheng*.

III. 2. 2. Cheng *and Natural Movements*

In many places, Wenzi describes *cheng* as an element that affects not merely humans, but Nature as well.[5] This mystical inclination reveals the second feature of his *cheng*. One of his passages reads that

> The sage emulates this (Heaven): when he promotes blessings, no one sees how he does it, yet blessings arise; and when he removes calamities, no one sees how it happens, yet calamities disappear. It cannot be found out by inquiry, yet when examined it is not unreal.... Silent and voiceless, yet moving the world tremendously with a single word—such is one who moves evolution by means of the celestial mind (*tianxin* 天心). Thus when purity and *cheng* form within, its energy moves Heaven: auspicious stars appear, yellow dragons descend, phoenixes arrive, flavorful springs emerge, fine grains grow, the

---

[5] The *Wenzi* and the *Huainanzi* share a number of similar, even identical ideas, phrases, and passages. Wang Liqi 王利器, the compiler of the *Wenzi*, believes that the *Wenzi* is written earlier than the *Huainanzi*, so it is the latter that copies the former, not the reverse (*Wenzi*, 9).

> rivers do not overflow, and the oceans do not have tidal waves. (*Wenzi*, 62-3)

The *Cheng* that the sage possesses is a "celestial mind" identical to the essence of Heaven. This identity enables him to move Heaven in a manner as one bird's singing invites echos from other birds, or as one musical instrument's sound is resonated by other instruments. Thanks to the assistance of Heaven, he can change his society as easily as Heaven changes all natural phenomena: he is silent, but effective; the changes are beyond ordinary people's understanding, but surely demonstrated. It is noteworthy that the sage functions as an intermediate between Heaven and humanity. He is not an observer (like an astronomer, or geographer) with sole naturalistic interest, but an agent working actively to harmonize the two sides.

As a matter of fact, Wenzi's belief in the "interconnection of Heaven and humans" (*Wenzi*, 63) is rooted in the remote antiquity, and has been held long before him, implicitly or explicitly, by both Daoists and Confucians. For example, when in personal danger in the place of Kuang 匡, Confucius said, "Since the death of King Wen, is not the course of culture (*wen* 文) in my keeping? If it had been the will of Heaven to destroy this culture, it would not have been given to a mortal [like me]. But if it is the will of Heaven that this culture should not perish, what can the people of Kuang do to me?" (*Lunyu*, 9.5) In Wenzi's time, the belief became even more popular among scholars. For instance, DONG Zhongshu writes,

> In ancient times those who created writing took three horizontal lines and connected them through the center to designate the king (*wang* 王). The three horizontal lines represent Heaven, Earth, and Humankind while the vertical line that connects them through the center represents comprehending the Way. As for the one who appropriates the mean of Heaven, Earth, and humankind, and takes this as the thread that joins and connects them, if it is not one who acts as a king then who can be equal to this [task]? Therefore one who acts as a king is no more than Heaven's agent. He models himself on Heaven's seasons and brings them to completion. He models himself on Heaven's commands and causes the people to obey them. He models himself on Heaven's numerical and categories and initiates affairs. He models himself on Heaven's Way and sends

> forth his standards. He models himself on Heaven's will and always returns to humaneness. (Dong, 328-9)

Despite the fact that what Dong emphasizes is not the sage/king's influence on Heaven but his emulation of Heaven, his message is still consistent with the *Wenzi* at one point. It is that there exists a connection between Heaven and humans, and the sage/king should and could function as intermediate to combine the two realms together.

Later, the supernatural power associated with the sage's *cheng* further evolves to the worthy person who partially or temporarily possesses *cheng*. The *Liezi*, another Daoist classic compiled in the Jin 晉 dynasty (265-420), consists of several interesting stories in this regard. One of them tells us that once on a trip, Confucius rested his horse at a bridge over the river and looked at the view. There was a waterfall more than two hundred feet high, and the river stretched with ten miles of whirlpool. Fish and turtles could not swim there, crocodiles could not live there, but there was a man just about to ford it. Confucius sent a student to stop him. However, the man took no notice, crossed over and came out. Confucius was rather surprised, "What a skill! Do you have some special art? How is that you are able to get through?" The man replied, "When I first enter, I start by being loyal and true to the water, and when I come out, I continue to be loyal and true to it. Throwing my body into the current, I do not dare to act selfishly. That is how I am able to get out again once I am in." After hearing the answer, Confucius said to his students, "Bear it in mind, my children. By loyalty, truth, and *cheng* we can make friends even with the water, not to mention humans" (*Liezi*, 238-9).

Another story is even more familiar to Chinese readers today. This popularity partially comes from the fact that MAO Zedong 毛澤東 (1893-1976) retold the story in the seventh convention of the Communist Party of China (1945) to encourage his comrades to overcome all difficulties for the establishment of a new China. However, he reinterpreted "God" (*di* 帝) in the text as "the Chinese people" in general, and did not mention the term *cheng* as the original text did.

The mountains Taihang 太行 and Wangwu 王屋 are seven hundred miles square and seven hundred thousand feet high. They stood opposite the house of Mister Simple (Yugong 愚公) and made his family take a long way to come and go. This vexed him constantly until one day when he was nearly ninety. The whole family was called together by the old man to discuss his proposal to level the mountains so that there could be a clear road straight down to wherever they wanted to go. His proposal was accepted after a minor argument, and the whole family and some of their neighbors started the work the next day. Taking his son and grandson as porters, the old man broke stones and dug up earth. He did not come home until the hot season had given way to the cold one. The spirits in charge of the mountains reported this event to God. "God was moved by the old man's *cheng*," and commanded two giants to carry the mountains on their back and put them somewhere else (*Liezi*, 160-1).

In comparison with the sage's mission, the goals of the swimmer and the old man are simpler and more specific: to swim across the river, or to level the mountains. They both succeeded because their *cheng* finally "moved" the water or God. Although *cheng* in the two stories still refers to an inner state, its content changes from the "naturalness" and "non-action" of the sage, which the *Wenzi* holds, to single-mindedness for achieving what one desires, and an unwavering persistence on what one believes in. The two men did not expect any sympathy or assistance from outside, but paradoxically, it fell on them as surprisingly as timely rain does to a land in drought. In this sense, the *Liezi* breaks the sage's monopoly of *cheng*, secularizing it to be something accessible to ordinary people. It tries to convince them that *cheng* in their mind is as powerful as that in the sage; they will get help from Heaven, as long as it is kept in a pure and complete condition. The result from the *Liezi* is twofold: on the one hand, it opens a door through which *cheng* enters into folk society to be a popular notion even among uneducated people; on the other hand, it adds a superstitious component to the idea of *cheng*, which often lures them to unrealistically expect certain miracles.

III. 3. *Cheng* as the Reality of Things

As stated before, *cheng*'s second major use refers to the essential attribute or quality of a thing or things. Its pre-history lies in the term "*shi* 實" (reality) that appears frequently in the texts before the Warring States period, and its earliest unambiguous expression is in Zhuangzi's phrases: "*cheng* of Heaven and earth" and "*cheng* of the great man." Since the Qin-Han period, this usage becomes increasingly popular among scholars.

There are two things particularly noteworthy about *cheng*/reality used since the Qin-Han period. First, it is not the only term for the designation of essential attribute. Long before its coinage as a concept, for example, both "reality" and "nature" already assumed the same function. Mencius refers to "reality" as saying that

> The reality of humaneness is the serving of one's parents; the reality of rightness is obedience to one's elder brothers; the reality of wisdom is to understand these two and to hold fast to them; the reality of the ritual is the regulation and adornment of them; the reality of music is the joy that comes of delighting in them." (*Mengzi*, 4A27)

Meanwhile, he coined many phrases about "nature," such as "the nature of man," "the nature of the hound," "the nature of the cow" (*Mengzi*, 6A3). Roughly speaking, there is a distinction in his two terms: "reality" is primarily applied to inanimate things, while "nature" to animate things.

Instead of replacing or eclipsing these two time-honored terms, the occurrence of *cheng*/reality simply adds one more term to the list of those regarding essential attribute. One proof about its interchangeability with the term "nature" can be found in DONG Zhongshu. Dong writes about *cheng* that, "If in the endowment of vital energy (*qi* 氣) one is free from evil, why should the mind restrict anything? From the name of heart-mind I know *cheng* of man. Both humaneness and greed (*tan* 貪) are within the *cheng* of humans" (Dong 1992, 293). In the same vein, he uses the term "nature" by saying that, "The nature of man may be compared to a rice stalk, while goodness compared to rice. Rice comes out of the stalk, but not the whole stalk is rice. Similarly, goodness comes out of nature, but not the whole nature is good" (Dong 1992, 296). A conclusion derived from comparing Dong's two passages is that *cheng* and "nature" mean the same thing; their interchanging use vivifies the wording of argument, which may have a certain literary or aesthetic value, but adds nothing philosophically.

Also common to the scholars of that time is the interchanging use of *cheng* with "reality." For example, WANG Bi, a major Neo-Daoist philosopher in the Wei-Jin period, writes that:

> If one diligently acts simply for getting fame and earning profit, then the more well-known his name is, the farther he departs from his *cheng*; and the more profits he earns, the faster his mind runs away. [We often see that] fathers and sons, older and younger brothers value only their desires, but forget their integrity (*zhi*, 直). Their filiality isn't guided by *cheng*, their kindness isn't guided by reality." (WANG Bi, 199)

It is apparent that both *cheng* and "reality" in Wang refer to the same quality of people's hearts that account for their moral actions.

The second noteworthy point is that *cheng*/reality may be used without any distinction or indication to denote the essential attribute of the animate or the inanimate, or to that of an individual thing, or a category of things, or all things in the universe. The vagueness of *cheng*/reality becomes more ostensive if compared with Aristotle's classification of "substance," a term that may be roughly treated as the counterpart of *cheng*/ reality. "The word 'substance' gets applied to at least four things; for the essence and universal and the genus are all thought to be the substance of each thing, and so, fourthly, is the substratum" (Aristotle 1941, 784). It is a fact that, as with many Chinese terms, such a detailed analysis of *cheng*/reality has never occurred in the history of Chinese philosophy. Hence we can only depend on a careful examination of the context in which *cheng*/reality occurs to identify its exact referent.

Among the frequent users of *cheng*/reality, the most remarkable is GUO Xiang, another major Neo-Daoist philosopher in the Wei-Jin period. By means of his commentary on the *Zhaungzi*, Guo, at the first time in the history of Chinese philosophy, interprets *cheng*/reality as a concept concerning individual beings. As a distinctive feature, his *cheng* is often entangled with a concept family whose members include "self-fulfillment" (*zide* 自得), "self-growth" (*zisheng* 自生), "self-being-as-so" (*zi'er* 自爾), "self-transformation" (*zihua* 自化), "self-complacency" (*zizai* 自在), and "self-sufficiency" (*zizu* 自足). These terms all have one thing in common. It is the "self," rather than any external cause, that initiates these activities: "fulfillment," "growth," "being-as-so," "complacency," and "sufficiency." For a thorough understanding of his *cheng*, we need to examine it in reference with its connection with those terms.

On Zhuangzi's phrase, "*cheng* of the great man," Guo comments, "[The great man] is engaged in no artifice (*buwei* 不爲), and yet realizes his self-fulfillment. Therefore, he is called *cheng*" (*Zhuangzi*, 856). Here "artifice" primarily refers to discursive reasoning or deliberation, while "no artifice" to naturalness or spontaneity. Meanwhile "self-fulfillment" means that the great man fulfils his goal out of his own initiative or his dependence on himself. Hence, Guo's commentary conveys a message that, because of the "self" that *cheng* denotes, individuals naturally or spontaneously start their actions and attain their goals. However, as did in the cases of Rousseau and Mencius in the first chapter, we have to inquire: is the term "self" in Guo a concept for a category of things or for an individual being? Put concretely, does it mean the "self" of all birds or that of an individual bird, such as this eagle or that hawk? The answer can be found in his next commentary.

Guo writes about an ideal government that, "If officials do not interfere the business of people, then the people will peacefully accomplish their own works. If the people do not exchange with each other the capability (*neng* 能) that belongs to each 'you' or 'me,' then 'you' and 'I' in the world will each peacefully realize his/her self-fulfillment" (*Zhuangzi*, 461). Carefully picking up the terms "you" and "me" as indicators for each individual, Guo would convince his readers that every individual possesses his or her own "capacity" and each capacity represents an individualistic attribute that differentiates one person from another. An ideal government should allow each individual to develop in a unique way for his or her own "self-fulfillment," and to actualize what one potentially possesses.

The same idea lies also in Guo's commentary on Zhuangzi's chapter of "Free and Easy Wandering." There he refers to "ceremony" to discuss further the *cheng* of each individual and its significance for the harmony of the world.

> The cook, the boy impersonating the dead at sacrificial ritual, and the other officers of prayer each is content with his duty. Bird, animal and all individual things each is content with its endowment. Emperor Yao and [the hermit] XU You are tran-

> quil in their circumstances. This shows the perfect reality of the universe. When everything attains its own reality, why should it take any action? Everyone will realize its "self-fulfillment." (*Zhuangzi*, 26)

The key term here is "reality," which is interchangeable with *cheng*. Guo paints us a perfect order in the universe: on the one hand, each individual is satisfied with its position because this enables it to "attain its reality" or "to realize its self-fulfillment;" on the other hand, it is because that each individual realizes its "self-fulfillment," the universe itself attains a great harmony that Guo names as "perfect reality." From Guo's description people may conclude that since individual's "reality" or "self-fulfillment" is prior to the universal harmony, a ruler who cares about the realization of "perfect reality" should create a situation in which each individual is encouraged to develop his or her own "reality," and to respect other things doing the same. In my view, despite the distance of space and time, Guo's idea is actually close to what Rousseau and the German Romantics advocated in the eighteenth century Europe.

Ying-shih Yu writes about the relation of certain Western terms and their equivalents in Chinese history that

> Both 'individualism' and 'holism' are Western concepts whose introduction to Chinese intellectual discourse is a matter of only recent historical development. But this does not mean that as categories of analysis these two concepts are totally inapplicable to the study of early Chinese thought. As a matter of fact, we find in the long history of Chinese political and social thought a wide range of views which can be legitimately characterized as either holistic or individualistic. (Yu, 121)

An analysis on the concept of "self" in Mencius and Guo will footnote Yu's position. In Mencius, human "self" is a universalistic or holistic concept, referring to the good nature common to all humans, whereas the individualistic element or the uniqueness that features a particular person seems to be unessential or unimportant for describing humankind as a category of species.

This idea is further elaborated as the distinction between "universality" (*gong* 公) and "individuality" (*si* 私) by the Neo-Confucian thinkers. CHENG Yi says, "Where there is universality, there is unity (*yi* 一), and where there is individuality, there is multiplicity (*shu* 殊). People's mind/self (*xin* 心) is as various as their faces, it is solely due to this that each of them possesses his own individual mind (*sixin* 私心)" (Zhu 2000, 39). In an even plainer manner WANG Yangming claims,

> The mind of everybody is at first not different from that of the sage. Only because it is obstructed by his individuality (*youwo zhisi* 有我之私) and blocked by material desires, what was originally great becomes small and what was originally penetrating becomes obstructed. Everyone has his own individual mind, to the point where some regard their fathers, sons, and brothers as enemy. The sages worried over this. They therefore extended their humaneness that makes them form one body with Heaven, earth, and all things, to teach the world, so as to enable the people to overcome their individuality, remove their obstructions, and recover that which is common to the substance of mind (*xinti* 心體) of all humans. (WANG Yangming, 194-5)

The message from Cheng and Wang is that the universal mind/self, which is originally possessed by everyone, is identical to the essence of Heaven, whereas the individual mind/self reflects a person's desire, calculation, and deliberation. The development of universal mind leads to the unity of people and the prevalence of humaneness in the world, whereas that of individual mind will lead each person to pursue his or her own goals, even at the cost of their family members' interest (selfishness). Thus, the purpose of the sage's teaching, as well as people's self-cultivation, is to eliminate the individual mind or individuality for the complete recovery of the universal mind or universality.

Contrary to these mainstream Confucians, GUO Xiang provides us with another theory about universality and individuality, and a new path to universal harmony. For him, "self" or *cheng*/reality is an individualistic concept, designating a quality that Heaven endows uniquely to each individual. This endowment accounts for a variety of distinctness in individuals' appearance and mind and, at the same time, underscores natural equality among those physically and intellectually distinctive individuals. Praising one's "individuality" or uniqueness doesn't necessarily mean to embrace "selfishness," and having it develop is not necessarily at the cost of other individuals.

After all, Heaven is not a malicious magician who endows various attributes to a myriad of individuals simply for seeing them to conflict against each other.

Guo interpretes universality primarily as a state in which each individual is engaged in manifesting his or her own self, acting in terms of what best fits his or her natural composition. He believes that the practices signified by the terms: "self-fulfillment," "self-growth," "self-being-as-so," "self-transformation," "self-complacency," and "self-sufficiency"—are the only way by which individuals work together to create a harmony in the universe. Implying a notion of "individualistic *cheng*," Guo's effort, in my view, opens a new dimension for the idea of *cheng* as a whole. Although this dimension is neither fully recognized, nor enthusiastically promoted by later scholars in Pre-modern China, it may become popular there in the near future. To support my anticipation, I would like to examine the changing opinions on "individualism" in Europe.

According to Steven Lukes, the first use of the term individualism "grew out of the general European reaction to the French Revolution and to its alleged source, the thought of Enlightenment" (Lukes, 3). For conservative thinkers in England, France, and Germany at that time, "individualism" was partially responsible for social dissolution. It meant a dangerous idea fostering social and economic anarchy, a lack of the requisite institution and norms, and the prevalence of a self -interested attitude among individuals. However, after the 1840's, the Romantic idea of individuality, including the notions of individual uniqueness, originality, self-realization etc. was gradually accepted in Europe as the main content of individualism. In the view of Georg Simmel, this is a new interpretation of individualism, an "individualism of difference, with the deepening of individuality to the point of the individual's incomparability, to which he is 'called' both in his nature and in his achievement" (Simmel, 78). Nowadays, this becomes a dominant reading in Western society.

As described before, Confucian thinkers in pre-modern China often viewed "individuality" as an equivalent of "selfishness," which may cause an individual to pursue his or her political or economical gains at the expense of other individuals, even that of the entire society. In fact, this is still the main reading in contemporary China. For example, The *Sea of Words* (*cihai*, 《辭海》), an authoritative lexicon used by all educated Chinese, defines "individualism" in this way:

> Individualism (*geren zhuyi* 個人主義) refers to a thought that places personal interest before anything else.... More specifically, it means seeking private gains at the expense of public interest, harming others to benefit oneself, looking for nothing but personal profit, and cheating and outwitting one another, etc." (*Cihai*, 309)

This definition is similar to what European conservatives viewed as "individualism," but has nothing to do with what GUO Xiang and Romantics advocated. I believe that, along with the advancement of Chinese modernization, the change in Europe will repeat itself in China. As their counterpart in Europe, the Chinese people will gain a new understanding on individualism, and therefore accept it as a positive value.

III. 4. LI Ao and Buddhism

After the collapse of Han dynasty, the main Confucian notions of *cheng*, their connection with the sage and the way of Heaven, and its transformation of people become remote to Chinese scholars. LI Ao in the Tang dynasty turns this tide through his *Recovery of Human Nature*, an explanatory work of *Centrality and Commonality*. Of his accomplishment ZHENG Jingwang 鄭景旺, a Song scholar, acclaims, "LI Ao is truly superior to HAN Yu in both learning and vision. The three parts of his *Recovery* borrow nothing from the Confucian scholars since the Qin-Han times, but rather, transcend [them] to reach directly the mind of YAN Yuan" (ZHENG Jingwang, 319). In addition to accepting the traditional account of LI Ao's achievement, which appeals mainly to his "genius," modern scholars have pointed out another reason. FENG Youlan writes, "In formulating these ideas [in the *Recovery*], LI Ao seems to have been influenced by the Buddhist theory of cessation (*zhi* 止) and contemplation (*guan* 觀), which was developed by the Tiantai sect" (Feng, 1953, 423). He even further specifies *General Rules for Cessation and Contemplation of Tiantai Sect* (*Tiantai zhiguan tongli* 《天台止觀通例》), a Buddhist book authored by LIANG Su 梁肅 (753-793), as the direct source from which LI Ao acquires some of his basic thoughts.

To the study of comparative philosophy, LI Ao's work is valuable for exemplifying how a foreign philosophy joins to reshape an indigenous thought. Roughly, we can summarize the Buddhist influence on him as the following. First, the Buddhist goal, "recovering human nature" that LIANG Su set up, turns to be the purpose of Li's philosophical endeavor. Second, the fundamental antagonism between nature and emotions (*qing* 情) that Liang insisted, is uncritically accepted by Li; and its resolution becomes the basic theme of his work. Third, several key terms regarding nature, emotion, and their relation, which Liang provided, are not only used by Li in the same way, but also appear as crucial components of his own system. Finally, and most importantly, Buddhism in general and Liang's doctrine in particular brought to Chinese thought a new concept of "nature," which channels Li's thinking back to classical Confucianism, and inspires him to restore the original meaning of *cheng* in Mencius and *Centrality and Commonality*.

III. 4. 1. Nature and Emotion

Despite the fact that the two terms "nature" and "emotion" frequently appear in both Confucian and Buddhist texts, the thinkers of the two schools do not always agree with each other on their meanings. A comparison of "nature" and "emotion" in them will shed light on Li's intellectual debt to both schools, as well as his contribution in reinvigorating the tradition of mainstream Confucianism.

III. 4. 1. 1. Nature and Emotion in Classical Confucianism

Generally speaking, classical Confucians used the term "*qing*" mainly in two ways: emotion/feeling and reality/fact. In reference to non-human objects, such as animals or inanimate beings, it either, as one of the major uses of *cheng*, refers to the reality of a thing or things, or to a fact or objective state. In contrast, when it refers to human beings, depending on context, it may be alternatively read as "reality," "emotion," or their combination. In the *Analects*, "*qing*" occurs as a term only twice. The first reads

> If those above them love ritual propriety, then among the common people none will dare to be disrespectful. If those above them love what is right, then among the common people none will dare to be disobedient. If those above them love trustworthiness, then among the common people none will dare depart from the real (*qing*). (*Lunyu*, 13.4)

In the same vein, the second reads, "Master Zeng said, it is long since those above lost the way and the common people lost their cohesion. If you find the real fact (*qing*) in them, be sad and show pity rather than be pleased (at discovering such fact)" (*Lunyu*, 19.19). Apparently, "*qing*" in both cases denotes objective fact, evidence, reality, or existential condition.

"*Qing*" appears in the *Mencius* only four times, but its connotation, compared with that in the *Analects*, is more complicated. The first occurs in his debate with CHEN Xiang 陳象, a thinker who is devoted to a doctrine of eliminating social hierarchy and labor division. Mencius argues,

> That things are unequal is part of their nature (*qing*). Some are worth twice or five times, ten or a hundred times, even a thousand and ten thousand times, more than others. If you reduce them to the same level, it will only bring confusion to the empire. (*Mengzi*, 3A4)

In another passage, he uses "*qing*" in a similar way by saying that, "Thus an exemplary person is ashamed when his reputation is admired higher than his realty (*qing*) deserves" (*Mengzi*, 4B18). Despite its distinctive flavor of speculative thinking, "*qing*" in these two cases is close to its use in the *Analects*. In fact, there is a great number of textual evidence to prove that this was of popular use in Mencius' time. For example, by the same token, Zhuangzi coins many phrases, such as "reality (*qing*) of things" (*Zhuangzi*, 155), "reality of nature and life" (*Zhuangzi*, 327), and "reality of Heaven and earth" (*Zhuangzi*, 827). Invariably, they are interchangeable with "*cheng*" as reality.

Philosophically, the more important usage of "*qing*" in Mencius are the two other cases, in which "*qing*" connotes simultaneously both "emotion" and "nature/reality." When arguing for his thesis that "human nature is good," Mencius says, "As far as the natural tendencies (*qing*) are concerned, it is possible for one to be good; this is what I mean by being good" (*Mengzi*, 6A6). Similarly, he explains the contradiction between good nature and bad behaviors in humans by saying that,

> Could it be that anyone should lack the mind of humaneness and rightness? If one lets go of the innate mind, this is like taking an axe to a tree; being hewn down day after day, can it remain beautiful?.... One becomes fettered and destroyed by what one does during the day, and if this fettering occurs repeatedly, ... he will be at scant remove from the animals. Seeing this, one might suppose that he never had the capacity for goodness. But can this be a human being's natural tendency (*qing*)?" (*Mengzi*, 6A8)

Here I follow Irene Bloom to render "*qing*" in the above two cases as "natural tendency" (de Bary 1999, 147), rather than as "nature," which many translators did. The reason is that this "*qing*" cannot be fully expressed by the single English term "nature." Looking from an analytical point of view, "*qing*" consists of two elements: "emotion" and "nature," the combination of which distinguishes human beings from animals. As for Mencius, emotion is not something independent from or standing besides nature, but rather is an organic part of nature. Or as I phrased differently in the first chapter, according to him, humans' good nature is mirrored by their universal feelings/emotion.

Many well-known passages from the *Mencius* imply this idea of the fusion of emotion and nature, although they do not always contain the term "*qing*" itself. For example, Mecius often describes the content of human nature by referring to the "four hearts": the heart of compassion, the heart of shame, the heart of propriety, and the heart of right and wrong (*Mengzi*, 6A5). In terms of modern criterion, at least the first two should be identified as being closely associated with emotion, or they should be viewed as two kinds of emotion themselves. Another example is about his conversation with King Hui of Liang. The King substituted an ox he saw personally with a sheep he did not see for an animal sacrifice in the consecration of a bell, because he "cannot bear the ox's trembling, like one who, though innocent, is being led to the execution ground." Phrasing the King's feeling as "a heart that cannot bear to see the sufferings of others," Mencius encourages him to extend this to the people in the world: "The fact that the ancients so greatly surpassed others was nothing other than this: that they were good at extending what they did" (*Mengzi*, 1A7). These cases further elucidate Mencius' position on the relation of emotion and nature: they are the two aspects of the same innate tendency. The "four hearts," as for its ability to respond to external events intuitively, may be named as "emotion," while, as for its role to characterize the human being as itself, may be named as "nature." In final analysis, they are inseparable: there is no emotion beside nature and no nature outside of emotion.

In Xunzi, the occurrence of the term "*qing*" becomes more frequent. One of his passages reads, "That which is as it is from the time of birth is called the nature of human. The like and dislike, delight and anger, grief and joy of the nature are called emotion (*qing*)" (*Xunzi*, 412). Similar to Mencius, Xunzi holds that "emotion" is not something that conflicts with "nature," but rather that which is consistent with it, and even a part of it. In the meantime, more concrete than Mencius, he specifies six particular feelings, "like and dislike, delight and anger, grief and joy" as the content of emotion. These feelings, according to him, will be aroused because of outside stimulus, and will initiate humans to act rationally or irrationally.

Nevertheless, Xunzi's general position on human nature affects his view on emotion as well. According to him, "The basic nature of human is that which they receive from Heaven. The emotions are the substance (*zhi* 質) of the nature and the desires are the response of the emotions. It is inevitable for humans to feel that their desires can be satisfied and to seek to satisfy them" (*Xunzi*, 428). Based on this observation, he warns that, "Any man who follows his nature and indulges his emotions will definitely become involved in wrangling and strife, will violate the forms and rules of society, and will end as a criminal" (*Xunzi*, 434-5). By virtue of the ideas in the two forgoing passages, Xunzi presents a dilemma before his readers: on the one hand, emotion, as nature itself, is innately endowed by Heaven, and therefore cannot be completely eliminated by any conscious efforts; on the other hand, it is a negative element that threatens the order and stability of a society. As a resolution, he appeals to education and rituals for restraining the exercise of emotion.

In summary, according to classical Confucians, emotion and nature are inseparable, because the former is nothing but the substance, indicator, or reflector of the latter. Mencius regards emotion as positive for humane government because of his favorable evaluation on nature, whereas Xunzi views it negatively because of his concern that the indulgence of emotion will lead a society in disorder. However, despite the fundamental disagreement on its moral value, they have one thing in common, that emotion and nature always correspond with each other. They may both be good (Mencius) or both be evil (Xunzi), but are never antagonistic against one another. In fact, as for the issue of "nature" and "emotion," this is a key point separating classical Confucianism from Buddhism.

III. 4. 1. 2. Nature and Emotion in Buddhism

Compared with Classical Confucians, Chinese Buddhist thinkers devoted more energy on the topic of the relation between "nature" and "emotion." The doctrines they formulated not only became crucial parts in Li's theory, but also contributed to the formation of the entire social-ethical program of Neo-Confucianism.

According to Tiantai Buddhism, the Absolute Mind (*xin* 心), known as "Bhutatathata" (*zhenru* 真如), embraces the universe in its entirety, and brings all things in the world into their existence. At the same time, as Master Zhiyi 智顗 (535-579) says, "the Buddhas of the three ages (past, present, and future), together with sentient beings, all equally have this one pure mind as their substance." This mind is neither increased, nor diminished, so it is termed as "genuineness" (*zhen* 真). Meantime, all things, both ordinary and saintly, each has its own distinct appearance, but this genuine mind is devoid of either distinctness or appearance, so it is termed as "thusness" (*ru* 如) (Feng 1953, 361-2). This mind always contains two natures: the impure nature and the pure one. Because of its impure nature, the mind is capable of manifesting the impure things pertaining to the myriad beings in the phenomenal world, while because of its pure nature it is capable of manifesting the pure attribute of Buddha. Later, Tiantai masters often called the pure nature simply as "Buddha nature." Against this doctrinal background, Liang writes,

> What is meant by cessation and contemplation? They serve to guide the phenomena (*fa* 法) of multitudinous to change in such a way so as to bring them back to the Reality (*shiji* 實際). What is this Reality? It is the original state of the nature. The failure of things to recover their nature is caused by obscurity (*hun* 昏) and movement (*dong* 動). What illuminates the obscurity is called enlightenment (*ming* 明), and what halts the movement is called quiescence (*jing* 靜). Such enlightenment and quiescence are (respectively) the substance of cessation and contemplation. Regarded as causative agents they are called cessation and contemplation. Regarded as end results they are called wisdom (*zhi* 智) and calmness (*ding* 定). (Liang 1983, 257)

Liang's argument implies that people often confuse the phenomenal world with Reality because of the operation of the impure nature. This confusion or illusion, as for its darkening people's vision on Reality, can be termed as "obscurity" and, as for its arousing "emotions" in people and making their mind unrest, can be termed as "movement." The most noteworthy is the term "nature," which appears twice in the phrases of "original state of nature" and "to recover their nature." The first one simply means the "Buddha nature," while the second means the nature of all things. Following the Tiantai doctrine of Absolute Mind, Liang assumes that "Buddha nature" and the nature of things are essentially the same; they both are enlightened, quiescent, and permanent. Hence, to "recover their nature" means simply to rekindle the "Buddha nature" which is darkened because of "obscurity" and "movement," but always exists in things.

Liang phrases the path of returning to Buddha nature as "cessation" and "contemplation." According to him, by cessation, people realize that the phenomena do not have real existence; they appear to be real only because of people's illusions. By contemplation, they realize that although phenomena have no real existence, still they sustain temporary existence and perform some worldly functions. Hence they seem to exist, just as dreams or illusions created by magic. Together the two methods lead people to a conviction that all phenomena are essentially unreal, and therefore undesirable, hence they need to free themselves from the confusion and the consequence it causes, namely "obscurity" and "movement," to reunite with their own Buddha nature. Apparently, there exist in Liang's argument three antitheses: the pure nature and impure one, the obscurity and the enlightenment, and the movement and the quiescence.

Influenced by Liang's doctrine, LI AO articulates his antagonism of nature and emotion. In Li's point of view, while nature itself is originally in a state of "enlightenment" and "quiescence," it is often situated in "obscurity" and "movement" due to the disturbance of "emotion." The goal of humans is to clean up the obscurity and stop the movement so that the nature itself can be recovered. He says,

> That whereby a man becomes a sage is the nature. That whereby a man may betray his nature are the emotions. Joy, anger, grief, fear, love, hate, and desire: these seven are all the operation of emotions. When the emotions cause obscurity, the nature is thereby drowned. This is not the fault of the nature. Rather it is the coming and going, by turn, of the seven emotions that prevents human nature from gaining its fulfillment. (Li, 551)

The terminology used here, such as "nature," "enlightenment," "obscurity," "quiescence," and "movement" shows clearly his intellectual debt to Liang's foregoing statement.

Meanwhile, Li's theses about emotion, nature, and their relationship are actually mixed with various components from both classical Confucianism and Buddhism. First of all, as for Li, human "nature" is originally good, and is in the state of enlightenment and quiescence. This idea is in line with the common position held by both Mencius and Liang, although they have different views on the composition of nature. Secondly, Li's "emotion" designates the feelings of joy, anger, grief, fear, love, hate, and desire. This reminds us of what Xunzi claims. Thirdly, instead of describing "emotion" as a part of nature, Li interprets it (or those feelings) as a psychological element that disturbs or clouds the original state of nature. Herewith he departs from the tradition of classical Confucianism and joins the Buddhist circle. Finally, he unequivocally claims that emotion is antagonistic against nature, thus people need to refrain, and even suppress their emotion, in order to have their nature recovered. This antagonism between emotion and nature echoes Liang's idea on the relation of (pure) nature and illusion. Looking carefully on these four points, we may conclude that the Tiantai doctrine has permeated into

Li's theory of emotion and nature; his position is more inclined to Buddhism than to classical Confucianism.

Later in the Song dynasty, the antagonism is further advanced by the leading figures of the Neo-Confucian Movement. For example, CHENG Yi echoes Li's idea by writing that,

> From the essence of life accumulated in Heaven and earth, humans received the five agents (water, fire, wood, metal, and earth) in their highest excellence. His original nature is pure and tranquil. Before it is aroused, the five moral principles of his nature, called humaneness, rightness, propriety, wisdom, and trustworthiness are complete. As his physical form appears, it comes into contact with external things and is aroused from within, the seven emotions, called pleasure, anger, sorrow, joy, love, hate, and desire, ensue. As emotions become strong and increasingly reckless, his nature becomes damaged. For this reason the enlightened person controls his emotions so that they will be in accord with the Equilibrium (*zhong* 中). He rectifies his mind and nourishes his nature. This is therefore called turning the emotions into the nature. The stupid person does not know how to control them. He lets them loose until they are depraved, fetter his nature, and destroy it. This is therefore called turning one's nature into emotions. (Cheng and Cheng, 577)

Similar to Li, Cheng also believes that human nature is originally pure and tranquil. However, after having their physical forms constituted, humans start to come into contact with external things, which causes the arising of emotions. In essence, the emotions should be regarded as belonging to "human" or "human desire," whereas the nature belongs to the "principle of Heaven." Following the former, humans will eventually turn to be beasts; whereas insisting on the latter, they will keep being authentic humans. Historically, his argument lays a foundation for the entire social-ethical program of Neo-Confucianism: "retaining the principle of Heaven while eliminating human desires."

III. 4. 2. Nature and Cheng

It is widely accepted knowledge that the connotation of "nature" varies from one school of thought to another, and even in different stages of evolution of a single school. For instance, ZHANG Hengshou 張恆壽, a contemporary Chinese historian, notes that its meaning in Confucianism changes significantly in ancient and modern times.

> The [human] nature that Confucius and Mencius discussed and the Confucians in the Han dynasty interpreted simply refers to a psychological aspect of humans. Originally, it had no clear metaphysical significance.... However, it was used more broadly in Buddhism. The idea that Buddhists originally intended to express is that substance and phenomena are neither one thing, nor two things.... Since there is no Chinese term equivalent to "substance" in Indian language, [Chinese Buddhists] had to fill the blank with "nature," which they borrowed from Confucians, Laozi, and Zhuangzi. (ZHANG Hengshou, 394-5)

Zhang reveals the reasons why the term "nature" is introduced into Buddhist context, and why there is a difference in the Confucian understanding of nature and its Buddhist counterpart. However, his argument seems too general and even inaccurate to a certain extent. To depict the history in more detail, and thereby underscore my divergence from him, I would like to speak more on the issue.

In classical Confucianism, especially in the *Mencius* and *Centrality and Commonality*, "nature" is certainly a concept of psychology. However, due to its integration with *cheng*/transformation, it acquires a metaphysical significance as well. The marriage of nature and *cheng*/transformation was discontinued in a historical period from DONG Zhongshu to LI Ao. As a result, "nature" turned to be a sheer psychological concept, and its quality of goodness that Mencius once firmly insisted became doubtful, and even deniable. Due to the introduction of Buddhist "nature" into the discourse of indigenous Chinese thought, the interest in Mencius' *cheng* was rekindled among Confucian thinkers, because there is a profound affinity between Buddhist "nature" and Mencius' *cheng*. This intellectual current inspired LI Ao to reconnect "nature" with *cheng*/transformation, and to redefine the Confucian "nature" as a metaphysical concept. I will prove these points by analyzing briefly the relation of nature and *cheng* from Mencius to LI Ao.

In Mencius and *Centrality and Commonality*, (human) "nature" is certainly a psychological and anthropological concept, referring to the in-born trait of human being. For example, *Centrality and Commonality* states, "What Heaven endows to man is called (human) nature" (*Zhongyong*, 17). More obviously, when disputing against Gaozi's 告子 notion that "the whiteness of white feather is the same as the whiteness of white snow, and the whiteness of white snow is the same as the whiteness of white jade," Mencius asked rhetorically, "In that case, is the nature of a hound the same as the nature of an ox, and the nature of an ox is the same as the nature of a human?" (*Mengzi*, 6A3) His inquiry implies that each species has its own nature, and the variety of natures accounts for the existence of a myriad of things in the universe.

In the meanwhile, due to its direct association with *cheng*, nature itself also acquires a metaphysical significance. *Mencius* says, "*cheng* is the way of Heaven, while thinking to be *cheng* is the way of humans." Correspondently, *Centrality and Commonality* reads, "Only he who is possessed of absolute *cheng* can fully develop his nature. If he can fully develop his nature, he can fully develop the nature of others" (*Zhongyoung*, 32). In their view, as an ultimate source for the existence of a myriad of things and a universal principle accounting for the regularity in the universe, *cheng* embodies itself as the sage and his fully developed nature. Ultimately, this nature is an attribute possessed not only by the sage, but also by all humans. The only distinction is that nature in the sage is exhaustively actualized, whereas in ordinary people it may exist simply as potency, or in a state of dormancy.

This idea gradually lost its audience since the Han dynasty. As one of its consequences, the connection of nature and *cheng* is broken up: "nature," as Zhang indicates, was simply applied to the "psychological aspect of humans," while *cheng* is variously understood as governmental consistency, the reality of things, the source of mystical changes, and the honest attitude toward others. This certainly blurs the idea of "transformation," and even makes it unintelligible. About "nature," DONG Zhongshu inquires, the theorists in his time differed from one another on its meaning; however, why didn't they simply go to check the word "nature?"

> Doesn't the word nature mean "inborn" (*sheng* 生)? If it means what is in born, then the spontaneous endowments that one possesses at birth are termed "nature." Nature is the basic substance (*zhi* 質). If we investigate the basic substance of nature by applying the term "good," will that be correct? If not, how can we still say that the basic substance is good? The term "nature" cannot be separated from the basic substance. If it is separated from the basic substance by as much as a hair's width, then it has already ceased to be nature. This must be understood. (Dong, 291-2)

Dong interprets human nature simply as what is inborn, or what comes with one's birth. It is the "basic substance" from which human life unfolds. The nature in its entirety is not necessarily good, although it may contain goodness in itself. "The nature is like the rice stalk, and goodness is like rice. Rice emerges from within the stalk, but not all the stalk becomes rice. Likewise, goodness emerges from within the nature, but not all of the nature becomes good" (Dong, 296). Herewith he takes a position close to Xunzi to promote education and ritual for an orderly society. Obviously, he doesn't feel that people need to take *cheng* or heavenly way into account when dealing with the issue of "nature."

The introduction of the Buddhist concept of Buddha nature threw a new light on the Chinese term "nature" and its connection with *cheng*. Among the ideas about its multiple attributes, what particularly interests Chinese Buddhists, and thinkers from other schools as well, is "universality," a notion that Buddha nature is universally possessed by sentient and insentient beings. A historical survey shows that the group to which the concept refers was gradually enlarged to accommodate more types of being.

Dao Sheng 道生 (360-434) may be the first Chinese Buddhist to insist that Buddha nature is what all humans share. According to historical record, when the incomplete version of *Nirvana Sutra* first reached the Buddhist community,

> He analyzed the principle of the *Sutra* and entered deeply into its profound meaning. He then asserted that even "icchatikas" (whose primary interest is the gratification of their desires) could also become Buddha. At that time, (the complete version of) *Great Nirvana Sutra* had not yet arrived in our land, and he, with his single understanding, was the first to develop this

> unique view, in opposition to most people's opinion.... Then when suddenly the *Great Nirvana Sutra* reached the capital, people found that it indeed says that all icchantikas possess the Buddha nature. This is completely consistent to what Dao Sheng had claimed before. (Hui Jiao, 256)

The monks in China then recalled his prophetic words and admired him even more for his penetrating wisdom. There is no doubt that the shift of the monks' attitude toward Dao Sheng means also a wide acceptance of his view within Buddhist community.

Likewise, Xin Xing 信行 (540-594), the founder of the Sect of Three Stages (*sanjie jiao* 三階教) argued that all the multitudinous things in the phenomenal world were the manifestations of the one source of reality, namely Buddha nature. Because all humans, regardless of sect and station, in fact, all sentient beings, were looked upon as possessors of Buddha nature. They were worthy of respect, to be considered as future Buddha (Chen, Kenneth, 299). Compared with Dao Sheng, his concept of Buddha nature is more inclusive, embracing not merely humans, but all the other kinds of sentient beings.

A similar idea is in the *Platform Sutra*. Hui Neng 慧能 (638-713), the sixth patriarch of Chan sect, recalled his first conversation with Hong Ren 弘忍, the fifth patriarch.

> The monk Hong Ren asked, "Where are you from that you come to the mountain to make obeisance to me? Just what is it that you are looking for from me?" I replied, "I am from Lingnan 嶺南, a commoner from Xinzhou 新州. I have come to this long distance only to make obeisance to you. I am seeking nothing else, but just want to be a Buddha." The monk then reproved me, saying, "If you are from Lingnan, then you are a barbarian. How can you become a Buddha?" I replied, "Although people from the south and people from the north differ, there is no north and south in Buddha nature. Although my barbarian's body and your body are not the same, what different is there in our Buddha nature? (Hui Neng, 8)

In the same *Sutra*, Hui Neng further elucidated the relation of sentient being's self-nature (*zixing* 自性) and the Buddha nature. "Buddha originates from self-nature, thus do not seek for it from outside. If self-nature is clouded, Buddha will become a sentient being; whereas if self-nature is enlightened, a sentient being will become

Buddha" (Hui Neng, 66). His saying implies that self-nature and Buddha nature of sentient beings are not two separate entities, but are the same thing with two names. To become Buddha simply means to have one's self-nature fully enlightened or developed.

Lastly, Zhan Ran 湛然 (711-782), the ninth patriarch of the Tiantai sect further stressed that "even inanimate beings possess Buddha nature" (*wuqing you xing* 無情有性).

> There is no water without wetness. This wetness does not distinguish between the muddy and the limpid, yet the waves are of themselves either clear or turbid. Irrespective of their clarity or turbidness, there is for them only one undifferentiated nature.... If on the one hand we grant that what responds to causation remains itself immutable, yet on the other say that inanimate beings lack [the immutable nature], do we not fall into a self-contradiction?" (Feng 1953, 385)

LIANG Su once admitted that Zhan Ran's doctrine was the direct source from which he derived his own idea of "nature." Unlike the "nature" in the Confucians since the Han, his "nature" refers to an all-embracing entity, a sole reality that manifests itself in a myriad of things. As for humans, it represents their reality that may be darkened or clouded because of the interference of "emotion," but will never be "lost."

In the Sui-Tang period, the prevalence of the notion of Buddha nature helped to create an intellectual atmosphere, by which the Mencian *cheng* turned to be something familiar to both Buddhists and lay people. In scrutiny, Buddha nature is comparable to *cheng* in two crucial points: the universality and accessibility to all beings, and the absolute goodness by which people can properly exercise their moral evaluation and value judgment. In fact, as far as its connotation is concerned, it is closer to *cheng* in Mencius and *Centrality and Commonality* than the "nature" understood by the Han Confucians. This affinity between Buddha nature and *cheng* enables LI Ao to seek for the original meaning of *cheng* from the perspective of Buddha nature, and to spread the idea of *cheng* among his contemporaries who have already embraced the notion of Buddha nature.

Li says about *cheng* and "nature" that "*cheng* is the nature of the sage," and "there is no difference between the nature of the sage and that of ordinary people" (Li, 551). It is apparent that the message carried by these two sentences has nothing at odds with the idea of Buddha nature. The nature of the sage is termed here as *cheng*, referring to the attribute of the sage, just as Buddha nature is to that of the Buddha. Meanwhile, *cheng* of the sage is not something qualitatively different from the nature of ordinary people, but rather the same attribute equally possessed by both of them. This reminds us of Hui Neng's position of Buddha nature and self-nature. Similar to his idea about the Buddha and common people, the only distinction between the sage and ordinary people is that the nature in the former is fully developed, actualized, and enlightened, whereas in the latter it is still undeveloped, dormant, and clouded. As for Buddhists, the goal is to become Buddha by means of cessation and contemplation, while in Li it is to become the sage by self-cultivation.

However, being a Confucian thinker, Li's first concern is still the traditional Confucian issue: the relation between human nature and the way of Heaven. In a tone reminiscent of Mencius and *Centrality and Commonality*, he writes, "Absolute *cheng* is the way of Heaven;" "(human) nature is what is endowed by Heaven" (Li, 555). In fact, even these typical Confucian ideas can still peacefully co-exist with relevant Buddhist doctrines. For example, in Tiantai Buddhism, the absolute mind is the final account for the existence of Buddha nature, while in Li, Heaven plays the same role to that of human nature and *cheng*.

In brief, Li's position on *cheng*, the way of Heaven, and nature can be described as this: nature is a commonality shared by both the sage and ordinary people; *cheng* is another name of nature; and the "absolute *cheng*" is the nature in its state of full development. Nature or *cheng* comes from and is consistent to Heaven. Although what is presented here is basically a Mencian framework, it is not contradictory to the notion of Buddha nature that was popular in Li's time. This explains why his idea is widely welcome by the intellectuals from both Confucian and Buddhist circles.

III. 4. 3. Cheng *and Illumination*

In Li's point of view, the sage has a duty to direct ordinary people to recover their nature. "The sage is the one who first attains understanding" (Li, 551); "Heaven, in producing the people, has given to those who first attain understanding the duty of awakening those who are slow to understand; and to those who are the first to awaken the duty of awakening those who are slow to awaken" (Li, 557). Also, he believes that the sage's mission is principally accomplishable, because "the nature of everyone is good, and by following it, they may themselves become sages" (Li, 552). Now the question is, how does the sage fulfill this duty? Put differently, what is the way by which the sage transforms others? To specify the mode of the sage's operation, Li reinterprets two concepts from *Centrality and Commonality*, namely *cheng* and *ming*.

A well-known passage from the text states that, "It is due to nature that *ming* results from *cheng*. It is due to education that *cheng* results from *ming*. Given *cheng*, there will be *ming*, and given *ming*, there will be *cheng*" (*Zhongyong*, 32). Historically, most Chinese commentators read "*ming*" as "intelligence" or "enlightenment." Therewith they often expound the passage as that the person with absolute *cheng* naturally possesses intelligence, while the person accumulating his intelligence through education knows the desirability of *cheng*, and therefore strives consciously to pursue it.

In contrast, Li interprets *cheng* as the nature of the sage, and *ming* as his "illumination" that penetrates through people's obscurity to have them enlightened. He writes, "To know everything, to do everything, to be absolutely tranquil in the mind, and yet to have its light illuminate Heaven and earth—that is *ming* (illumination) of *cheng*" (Li, 554). Also, "*Cheng*, if uninterrupted, leads to 'vacuity' (*xu* 虛). Vacuity, if uninterrupted, leads to illumination; illumination, if uninterrupted, leads to an all-embracing illumination of Heaven and earth" (Li, 552). Sometimes, he even directly visualizes the relation between *cheng* and *ming* as the sun and its illumination of a myriad of things. "The sage is silently immovable. He reaches his destination without traveling; he is divine without uttering a word; he glows without making any shining." "*Cheng* is the nature of the sage. It is silently inactive, all-embracing and purifying, and casting lights through Heaven and earth. But, when acted on, it immediately penetrates all things" (Li, 551). The passages above contain an idea that the nature of the sage and its transforming power can be compared to "light source" and its "light." Like the sun, the sage naturally possesses an invincible moral force that will cast out just as the sun shines to warm and nurture all things on the earth.

The pairing metaphors of "light source" and "its light," as well as the relation they display are not a typical Confucian heritage, but borrowed from Daoism and Buddhism. In the *Zhuangzi*, LIE Yukou said, "If you cannot dispel *cheng* inside you, it oozes out of body and forms a radiance that overpowers people's minds" (*Zhuangzi*, 1037). The Daoists in the Six Dynasties further pushed this mystical thought forward. They held that the immortals were able to absorb the essence of the sun and moon and to project colored lights across long distances (Munro 1988, 83). The more direct source for Li's metaphors is in Buddhist texts. For example, Hui Neng once asked his audience, "What do 'calmness' (*ding* 定) and 'wisdom' (*hui* 慧) look like? [They look] like a lamp and its light. If there is a lamp, there must be light. If there is no lamp, there must be no light. The lamp is the substance of light, while the light is the function of the lamp" (Hui Neng, 30). What interests us in this passage is not only the appearance of the same metaphors, "light source" and its "light," but also the theorization of them as substance and function.

Li's illustration of *cheng* and illumination, and the sage and his transformation with the metaphors of light source and light, the sun and its shining, adds one more piece of evidence for the Buddhist influence. It highlights an idea of classical Confucianism that has been neglected, ignored, and even forgotten by the Confucian thinkers from the Han. It is that the transformation initiated by the sage is an automatic and natural process, and an ideal way to social harmony. All ordinary people are transformable so long as they model themselves on the sage to reserve or recover their nature or *cheng*.

Conclusion

In the historical period with which this chapter deals, compared with its classical form in the pre-Qin period, the idea of *cheng* became more complicated, encompassing more dimensions and uses. Among those new developments are two things particularly noteworthy. First, *cheng* was expanded into the field of government as being an efficient measurement for social order, and a useful means for politicians pursuing their goal. Second, the elements from Buddhism participated in the evolution of *cheng*, providing scholars with a new perspective to examine and evaluate relevant issues in classical Confucianism. As the result of their efforts, the original meaning of *cheng* was restored, and its connection with human nature was re-established. At the same time, however, an antagonism between *cheng* and emotion, which is strange to classical Confucians, entered into Chinese intellectual discourse. As will be seen in the next chapter, all these points were assimilated as crucial components to the philosophical system of Neo-Confucianism in the Song dynasty.

Chapter IV

The Heyday

In the Song dynasty, the tradition of transformation that LI Ao promoted reached its apex. Among the Neo-Confucian philosophers, it became common knowledge that *cheng* is a universal principle for all kinds of consistency, regularity, and predictability in human activities and natural phenomena. The sage embodies *cheng*, acting as "creator" of the social harmony, and the transformation that the sage initiates is the most reliable route toward its realization. Due to their writings and lectures, as well as a generally favorable political and intellectual atmosphere, this notion dominated the discourse on relevant issues. It was widely accepted by learned people and, through their activities, it strongly affected the contemporary academic life and political affairs. What the term "heyday" refers to is a state in which the notion of transformation is not only fully articulated, but also directly influences people's intellectual and political lives. This chapter plans to examine *cheng* in the writings of four Confucian masters, ZHOU Dunyi, ZHANG Zai 張載(1020-1077), CHENG Yi, and ZHU Xi. They agreed with each other on the basic notion of *cheng*; and, at the same time, they strove to enrich and popularize it in distinctive ways. To avoid unnecessary repetition that will likely occur when attempting to write comprehensively about their systems, in what follows I will simply focus my analysis on their "distinctiveness." The purpose is to highlight their unique contributions to the final formation of the idea of *cheng*.

IV. 1. *Cheng* in ZHOU Dunyi

One of the modes in which Chinese philosophy after the Qin-Han period evolved is the explanation of and commentary on ancient texts. The early examples are WANG Bi's explanation of the principles of the *Laozi* and the *Book of Changes*, GUO Xiang's commentary on the *Zhuangzi*, and much later, ZHU Xi's commentary on the *Four Books*. In these philosophical endeavors, the texts stand as "authoritative framework," which inspires the creativity of the later thinkers and, in the meantime, restrains it within a certain boundary. As a result of this twofold effect, the new ideas raised later are often entangled with old contents, and the new insights often appear in the clothes of old texts. This conclusion also applies to ZHOU Dunyi's *Penetrating the Book of Changes* (*Tongshu*, 《通書》), an interpretive work on the principle of the *Book of Changes*.

The *Book of Changes* has been ranked as the primordial source of traditional wisdom and the first among Confucian classics. It exhibits a paradigm of Heaven and earth and, especially in the *Grand Commentary* (*Dazhuan* 《大傳》), one of its ancient exegetical materials, structures a universal order that underlies the myriad things. Serving as a philosophical background, this text enables Zhou to identify the cosmological origin of *cheng*, to explore its universality manifest in both Heaven and humans, and to concretize the procedure that the transformation undertakes. Because of his effort of founding *cheng* on a cosmic basis, and defining it as the "substance" that lies and effects in all the other Confucian virtues, he evokes among his successors a strong interest in and diligent study on *cheng*. For this reason he is generally praised as the true initiator of Neo-Confucian Movement.

IV. 1. 1. The Cosmological Origin

As discussed before, both the *Xunzi* and *Centrality and Commonality* began their doctrines of *cheng* with a statemet on the ethical *cheng*, and then read it into Nature to formulate the cosmic *cheng*. Finally, from the commonality between the two, they derived the universal *cheng* as a general principle. In contrast, due to the wide acceptance of the "universal *cheng*" and the prevalence of the cosmological view represented by the *Grand Commentary* in the Song dynasty, Zhou chooses to unfold his own system with a new start.

According to Zhou, the ultimate source for the creation of the entire universe is the "Creative" (*qianyuan* 乾元), a term he borrows from the *Grand Commentary*. It is the "creator" in the sense of Ames and Hall and its "creativity" represents what MOU Zongsan calls the "principle of actualization." The first chapter of the *Penetrating* says that,

> "Great indeed is the sublimity of the Creative, to which all beings owe their beginnings" (*Yijing*, 53). It is the source of *cheng*. "The way of the Creative works through change and transformation, so that each thing receives its true nature and destiny" (*Yijing*, 54). In this way, *cheng* is established. *Cheng* is pure and perfectly good. Therefore "the successive movement of *yin* and *yang* constitute the Way. What issues from the way is good, and that which realizes it is the individual nature" (*Yijing*, 514). "Origination" and "flourishing" characterizes the penetration of *cheng*, and "advance" and "firmness" are its completion. (Zhou, 31)

In this passage, the quoted sentences are from *Yijing*, or the *Book of Changes*, while the others are Zhou's interpretation of their meanings. It tells that, the Creative originates *cheng*; and due to the transformation and change from the Creative, *cheng*, as well as the nature of myriad things, are formed. In light of this description, *cheng* is among all creatures of the Creative. It is "pure" because it possesses no physical qualities, such as weight, color, or taste; also, it is "perfectly good" because its formation is directly related to the Way, having nothing to do with human consciousness or activities. Different from other "particular" natures, such as "tree-ness" or "dog-ness," with which only trees or dogs share, *cheng* is the most general concept signifying the nature/reality of all kinds of being. Meanwhile, it penetrates the entire life cycle of all beings through four phases represented respectively by the terms: "origination," "flourishing," "advance," and "firmness." Zhou's message is that *cheng* is not reality/nature in a regular sense, but something that generalizes the commonness of all kinds of nature/reality, which exists in anywhere, anytime.

Like almost all Confucian philosophers, what interests Zhou the most is not the structure or composition of *cheng*, but its social and moral significance. After a short description of *cheng*'s cosmic origination, he moves on to bridge the Creative and moral virtues with *cheng*.

> *Cheng* is the root of the five constant virtues (humaneness, rightness, propriety, wisdom, and trustworthiness) and the source of all activities. When quiescent, it is in the state of non-being (*wu* 無), and when active, it is in the state of being (*you* 有). It is perfectly correct and clearly penetrating. Without *cheng*, the five constant virtues are not as what they are now, and they will be depraved and obstructed. Therefore, with *cheng* little effort is needed (for social achievement). This seems extremely easy, but is difficult to put into practice. (Zhou, 32)

Along with the tradition of treating *cheng* as the way to exercise the three universal virtues: "wisdom," "compassion," and "courage" (*Zhongyong*, 28), Zhou further describes it as the "foundation" of the five constant virtues. This is not a mechanical relationship in which the five virtues are founded on *cheng*, but rather an organic one in which *cheng* penetrates through and exists in all of them. Strictly speaking, *cheng* is not an entity independent of the five virtues, but a common reality shared and expressed variously by the virtues. Each virtue manifests *cheng* in its own way; and they are regarded as "virtue" simply because of *cheng*'s existence in them. Put differently, without *cheng* there will be no virtues to better people's life, and no standards to judge and evaluate their activities. According to Zhou, *cheng* acts on people in a subtle way. On the one side, it is "quiescent" because it doesn't start any striving directly, but instead exercises its influence through the five virtues. In this sense, its operation can be phrased as "non-action." On the other side, it is "active" because it is not a void name or imaginary entity, but a real force that effects in a society through the five virtues. As far as this point is concerned, it can be named as "being."

The unity of quiescence and activity signifies a perfect pattern by which the sage accomplishes the work of transformation. Similar to LI Ao, Zhou also views the sage as the embodiment of *cheng*: "*Cheng* is the foundation of the sage" (Zhou, 31); "the sagehood is nothing but *cheng*" (Zhou, 32). He compares the sage's transformation of people to the Creative's creativity in the universe: the sage's *cheng* manifests in consistent conducts, while the Creative convinces people of its presence through regular and predictable movements in cosmos; the sage transforms people by inspiring and encouraging them to develop their good nature, while the Creative accomplishes its transformation of a myriad of things by silently creating and nourishing them.

To describe the essence of the sage and the feature of the sage's transformation more sufficiently, Zhou borrows two phrases from the *Grand Commentary* and says that, "what is 'absolute quiescent and inactive' is called *cheng*; what 'immediately penetrates all things when responding to them' is called divinity (*shen* 神)" (Zhou, 33). *Cheng* as the essence of the sage is "absolute quiescent and inactive." Meanwhile, its transformation is as powerful and effective as "divinity" is to all things. Here "divinity" is metaphorically used to signify a manner in which Heaven and the sage affect us evidently, but leave us no clue to how it exercises. I would like to clarify this term by referring to the two concepts of Aristotle, "effective cause" and "final cause."

According to Aristotle's distinction, when I push this chair to move it, my action is both effective (the chair is moved) and understandable (other people have the same experience). Here I (or my action of moving) am (is) the effective cause of the chair's motion. Meanwhile, "since that which is moved and moves is intermediate, there is something which moves without being moved, being eternal, substance, and actuality. And the object of desire and the object of thought move in this way; they move without being moved." This "unmoved mover" is the "final cause" of all motions in the cosmos, and it exercises in a manner very close to that of "divinity." In concrete, "For the final cause is (a) some being for whose good an action is done, and (b) something at which the action aims; .... The final cause, then, produces motion as being loved, but all other things move by being moved" (Aristotle, 879). As in Aristotle, the final cause is often interchangeably used with "God," whereas Zhou likes to associate "divinity" with Heaven and the sage. He says that,

> As the Way of Heaven operates, all things are in harmony (*shun* 順). As the virtue of the sage is cultivated, all people are transformed. The great harmony and great transformation leave no

> trace, and no one knows how they come to be: this is called divinity. (Zhou, 36)

Unlike other causes of motion that we know from daily life, *cheng* of the sage doesn't "propel" people for its goal, but instead, simply "attracts" them with its own existence. This explains why people voluntarily follow the sage to transform themselves, and why the sage can accomplish the mission as certain as the final cause/God effects on things. Zhou's idea of *cheng* and divinity clearly shows his optimistic conviction for the success of the sage's endeavor.

IV. 1. 2. Moral Hierarchy

For elucidating the procedure of transformation, Zhou proposes a theory, which I would call the "graded transformation," or the "moral hierarchy in transformation." Its core idea is that, as a huge social project, the transformation needs not only the initiation of the sage, but also the active participation of all members in a society, especially the educated ones. A passage from him reads,

> The sage institutes education so as to enable people to transform their evil by themselves, to arrive at equilibrium and rest there. Therefore those who are the first to be enlightened should instruct those who are slower in attaining enlightenment, and the ignorant should seek help from those who understand. (Zhou, 34)

To find the "lost" heart, to recover the nature, or to preserve the inner state of *cheng* is a work that must be done by people themselves. In this sense, people are the real agents for their own transformation, although they need a "light" from the sage. Zhou believes that, even though people are all transformable by nature, they vary in moral life: some are clear, others are clouded; some are in quiescence, others are in disturbance. This divides them as higher or lower. The goal of education is to encourage a co-operation between the two groups of people, letting the lower catch up with the higher, and the higher assist the lower. Different from LI Ao and the Buddhist philosophers, Zhou's "light source," or the sage's *cheng*, doesn't throw its light directly on everyone, but enlightens educators first, and through their transmission, eventually reaches people in the lower status. The educators are actually the mediator for the transformation in a society.

There is a graded transformation even among the educators themselves. Zhou asserts, "The sage aspires to attain [the status of] Heaven, the worthy aspires to attain [that of] the sage, the gentleman (*shi* 士) aspires to attain [that of] the worthy" (Zhou, 35). Here the "worthy" refers to the persons like Yi Yin 伊尹, the legendary minister of the State Qi, and YAN Yuan, the best student of Confucius. The "gentleman" refers to the "true Confucians" (*zhenru* 真儒) who usually live among people and instruct them on a daily basis. As Munro describes, "Their job is to transform and nurture the people and to be examples for other literati. Such true Confucians may be found teaching in schools rather than serving as prefects" (Munro 1988, 170). Moreover, Zhou holds that the path to the sagehood is open to everyone. As for the educators, the more they persist on their self-cultivation, the higher the status they may attain. "When one desires what Yi Yin desires, and learns what YAN Yuan learns, [there may come two consequences—] if he exceeds them, he will become a sage; while if he attains their state, he will become a worthy" (Zhou, 35). In essence, both "educator" and "student" are relative concepts, denoting the twofold role that every individual plays in the social project of transformation. For example, the sage is an educator in terms of teaching the worthy and others, while he is also a student who needs to emulate the way of Heaven.

The transformation will eventually lead people to a state of "equilibrium," a term Zhou borrows from *Centrality and Commonality*, but reads into it something new. A comparison between its uses in the two texts will show Zhou's position on three important concepts in Chinese philosophy: "emotion," "equilibrium" and "harmony." *Centrality and Commonality* reads, "Before the emotions of pleasure, anger, sorrow, and joy are aroused it is called equilibrium. When these emotions are aroused and each and all attain due measure and degree, it is called harmony (*he* 和)" (*Zhongyong*, 18). Here "emotions" are viewed as the source that generates all the moral actions, a positive quality that characterizes humans as what they are. And, "equilibrium" is basically a neutral term that simply denotes a state accommodating the potency of all emotions. The goal for each individual is to reach "harmony," so that a person's emotions can not only be aroused properly, but also initiate the right actions to the right target. In contrast, Zhou's "equilibrium" means "harmony, and attaining due measure and degree. It is a universal path in the world, and is that to which the sage is devoted" (Zhou, 34). In his framework, "equilibrium" connotes a state that seems closer to "harmony" than to "equilibrium" in *Centrality and Commonality*. At the same time, there seems no room for "emotion," let alone its connection with Zhou's "equilibrium." In my view, the absence of "emotion" hints that Zhou is reluctant to regard "emotion" as a positive element in his social project of transformation. In fact, his stance forebodes the general tendency of Neo-Confucian Movement—denying that "emotion" may play a constructive role in human life, and even treating it as opposed to human nature or *cheng*.

The idea of "graded transformation" reflects the collective consciousness of Confucians as an intellectual-political group, and displays a social program in which they should and could participate. Now, to enlighten people is no longer a mission ascribed only to the sage; it becomes a collective cause that needs the effort of educator at all levels. This idea not only encourages Confucians to be more sincere in self-cultivation for the attainment of higher status, but also urges them to be more active in transforming the populace. The combination of these two sides results in the emergence of a large number of Confucian communities in the Song period, which sometimes have an organizational base in academies. They are philosophical centers from which the ideas of *cheng* and transformation spread to the entire society. Their members often constitute some political factions, and even directly take part in social reforms. Since the end of the Han dynasty, Chinese intellectuals have never been so organized and so active in philosophical discussion and in political affairs.

IV. 2. *Cheng* in ZHANG Zai

ZHANG Zai, the second major figure in the Neo-Confucian movement, attains his final position through a long and winding path. According to the *History of the Song Dynasty* (*Songshi*, 《宋史》), as a youth, he "delighted in discussing military matters." Due to the advice and encouragement from Fang Zhongyan 范仲淹 (989-1052), a well-respected politician and scholar, he began his study on *Central-*

ity and Commonality. Not being wholly satisfied by the text, "he turned to delve in the doctrines of Buddhism and Daoism for several successive years. Yet he could not acquire the anticipated understanding in these texts either, so again he shifted back to the six classics of Confucianism." Inspired by discussions with CHENG Hao and CHENG Yi about the *Book of Changes* and the learning of Dao (*daoxue* 道學), he finally concluded that, "the truth of our school is self-sufficient, why do we need to search else where?' And with this idea, he completely discarded his heterodox learning and turned to be a pure Confucian thinker." After serving at governmental positions for several years, he retreated to farm and taught in his hometown. "Wearing shabby clothes and eating only vegetable, he taught his students to strive to become sage. He claimed that it had been a major error from the scholars since the Qin-Han period that they understood people, but not Heaven, sought only for being the worthy person, but not the sage. Hence, he established his own doctrine that took what is in the *Book of Changes* as the principle, and what is in *Centrality and Commonality* as the substance. It encouraged people to respect Confucius, value the virtue, enjoy what Heaven endowed, and feel ease with destiny" (ZHANG Zai, 385-6).

His biography interests us for several reasons. First, thanks to his diligent study of Buddhism and Daoism, Zhang is qualified in comparing them with Confucianism, and thereby his conclusion in favor of the latter sounds convincing to his audience. Second, being the major source of his philosophy, the *Book of Changes* and *Centrality and Commonality*, including their central theme—the unity of Heaven and humans—tremendously influenced his approach to philosophical issues. Third, the goal he sets for learning is not becoming a worthy person, but becoming a sage or attaining sagehood. These points jointly shaped his notion of *cheng*, and provided us with a clue for its understanding.

IV. 2. 1. The Union of the Way of Heaven and Human Nature

A saying of Zigong, one of Confucius' star students, is recorded in the *Analects*, "Our Master's view concerning culture and the outward insignia of goodness, we are permitted to hear; but about human nature and the way of Heaven he will not tell us anything at all"

(*Lunyu*, 5.12). His comment implies that "human nature and the way of Heaven" signify the objects of the highest wisdom, to which even the Master himself is always reverential and cautious. In my view, Confucius' avoidance of discussing them may result from a concern related to both his religious skepticism and earnest interest in earthly issues.

In reply to a student's question about serving ghosts and spirits, Confucius asked rhetorically, "Till you have learnt to serve humans, how can you serve ghosts?" Likewise, when answering a question about the dead from the same student, he said in the same tone, "Till you know about the living, how are you to know about the dead?" (*Lunyu*, 11.11). In another place, when questioned by another student about wisdom, he responded, "Devote yourself earnestly to the duties due to humans, and respect spiritual beings but keep them at a distance. This may be called wisdom" (*Lunyu*, 6.20). These sayings reveal Confucius' profound doubt on the limitation of human intelligence, as well as his preference to do things at hand first. The knowledge on the supernatural beings, the transcendent world, the way of Heaven, and even human nature is something that can be neither proved nor disproved by any empirical means. The Master worried that an attachment to them might distract students' attention from the practical issues pertaining to people's conducts and social institutions.

Interestingly, the two themes that the Master refused to comment about—the way of Heaven and human nature—become the central topic of *Centrality and Commonality* and the *Grand Commentary*. This tradition is channeled through LI Ao to the Song Neo-Confucians, including ZHANG Zai himself. One of the features of Zhang's philosophy is that he does not view the way of Heaven and human nature as two separate subjects, but rather two aspects of the same *cheng*. He writes that, "Rightness and destiny are united in principle. Humaneness and wisdom are united in sagehood. Movement and tranquility are united in divinity. And human nature and the way of Heaven are united in *cheng*" (ZHANG Zai, 20).

Methodologically, he often expounds the content of *cheng* by presenting a parallel relationship between the way of Heaven and human nature. Taking the tradition of *Centrality and Commonality*, he argues that "ceaselessness," one of the most distinctive attributes of *cheng*, is identifiable in the two domains. "The way by which Heaven unceasingly lasts is called *cheng*. The reason why the humane man and filial son can serve Heaven and develop themselves is simply that their humaneness and filial piety are also unceasing" (ZHANG Zai, 20). In another place, he equates *cheng* with "ceaselessness," explaining how it integrates Heaven and humans as a unity.

> The absolute *cheng* is the nature endowed by Heaven; the ceaselessness is the mandate coming from Heaven. When humans attain the absolute *cheng*, their nature is fully developed, their divinity is fully revealed. When they attain "ceaselessness," their lives run in accordance with the course of Heaven, and their transformation can be anticipated." (ZHANG Zai, 63)

Zhang's approach to unify the way of Heaven and human nature with *cheng* is showed also in his position on *cheng* and *ming*. As discussed before, these two terms were first tied together in *Centrality and Commonality*, signifying the two directions from which the sage and the worthy attain the same goal—being an ideal person with both *cheng* and enlightenment. In LI Ao, however, they were reinterpreted as a light source and its light (illumination): *cheng* is the reality of the sage, while *ming* is the light that the sage cast on people for their transformation. Viewing from a different perspective, Zhang regards *cheng* as the same reality in both the way of Heaven and human nature, and *ming* as the same knowledge about *cheng*. "When the the way of Heaven and human nature function differently, there cannot be *cheng*. When the knowledge of the way of Heaven and that of human nature are divergent, there cannot be *ming*" (ZHANG Zai, 20). He believes that, since the way of Heaven and human nature possess the same *cheng*, they must function in the same manner (transformation), and the learnings about them, if fully accomplished, must reach the same end.

To show his audience the shortest way to *cheng*, Zhang further argues that, "there is no distinction between the way of Heaven as being great and human nature as being small," (ZHANG Zai, 21) so we'd better focus our attention on human nature and human life, instead of dreaming or guessing what happens to the way of Heaven. After all, the things at hand possess the same *cheng* as the way of Heaven does, and they are reachable and verifiable. For the same purpose, he reinterprets two phrases *Centrality and Commonality*. "By '*cheng* resulting from *ming*' is meant to obtain the full development of one's nature (*jinxing* 盡性) through thorough investigation of the principle (*qiongli* 窮理), and by '*ming* resulting from *cheng*' is meant to obtain a thorough understanding of the principle through fully develop one's nature." Here he suggests a two-way journey for the final attainment of both *cheng* and *ming*: to know the principle of things by fully developing one's nature/*cheng*, and to develop one's nature/*cheng* by thoroughly knowing the principle of things. In fact, they both are related to daily life, and both depend on daily practice for their success.

IV. 2. 2. **Cheng** ***as the Ultimate Realm***

Zhang's philosophy of *cheng* shows a religious inclination that is distincetive and rational. To verify this thesis, I would first borrow George Mavrodes' suggestion to define what "religion" means, and then employ Max Weber's criterion to evaluate the degree of rationalization that Zhang's philosophy attained.

In Mavrodes' view, religion contains a view of ultimate nature or reality (perhaps, but not necessarily, God as a creator), a source of human values derived from the reality (God is love, so love is a value) and practices (worship, prayer) that link humans to the reality. It emphasizes the existence of a spiritual or transcendental experience that follows the linkage and efforts to cultivate it (fasting, meditation). Finally, those who share the above beliefs will organize to be a community in which they can provide support to each other or acknowledge the legitimacy of this community.[6] Meanwhile, according to Weber, "To judge the level of rationalization a religion represents, we may use two primary yardsticks which are in many ways interrelated. One is the degree to which the religion has divested itself of magic; the other is the degree to which it has systematically unified the relation between God and the world and therewith its own relationship to the world" (Weber, 226). In an attempt to prove the aforementioned thesis, I will examine Zhang's position on two

---

[6] This definition is derived from George Mavrodes of the University of Michigan, and was conveyed to me through Professor Donald Munro.

issues: the source of YAN Yuan's joy, and the relation of the ultimate realm and the world.

IV. 2. 2. 1. The Joy of YAN Yuan

The *Confucius' Analects* contains two passages concerning poverty and joy. The first is about the Master himself: "With coarse rice to eat, with water to drink, and my bent arm for a pillow;—I have still got joy (*le* 樂) in the midst of these things" (*Lunyu*, 7.16). The second refers to YAN Yuan: "With a single bamboo bowl of rice, a single gourd of water, and living in a shabby lane, while others could not have endured the distress, he did not allow his joy to be affected by it" (*Lunyu*, 6.11). What characterizes the two passages is a sharp contrast between poverty in material life and joy in spirit. Obviously, since both the Master and Yan are poor in materialistic sense, their joy must come from a source independent of financial wealth and physical comfort. Later, to locate the source of joy, and therewith to enjoy the same experience become a compelling topic in Confucian tradition.

YANG Xiong 揚雄 (53 B.C.E.-18 C.E.), a Confucian scholar in the Han dynasty, writes, "Someone asked, 'If I am a person wearing clothes decorated with pearls and possessing gold, is there anything more joyful than my joy?' I replied, 'the joy of those who wear clothes with pearls and possess gold is not as joyful as what YAN Yuan experienced. YAN Yuan's joy comes from inside (*nei* 內); while their joy comes from external sources (*wai* 外)'" (YANG Xiong, 41). Yang distinguishes two views about joy: one looks it as material pleasure and seeks for its satisfaction from external world; while another regards it as an inner experience, and strives to find it from one's inner realm. However, his analysis stops here, failing to further identify what the realm is.

Among the Song Confucians, ZHOU Dunyi first touches the same topic. He inquires that,

> Wealth and honor are what people love. YAN Yuan doesn't love to seek them but instead staying in peace with poverty. What is the idea? In the world, there are the highest [honor] and the greatest [wealth] to love and seek, which are different from [ma-

> terial] wealth and honor. [Yan takes his own way, because] he sees what is great and ignores what is small. (Zhou, 38)

Based on his own criterion about the great and the small, Zhou claims that the wealth and honor in common sense is actually trivial in comparison with what Yan cherishes. Similar to all normal people, Yan doesn't enjoy poverty itself. Because poverty is a hard condition to live in, it itself cannot bring him any pleasure or happiness. Meanwhile, unlike other people, he is able to stay in peace with poverty, rather than being discontent and complain about it. With a chain reasoning, which we already met in Mencius, Xunzi and *Centrality and Commonality*, Zhou explores the reason why poverty and happiness can co-exist in Yan.

> Since he sees the greatest, his mind is at peace. His mind being at peace, he has no discontent. Having no discontent, he treats worldly wealth, honor, poverty, or humbleness in the same way. As he treats them in the same way, he can transform and equalize (*qi* 齊) them. This is why YAN Yaun has been regarded as second to the sage. (Zhou, 38)

The key to understand the co-existence lies in the terms "transform" and "equalize." On them, ZHU Xi comments, "They mean that YAN Yuan 'diminishes' (*xiaohua* 消化) the consciousness of wealth, honor, poverty, and humbleness, and therefore reaches the state of 'equalization.' The equalization means also Oneness" (Zhu 1986, 2409). In his reading, "equalization" refers to a state of mind in which the differences between wealth and poverty, honor and humility are all melting away. Modern scholars often point out that ZHU Xi borrows the idea of equalization from Zhuangzi, although he has never mentioned this. For instance, Wing-tsit Chan questions, "There is nothing wrong in accepting the word (*qi*) in its ordinary meaning 'to equalize.' Is it because ZHU Xi didn't want to associate Master Zhou with Zhuangzi's doctrine of equality of things?" (Chan, 475). Chan's inquiry suggests that we should understand "equalization," as well as the co-existence of happiness and poverty from Zhuangzi's point of view.

History has recorded that both ZHOU Dunyi and ZHANG Zai were diligent students of Daoism before they turned to be Confucians. Chan's question is constructive in the sense that the relevant idea from Zhuangzi may not only throw a light for our understanding of the term "*qi*" in Zhou, but also help us to comprehend Zhang's religious inclination as well. It is Zhuangzi's position that the difference among things is ultimately deceiving.

> Let's take, for instance, a large beam and a small beam, or an ugly woman and Xi Shi 西施 (a famous beauty in ancient China), or generosity, strangeness, deceit, and abnormality. *Dao* identifies them all as one. What is division [to some] is production [to others], and what is production [to others] is destruction [to some]. Whether things are produced or destroyed, *Dao* again identifies them as one. Only the intelligent knows how to identify all things as one. (*Zhuangzi*, 70)

In terms of Zhuangzi's analysis, there are two kinds of wisdom: the small understanding (*xiaozhi* 小知) and the great understanding (*dazhi* 大知). The first is associated with the point of view of ordinary people, while the second with that of Dao. One of them looks the difference in people's physical life as distinctive and significant, while another regards it as trivial, and even negligible. It is ZHOU Dunyi's opinion that Yan's joy come from his ability to reach the height of Dao, and to "equalize" wealth and poverty, honor and humility.

The topic of "joy" also strongly interests ZHANG Zai. However, unlike Zhou, the source of joy for him is not "equalization," but *cheng*, or the unity of the way of Heaven and human nature. In his view, "joy" is a "heavenly virtue," and emulating Heaven means to practice the virtue in human life. Hence, Yan's joy reflects not only his personal character, but also what results from his effort to unify himself with the way of Heaven. Zhang says, "Peace and joy are the beginning of the Way. Because it is peaceful, it can be great, and because it is joyful, it can be lasting. The nature of Heaven and earth is nothing other than being great and lasting" (ZHANG Zai, 24). With the same tone, he talks about "joy" in humans, "When reaching the high, we are joyful for what Heaven endows; being joyful for what Heaven endows, we do not complain. When coming down to learning, we are serious with ourselves; being serious with ourselves, we have nothing to worry" (ZHANG Zai, 35). There are four seasons in Heaven and earth. Because of the change of hot and cold weather, plants and animals grow and reproduce things of their own kind.

Likewise, there are fortune and misfortune in human life. Because of personal experience of them, we develop ourselves to be real humans. Having established joy as a feature common to the way of Heaven and human nature, Zhang has enough reason to question, why shouldn't Yan be joyful to accept both pleasure and suffering, and why shouldn't we follow him to enjoy what occurs to our life?

IV. 2.2.2. The Highest Realm in Confucianism and in Buddhism

Zhang's defining "joy" as a "heavenly virtue," which natural movements and Yan's mundane life both display, exemplifies the general Confucian approach toward crucial topics in religion—the relationships between this world and the transcendent realm, and between the moral effort and its attainment of supreme goal. As Weber phrases, Confucianism is a "system of radical world optimism" and a "rational ethic" (Weber, 235, 227). Unlike other world religions, completely absent in the system are the tensions between Nature and deity, ethical demand and human shortcoming, consciousness of sin and need for salvation, conduct on earth and compensation in the beyond, and religious duty and socio-political reality. From Zhang's doctrine we derive that this state of "tension free" comes from a fundamental conviction: Heaven and humans both possess *cheng* as their reality; people can reach the way of Heaven by cultivating their own nature. His comparison of the highest realms in Confucianism and Buddhism explains the conviction clearly.

Zhang writes that, "'the realm of reality'" (*shiji* 實際) in Buddhist lexicon is named by the people who understand the Way (meaning, Confucians) as *cheng*, or "heavenly virtue (*tiande* 天德)." He believes that, although Buddhists, as their Confucian counterparts, recognize the existence of the highest realm, they fail to understand what the realm is. It is because

> When talking about the realm of reality, Buddhists always regard human life as fantasy, human activities as useless warts, and the human world as a dirty pond. Instead of appreciating life, they condemn it; instead of protecting life, they discard it. Even if they may be aware of the realm of reality, the Buddhists are still the people who value *cheng*, while disliking *ming* (enlightenment). (ZHANG Zai, 65)

We know from Weber's analysis that, as in the case of Judaism, Christianity, and Islam, there exists a sharp tension between the "realm of reality" and the "illusion of worldly phenomena" in Buddhism as well. For Buddhism, Heaven and humans, transcendental realm (Nirvana) and mundane society are two separate domains; the attainment of the former means diminishing and even annihilating the meaning of the latter. On the contrary, Zhang's doctrine is totally free from this tension, because his *cheng* exists in both domains, and is a principle integrating them together. It is both the highest realm to which humans must pursue, and the nature of humans that they must preserve. In fact, pursuing the highest does not mean to look for an entity beyond the human world, but rather to be engaged in daily practice and to reveal *cheng*/reality of life from this engagement. *Cheng* is the highest in the sense that it generalizes the reality of all particular beings, while it is also the nearest in the sense that it functions in everything around us and in our life itself.

In correspondence to the twofold trait of *cheng* (the highest and the nearest), following the teaching of *Centrality and Commonality*, Zhang suggests his readers to take a two-way journey—"reaching *cheng* through *ming*" and "reaching *ming* through *cheng*"—for *cheng's* final attainment and for its final prevalence in the world. He specifically remarks that this "*ming*" refers to a "genuine knowledge of the virtue of Heaven, not petty knowledge of hearing and seeing (namely empirical knowledge)" (ZHANG Zai, 20). It may not directly satisfy people's needs and wants, but can ultimately serve for the attainment of the unity of Heaven and humans. Thus, the first way means to attain *cheng* by learning about its content and desirability, while the second way involves comprehending the meaning of things and events from the stance of *cheng*, instead of that of daily lose or gain. Zhang optimistically concludes that through the two-way journey, "Confucians are able to unify Heaven with humans, become the sage by pursuing knowledge, and apprehend [the reality of] Heaven without missing [that of] humans" (ZHANG Zai, 65). Compared with the Buddhist journey to the "realm of reality," Zhang's solution is definitely more attractive to the people who tend to find the greatest and the highest in this life and in this world.

After studying Zhang's position on the transcendental realm and the world, we can start to discuss his attitude toward "magic," ghost and spirit, which Weber holds as the second "yardstick" to judge the rationalization of a religion. First of all, I would like to note that Zhang's doctrine provides no room for an anthropomorphic deity, such as the early Christian God, or the Heaven found in the Western Zhou 西周 (1122?-771 B.C.E.). It is true that he has been a powerful advocate for the sacrificial rites, especially those in which people serve their ancestors. Nevertheless, when reasoning these time-honored ceremonies, his approach is always rational, instead of magical. For him, the sacrifice is primarily a way to commemorate the dead. Its main purpose is not to link his contemporaries with their ancestors' spirits, but rather to "rectify custom and habit, and make people know the root of their kinship" (ZHANG Zai, 258). By means of these activities, according to him, people's consciousness of belonging to a family or kinship is solidified, and their willingness to help each other is strengthened. This consideration is actually very close to modern idea about the necessity of rituals, such as celebration of national day, or a chorus of national anthem before a college football game begins.

Regarding the issue of ghost and spirit, Zhang may be more rational even than other leading figures in Neo-Confucian movement. For example, ZHU Xi often holds a vague position on the existence of ancestors' spirits. Sometimes, he even suggests hesitantly that people belonging to the same clan might share a similar "material energy," which will remain even when a person died. Because of the affinity of the "material energy," there may be a "communication" (*ganton* 感通) between the ancestors' spirits and the descendants who offer sacrifice (Zhu 1986, 37). To my knowledge, there is no trace of this kind of idea in Zhang's work.

Back to the features that Mavrodes ascribes to religion, we can find that almost all of them are present in Zhang's doctrine. *Cheng* signifies an *ultimate reality*, to which people are dutifully to pursue. It is also the *source of human values*. Any human qualities, if they are contrary to *cheng*, should not be regarded as "virtues." The essential identity between the way of Heaven and human nature assures that everyone is potentially capable of reaching "the highest and the greatest" through moral *practice* and daily activities. Confucians, especially those in the Song-Ming period who share the above notions, are often organized as a solitary *community* in which they support each other to confirm the legitimacy of the notions and the community itself. In brief, these are the foundation based on which I argued that Zhang's doctrine had a distinctive "religious inclination."

IV. 3. *Cheng* in CHENG Yi

CHENG Yi, the third major thinker about *cheng* in the Song Confucians, is Zhang's cousin, and CHENG Hao's (1032-1085) younger brother. Because of the close family tie and common philosophical interest, there are many discussions and correspondences among them. Those intellectual contacts result in their influence on each other, and have left the historians of Chinese philosophy a difficult task in identifying the initiator of some key ideas. Also, there exists an evident intellectual affinity between CHENG Yi and ZHU Xi, thus their doctrines are often linked together by scholars as the "Doctrine of Principle from CHENG and ZHU (*Cheng-Zhu lixue* 程朱理學)." As for the issue of *cheng*, CHENG Yi's contribution mainly lies in his analysis on the relation between "no irregularity" (*wuwang* 無妄) and "no deception" (*buqi* 不欺).

It is his definition that, "No irregularity is what is meant by *cheng*. No deception is secondary to this" (Cheng and Cheng, 92). Before going into its detailed examination, I would like to point out two things. First, for him, "no irregularity" is *cheng*'s basic meaning, while "no deception" is a derivative one. With the clarification of the former the meaning of the latter, as well as that of his *cheng* as a whole, will become apparent. Secondly, "no deception" alludes to a passage from the *Great Learning*, "[the phrase] 'making the will sincere' (*chengyi* 誠意) means allowing no self-deception" (*Daxue*, 7). Hence, his "no deception" actually means "no self-deception," rather than "no deception of others."

IV. 3. 1. "No Irregularity"

James Legge interpreted CHENG Yi's "*wuwang*" as "freedom from all moral errors" (Legge, 415), a term referring to people's moral inclination and activities. Putting CHENG Yi's two definitions under consideration, his readers may question that, what is the relation between "freedom from any moral errors" and "no deception?" Are they both ethical concepts? Why is the former, according to CHENG Yi, more fundamental than the latter? Needless to say, these are all legitimate questions, which reveal the shortcoming of Legg's interpretation.

A. C. Graham did a better job in interpreting the meaning of "*wuwang.*" He indicated that it was "one of the hexagrams of the *Book of Changes.*" "*Wang* is license, arbitrariness, irregularity—a course not in accordance with any principle. Heaven and earth are *wu* [no] *wang*, following principle without irregularity" (Graham 1958, 68). Based on this account, he rendered it with another name, "no irregularity." Along with Graham's line of thinking, I would like to examine further some representative ideas concerning "no irregularity" in the history of Chinese philosophy in order to demonstrate its full meaning and its connection with "no deception."

"No irregularity" is the name of the twenty-fifth hexagram in the *Book of Changes*, which the sign ䷘ symbolizes. Here the upper three lines represent the Creative/Heaven (*qian* 乾), while the lower three lines the Arousing/Thunder (*zhen* 震). Its "Judgment" (*guaci* 卦辭) explains, "No irregularity. Supreme success. Perseverance furthers. If someone is not as he should be, he has misfortune, and it doesn't further him to undertake anything" (*Yijing*, 245). Its "Image" (*guaxiang* 卦象) reads, "Under Heaven thunder rolls: all things attain the natural state of no irregularity. Thus the kings of old, rich in virtue, and in harmony with the time, fostered all beings" (*Yijing*, 247). Because of the common knowledge that the hexagram itself appeared earlier than its "Judgment" and "Image," people can easily conclude that "no irregularity" originally referred to an astronomical phenomenon, and later acquired a philosophical significance.

On the "Image" WANG Bi comments, "Under Heaven thunder rolls, so there is no being in irregularity." "Because no being dares to be irregular, each of them completes its nature" (WANG Bi, 342-3). According to him, by means of its awe-inspiring sound, the "thunder," which signifies the command of Heaven, intimidates all beings below to avoid taking any irregular actions. Each being acquires or preserves its nature due to its reverential submission to Heaven's command. This commentary connects Heaven's command with the completion of each being's nature: "thunder" demands each being to act regularly and consistently as Heaven orders, and to act as that is the only way by which individual being sustains its life and nature.

Following the idea showed in the "Judgment" and the "Image," ZHOU Dunyi extends the relation of Heaven and a myriad of beings, which WANG Bi explored, to the human world. He discusses "no irregularity" in humans and its relation with *cheng* by saying that,

> To be correct in one's person means to be *cheng* in one's heart. And to be *cheng* in one's heart means to turn back from evil activities. Evil activities represent irregularity. When one turns back from it, there will be 'no irregularity' in him. Since there is no irregularity, one becomes [a person with] *cheng*. (Zhou, 41)

Despite the fact that the terms of "Heaven" and "thunder" do not explicitly appear in his statement, they still stand as a background against which humans exert their regular activities. As for Zhou, "no irregularity" primarily means an attribute of Heaven to which humans must emulate. In modeling their actions on the regularity of Heaven, humans avoid doing anything inconsistent or irregular. This also means that it is possible for them to reach the same "no irregularity." *Cheng* in Zhou's context mainly refers to a state in which one resides in "no irregularity," and hence refuses to commit any "evil activities."

The next account on "no irregularity" comes from CHENG Hao, CHENG Yi's older brother. He inquires,

> "Under Heaven thunder rolls: all things attain the natural state of no irregularity." How can heavenly nature (*tianxing* 天性) be irregular? The sage is "rich in virtue, and in harmony with the time, fostered and nourished all beings." He lets each being acquire its own nature.... In [the hexagram of] 'no irregularity,' the Arousing/ Thunder is below, while the Creative/ Heaven is above. Since the movement is aroused by Heaven, how can there be irregularity? However, if a movement is aroused by human, there may be irregularity. (Cheng and Cheng, 121)

CHENG Hao differentiates two groups of things. On the one side are those in the category of Heaven: the movements aroused by Heaven, the sage in harmony with Heaven, the nature endowed by Heaven, and "no irregularity" that characterizes the heavenly movements. On the other side are those in the category of human: humans as social beings, the movements aroused by them, the wants and desires contrary against their heavenly nature, and irregularity that frequently occurs in their activities. Furthermore, he analyzes the traits of the two groups, pondering over a series of interrelated questions: why there exists a difference between the two groups, what is responsible to human's divergence from Heaven, and where is the source in human that causes the irregularity? His ideas concerning those questions become an intellectual background against which CHENG Yi proposes his concept of "no deception" as the secondary definition of *cheng*.

IV. 3. 2. "No Deception"

In a similar tone with his older brother, CHENG Yi claims, "No irregularity is perfect *cheng*. Perfect *cheng* is the way of Heaven" (Cheng and Cheng, 822). In many places, he simply treats "no irregularity" and *cheng* as interchangeable, and even applies them as synonymous with one another. In the meanwhile, as Graham points out, CHENG Yi believes that "man has integrity (*cheng*) as long as he does the same [no irregularity]" (Graham 1958, 68). His line of thinking is still the same: "no irregularity"/*cheng* is the way of Heaven; humans are potentially able to act in tune with Heaven; the key is to find the path for their attainment of "no irregularity," or for the unity of Heaven and humans. To identify the source of human irregularity, CHENG Yi closely examines the problem of "deception," which frequently occurs in human deeds and words. In order to elucidate his position clearly, this time we will start with ZHANG Zai's discussion on human nature.

Zhang writes, "With the existence of physical form, there exists physical nature (*qizhi zhi xing* 氣質之性). However, if one is good at examining himself, then his nature of Heaven and earth (*tiandi zhi xing* 天地之性) will be preserved. Therefore in physical nature there is that which the exemplary person denies to be his (original) nature" (ZHANG Zai, 23). This short passage contains three concepts: the "physical nature," the "nature of Heaven and earth," and the "original nature." According to Zhang, physical nature is an innate property that forms when one is born into the world. It consists of two parts: one is the "nature of Heaven and earth," another is related to material force. A Confucian exemplary person regards the first as human's "original nature" because it conforms to the "heavenly principle," but strives to eliminate the second because it is the source of human desires. With his coinage of the term "physical nature," Zhang admits that, for humans, both heavenly principle and human desires are natural factors, which are not inserted from outside, but something rooted in human heart.

Along with Zhang's line of thinking, CHENG Yi further reveals the psychological trace from the negative part of physical nature to the rise of human desires. He writes that

> All human desires grow out of nourishing and sustaining life. But when these fundamental needs are carried too far, they are harmful. When ancient kings regulated our fundamental needs, they did so according to the heavenly principle, but when people of later generations succumb to things that are secondary, it is because of their human desires. (Zhu 2000, 75)

CHENG Yi distinguishes two kinds of things in human life: "fundamental needs" and "secondary desires." The first comes from the "original nature," having nothing at odds with the heavenly principle, whereas the second is initiated by the negative part of physical nature, and will eventually harm both people and Nature.

However, "secondary desires" are not absolutely independent from the "fundamental needs;" instead, they develop, consciously or unconsciously, from the latter. CHENG Yi explains this point with following examples. Lofty buildings and richly ornamented walls grow out of houses for shelter. Pools of wine and forests of meat grow out of daily drink and food. Harshness and ruthlessness grow out of the proper punishment of criminals. And the excessive use of troops to prolong war grows out of legitimate expeditions. In these four cases, the first parts are "secondary desire," while the second the "fundamental need." When the effort to satisfy the fundamental need goes over the Mean, it serves for the "secondary desire." CHENG Yi says, "The meaning of the hexagram '*sun*' 損 (decrease) is to reduce mistakes so as to abide in the Mean, and to reduce what is superficial and secondary so as to abide in the substantial and the fundamental. All the harm in the world comes from the superiority of the secondary."

The "decrease" symbolizes a conscious moral action that "no deception," the second meaning of his *cheng*, exerts. CHENG Yi argues that,

> One doesn't seize a thing called *cheng* from outside, and then preserve it. People today are slaves to the evil outside, yet try to seek the good from the evil and preserve it. How can they enter into virtue this way? If one is simply on guard against [inner] depravity, his *cheng* will naturally be preserved. This is why Mencius said that all goodness of nature comes from within. (Zhu 2000, 68)

Cheng in this passage is used in the sense of "no irregularity," referring to the "original nature," or the "nature of Heaven and earth." Meanwhile, to guard "against depravity" is another expression of the "decrease" or "no deception." As an imperative from one's "original nature" it always warns people not to cross the Mean, and not to fool themselves that they don't know where the Mean is. In fact, people's attempts of fooling themselves fall in the category of self-deception, and they must fail for the following reason.

The existence of original nature, according to Cheng, categorically makes it impossible for humans to have no awareness at all when doing something morally wrong. As the *Great Learning* refers to our everyday experience, when smelling a bad smell, we intuitively hate it; when seeing a beautiful thing, we intuitively love it. We can consciously conceal the hatred and love from others, but when doing so, we clearly know that we are deceiving. Similarly, in moral life, when lying or committing a wrong action, we certainly know that we are saying or doing something wrong. Our original nature functions as an evaluative mind that always notifies us when our thinking and action become irregular, or contrary to *cheng*/"no irregularity."

A common flaw in humans is that, on the one hand, we know we are undertaking a conduct morally wrong; on the other hand, we try to shift our attention to other things, including the benefits from wrong doings, or look for some excuse to release ourselves from the burden of guilt. Nonetheless, no matter where we shift our attention to and what excuses we try to find, still we are persistently haunted by a thought: I am doing something wrong; I am trying to cover the wrongness with unconvincing reasons; this try is self-deceptive; I cannot succeed in this game because the evaluative mind is always there to remind me of my self-deception. This vicious circle can go on and on: the more we commit self-deception, the more we feel frustrated. In fact, Cheng's "no deception" is simply designed for saving us from this awkward state. It is an ethical imperative to command people stopping self-deception ("on guard against depravity," as he phrased), and an advice to persuade people facing bravely their original nature ("no irregularity"). An action in accordance with the imperative or advice is that with *cheng*, and its goal is nothing but the unity of "no irregularity" and "no deception." It is Cheng's belief that, as the source of human irregularity, desire is closely related to "self-deception;" and a conscious action with the imperative of "no deception" is the only way to get rid of "self-deception" as well as the desire as such.

In brief, the relation between Cheng's two definitions can be summarized like this. "No irregularity" signifies the way of Heaven that is present as both the ultimate cause for regular movements in cosmos and the heavenly nature in humans. Meanwhile, "no deception" is both a genuine trust in one's own words and deeds, and an imperative for people's avoidance of self-deception, aiming to harmonize their activities with their heavenly nature. The former is primarily a concept of ontology, while the latter that of ethics. Moreover, "no irregularity" assures that there is no chance for the success of self-deception, and therefore, lays a foundation for the implementation of "no deception." These are the reasons by which Cheng claims that "no irregularity" has a priority over "no deception," or "no deception" is secondary to "no irregularity."

IV. 4. *Cheng* in ZHU Xi

The fourth leading figure in the Song Neo-Confucian movement is ZHU Xi, an encyclopedic thinker in Chinese classic learning. Synthesizing the achievements of his predecessors, especially those in the Song dynasty, he forms a comprehensive system of *cheng*. It integrates almost all contents that we have discussed before, and, in certain sense, signifies the completion of the adventure of the idea of *cheng* itself. To avoid some unnecessary repetition, instead of trying to describe his entire system, I would simply concentrate my investigation on two issues: his definition of *cheng*, and his emphasis on "completeness," one of the qualities of *cheng*.

II. 4. 1. Completeness

Among Western Sinologists, Graham and Munro made remarkable contributions to the study of *cheng*. Through their research respectively on CHENG Yi and ZHU Xi, they both underscored the "completion" or "completeness" as an outstanding attribute of *cheng*, and thereby proposed to translate the term as "integrity." In his monograph on the Cheng Brothers in 1958, Graham notified his readers of a statement from CHENG Yi that "'*Cheng* is self-completion.'—Thus if you serve your parents with complete *cheng*, you are a complete son; if your ruler, you are a complete minister" (Cheng and Cheng, 203). This observation further led him to define it in 1989 as that, "*Cheng* 'integrity' derives from *cheng* 'become whole,' used in contrast with *sheng*, 'be born' of the maturation of a specific thing. Graphically it is distinguished by the 'speech' radical, marking it as the wholeness or completeness of the person displayed in the authenticity of his words" (Graham 1989, 133). Similar to Graham, Munro concluded his study of ZHU Xi's *cheng* in 1988 by saying that "My translation of *cheng* as 'integrity' rather than 'sincerity' comes from the term's sense as a completeness that contains all natural attributes, none of which is fraudulent or missing." He further explained the meaning of completeness as that, "One form of being complete is having a beginning and end. Going through all the stages for which one is prepared is therefore a form of completeness. Things that go through such a process are thereby complete and can be said to have integrity" (Munro 1988, 119-20). Checking the context in which the two scholars proposed their ideas on *cheng's* completeness, we can find that they both start with two passages from *Centrality and Commonality*, and both referred to ZHU Xi's interpretation on them. Here I would like to footnote their works by elucidating further the passages and ZHU Xi's interpretation.

The passages are what have been discussed in the second chapter: "*Cheng* is the beginning and end of things; without *cheng* there is nothing," and "Perfect *cheng* is unceasing" (*Zhongyong*, 34). The first reminds us of an image of a life process or life cycle, such as a person completes his entire life year by year, or a plant actualizes its entire potentiality phase by phase. The second primarily refers to the image of a river, comparable to what is recorded in the *Analects*, "Standing by a stream, the Master said, 'passing on like this, it never ceases, day or night'" (*Lunyu*, 9.16). In *Centrality and Commonality*, they are originally applied to describe the constancy and universality of *cheng* and its potency to create a myriad of things in the universe. In addition to retaining these original connotations, Zhu's interpretation highlights an implied meaning of completeness, and relates it to human affairs. He tells his student that,

> That "*cheng* is the beginning and end of things" refers to the real principle in things. It means that *cheng* lasts from a thing's beginning to the end, without any discontinuation. It has been so since the beginning of Heaven and earth until the total annihilation of things and humans. As for the mind of humans, when they are sincere and honest, without any falsity, what they possess, from beginning to the end, is simply this principle; whereas when there is discontinuation in their sincerity and honesty, what they possess will not be *cheng* any more. For instance, the sage (Confucius) is absolute *cheng*. It means that *cheng* penetrates his entire life, from his birth to death. [By contrast,] in YAN Yuan, "there is nothing contrary to humaneness for three months" (*Lunyu*, 6.5). It means that his *cheng* lasts from the beginning of the three-month period to its end. After the period, *cheng* is discontinued in him. (Zhu 1986, 1578)

What particularly interests us here is Zhu's distinction of *cheng* and its completeness at three levels. First, *cheng* as a heavenly principle penetrates through the dynamic process of things. It causes the process continuously to move forward, and enables the things gradually to actualize their potentiality. This is applicable to the entire natural world, from the formation of Heaven and earth to their doom, from the birth of myriad things to their end. Because of *cheng*, the sun and moon consistently exist as themselves, and their movements are constantly regular and predictable; a peach tree is always a peach tree, which will neither blossom the flower of apricot, nor bear the fruit of apple. Through their regularity, consistency, and predictability, natural phenomena perfectly exemplify the completeness of *cheng*. Secondly, the sage like Confucius is envisioned as someone whose *cheng* is maintained as complete as that in natural phenomena. This is the reason why he is called "absolute *cheng*" or "absolute *cheng* in the world." Thirdly, and the most important, the ordinary people should emulate the sage for the completeness of their own *cheng*, although this may be rather difficult. Taking YAN Yuan as an example, Zhu contends that, within the three months in which he did nothing contrary to humaneness, he is as perfect as Confucius. However, as the result of the discontinuity of his *cheng* afterwards, he turns to be a person with certain moral flaws. His maintenance of perfect *cheng* in the three months proves that it is possible for people to abide by *cheng*, while his failure afterwards reminds us that self-cultivation for the completeness of *cheng* is a life-long effort.

As John Berthrong indicates, "The special distinction of [Zhu's] *cheng* is that it points to its own self-actualizing activity in the life of a person seeking to become a sage" (Berthong, 47). By characterizing *cheng* with completeness, Zhu underscores *cheng*'s presence in the entire process in which things accomplish their self-development. Meanwhile, he applies the completeness that is found in Nature to human affairs, encouraging people to complete their *cheng* for being compassionate and upright all their lives. After all, a tree that is cut off in any of its first three phases is not a perfect tree, because it fails to actualize its full potentiality. Similarly, a person who stops holding his *cheng* at certain point is not a perfect human being, because he doesn't fully develop his nature that Heaven endows.

IV. 4. 2. The "Real Principle" and the "Principle of Realities"

ZHU Xi defines *cheng* in two ways: "*cheng* is '*zhen*' 真 "*shi*" 實 and "no irregularity;' it is the reality of the way of Heaven" (Zhu 1983, 31). "*Cheng* is a *shili* 實理; it also means 'sincerity'" (Zhu 1986, 1563). Here I intentionally left the four Chinese characters (*zhen*, *shi* and *shi li*) in the form of romanized Chinese for the sake of convenient analysis. A clear description of their meanings and interrelationship will help to clarify the content of Zhu's *cheng*.

As for the first definition, linguistically there are two possible readings: "*cheng* is 'truth,' 'reality,' and 'no irregularity';" and "*cheng* is 'true reality' and 'no irregularity.'" Traditionally, as exemplified by

Legges' translation, most Western scholars have accepted the first one, treating *cheng* as possessing three attributes: "truth," "reality," and "no irregularity." Disagreeing with them, I prefer the second one, which contains only two attributes: "true reality" and "no irregularity." My interpretation has a textual support in Zhu's Commentary on ZHOU Dunyi's *Penetrating*: "*cheng* means '*zhishi*' 至實 (perfect or absolute reality) and 'no irregularity" (Zhu 2001, 97). This seems more consistent with the second reading than with the first.

The term "no irregularity" in Zhu is principally in line with that in CHENG Yi, designating mainly a manner in which Heaven operates, and a heavenly standard in accordance with which humans adjust their actions. However, his use of another term "true reality" is relatively complicated, needing more explanation. Superficially, it is the same as what is understood by the philosophers in the tradition of *cheng*/reality, such as DONG Zhongshu, denoting an attribute similar to Aristotle's "essence." That "is what a thing in 'itself,' that on which its identity depends and a change in which would make it a different thing" (Ackrill, 126). Surely, Zhu's *cheng*/reality would be an abstract and static concept, if this were the case. However, thanks to the introduction of "completeness," he adds a new element to the old *cheng*/reality, and makes it a concrete and dynamic one. Let me explain this point with an example.

When examining the human mind, we may possibly claim that "thinking" is its *cheng*/reality because it is consistently done by humans, and can consistently characterize their mind. However, we can further question: how many components are involved in "thinking?" and how do they form (develop and construct) to be "thinking?" An answer to these questions may change "thinking" from an abstract concept to a concrete one that accommodates a variety of conceptual determinations within itself. With this approach, Hegel explains the concreteness of Idea as saying that, "Philosophy deals with the region of thought, and has therefore to deal with universals; its content is abstract, but only as to form and element. In itself the Idea is really concrete, for it is the union of different determinations" (Hegel, 24). Zhu expresses the similar notion with much plainer wording. "Its [thing's] origin is *cheng*, and its final point is also *cheng*. If there is *cheng*, then there is something, and if not, there is nothing.... For example, a plant from its germination until it withers, dies, and falls to the ground is following a real principle [*cheng*]" (Zhu 1986, 1578). In his point of view, the entirety of a plant's life is composed of four phases that the *Book of Changes* phrases as "origination," "flourishing," "advantage," and "firmness." Each of them has its own *cheng*/reality that differentiates it from others; while together they stand as four components to constitute *cheng*/reality of the plant as a whole. In this sense, *cheng*/reality seems comparable to Hegel's Idea. In addition, it is also a dynamic concept that evolves to assimilate all determinations unfolding in a sequence of time. The four phases exhibit themselves one by one to complete the wholeness of the plant. It is only in a time when the four determinations are all manifest, can people say that *cheng*/reality of the plant is complete.

Zhu's second definition is that "*cheng* means '*shili*;' it also means 'sincerity'" (Zhu 1986, 102). As noted in the first chapter, "sincerity" is a widely accepted definition for *cheng* since the Han dynasty; whereas *shili* is a relatively late one, introduced first by CHENG Yi. As a phrase, *shili* is composed of two terms: "*shi*" (real, realness, reality) and "*li*" (principle). Occasionally, Zhu also claims, "*cheng* is just *shi*; *cheng* is also *li*." "What is called *cheng* means that there is really such a principle (*shi you ci li* 實有此理)" (Zhu 1986, 102). We can conclude by comparing these sayings that Zhu's *cheng* is related to both *shi* and *li*, and a clarification of their meanings and relation may help to reveal its full content. Linguistically, it is permissible to read *shili* as either "real principle," which most scholars did, or "principle of realities." In what follows, I will first deal with the term "principle," and then explain why a full understanding of Zhu's *cheng*/*shili* needs to combine the two readings.

About "principle" Munro writes, "Originally standing for the grain in wood or jade, on which the carver should be mindful, '*li*' (principle) refers to natural patterns in things or events" (Munro 1988, 5). Unlike ZHOU Dunyi, who views the Grand Ultimate as the sole creator in cosmos, Zhu reads "principle" as both the creative source due to which a thing or a category of thing appears, and the reality that characterizes the thing or the things. In defining *cheng* with "principle," he transfers "creativity" from the latter to the former. Now, similar to "principle," *cheng* stands as not only a reality that signifies the essential attribute, but also a creative source that results in the transformations in natural phenomena and human society. In many places, Zhu even interchangeably applies "principle" and *cheng*.

Both interpretations of "*shili*" as "real principle" and "principle of realities" can equally find strong textual supports. As for the first one, we read in Zhu that

> The bricks of these steps have within them the principle that pertains to bricks.... This bamboo chair has within it the principle pertaining to bamboo chairs. The "house" is simply a principle, but [empirically] there are halls and rooms; the "plant" is simply a principle, but [empirically] there are peach and plum; the "human" is simply a principle, but [empirically] there are persons such as Mr. Zhang and Mr. Li. (Zhu 1986, 102)

Here the terms "principle of brick," "principle of human," etc. fall in the category of "genus" that designates the commonness of a class of things. Thanks to the existence of a variety of principles, there are various classes of things.

However, Zhu rarely uses the term like "*cheng* of apple," or "*cheng* of brick," because he is aware of an important distinction between *cheng* and the "principles" mentioned above. The principle of apple simply characterizes all empirical apples, whereas *cheng* features the reality of all things in the universe, which include, but not to be limited to, the apples. We see the motion of heavenly bodies manifesting *cheng*, the plant completing *cheng*, and the moral behavior practicing *cheng*; also we see the apple reflecting *cheng*. In brief, it seems to Zhu that *cheng* is a principle, but not a "principle" in the sense of that of apple. In my view, this may be a reason why he follows CHENG Yi to name *cheng* as the "real principle." *Cheng* as a principle is "real," rather than false, void, or empty, although it doesn't only represent a class of brick or a class of apple. It is really responsible for the existence of all things, although they do not appear in uniform style, manner, and pattern.

Furthermore, we need to clarify Zhu's position on the relationship between *cheng* and various "principles." This refers to the second reading: *cheng* is a "principle of realities." According to him, "*Cheng* means perfect reality and no irregularity. As a pure principle granted by Heaven, it is received by a myriad of things. All people possess *cheng*. The sage has his sagehood for the reason that he completes *cheng*.... *Cheng* is just the so-called Grand Ultimate" (Zhu 2001, 97). Based on his equation of *cheng* and the Grand Ultimate, we can logically infer that *cheng* is related to various "principles" in a way just as the Grand Ultimate to them.

Regarding the relationship between the Grand Ultimate and various "principles," Zhu says, "The principles of all the myriad of things, brought into a whole, that is the Grand Ultimate. The Grand Ultimate is simply a *shili* that penetrates through everything" (Zhu 1986, 2357). This tells us that the Grand Ultimate with which *cheng* is synonymous is a *shili*, or a "universal principle" encompassing the "principles of all the myriad of things." Alternatively, as FENG Youlan indicates, "it consists of the principles of all things in the universe" (Feng 1953, 537). Thereby it is reasonable to think that Zhu's *shi* at the present context is actually a plural noun, referring to "realities" of all categories of things, while *li* denotes a universal principle, the Grand Ultimate, or *cheng*, which relates to all empirical things by the intermediary of various realities or principles.

Now let's summarize our discussion on Zhu's second definition that "*cheng* is *shili*." *Cheng* is a "real principle," although its application is not particularly limited to a class of empirical things. Meanwhile, it is the "principle of realities" because it generalizes the essence of various realities, and assures the existence and movements of all empirical things. Incorporating the two readings, we may acquire comprehensive knowledge of what his *cheng* is.

Conclusion

Treating *cheng* as a focus of their philosophical studies, the Song Neo-Confucian philosophers collaboratively and continuously explored its natural and social significance. ZHOU Dunyi regards *cheng* mainly as a "creature" of the Grand Ultimate, instead of "creator" itself, describing it as the "root" of all human virtues, and the principle that manifests itself through those virtues. As for *cheng*'s transformation, he designs a moral hierarchy consisting of three levels: the sage, the worthy, and the ordinary people. He contends that the transformation is a social mission relevant to all Confucian intellectuals. For its accomplishment, those who are at the first two levels must work as both educators and students, to model themselves on

Heaven (the sage) or on Heaven and the sage (the worthy), while to teach the people below. ZHANG Zai views *cheng* as the union of the way of Heaven and human nature, arguing that the path to Heaven simply lies in people's daily life, and whoever concentrates on cultivating or developing his or her nature will become a sage. His doctrine fills the gap between Heaven and humans, and melts off the tension between transcendental realm and human mundane world. Next, CHENG Yi explores the two meanings of *cheng*, "no irregularity" and "no deception," explicitly ranking them as the fundamental and the secondary. This further narrows down the effort of moral cultivation to denying any attempt of self-deception. He hopes that people can preserve their heavenly nature by guarding against self-deception, and thereby eventually achieves the unity with Heaven. Finally, similar to his role for Neo-Confucian philosophy in general, ZHU Xi is also a great synthesizer for the theoretical elements pertaining to the idea of *cheng*. For him, *cheng* is "true reality," "real principle," "principle of realities," as well as "sincerity." As being descriptive and prescriptive at the same time, it generalizes the reality of Nature and human, explains why things in the two domains appear as they are, and commands all humans to act for the unity with Heaven through life-long self-cultivation.

Chapter V

The Modern Fate

In 1313, ZHU Xi's commentary on the *Four Books* was decreed by the Yuan dynasty (1271-1368) as orthodoxy for the civil service examinations. Accordingly, his system of *cheng* in the commentary also became an authoritative interpretation. Until the turn of nineteenth and twentieth century, with a few exceptions, most scholars had been reasserting what Zhu said. This actually signified the end of *cheng*'s evolution, and mirrored from a particular angle that the vitality of traditional Chinese thinking was beginning to fade away.

In the meantime, its Western counterpart moved into a new phase, challenging it with accelerating pressure in two ways. First, with a different world map, it proved that the Chinese "*tianxia*" 天下 ("all under Heaven" or the "world") was essentially a concept of locality, rather than that of a universal culture, as the Chinese had perceived for thousands of years. Secondly, it introduced into China a new conception of Nature, which, unlike the Chinese one, presupposed a separation of Nature and humans. These two doctrinal challenges, as well as the military and material force that accompanied them, posed a fatal threat to the validity of traditional Chinese social and ideological structures. As a result of tremendous changes in social and intellectual life, Zhu's system of *cheng* withdrew into a deep shadow, turning into a historical legacy.

In what follows, I will place the idea of *cheng* in the context of world civilizations to reveal the intellectual reasons for the eclipse of Zhu's system. Also, I will distinguish the living from the dead in the system, and thereby analyze and evaluate different stances toward this philosophical relic. Finally, I will discuss the "crisis of sincerity and trustworthiness" (*chengxin weiji* 誠信危機) that has occurred in China since the mid-1990's to counterevidence the necessity of studying and promoting "ethical *cheng*" in a society.

V. 1. The Stagnation

From the fourteenth century to the beginning of the twentieth century, China witnessed the rise and decline of three dynasties. In spite of the replacement of regimes, Zhu's system had never encountered serious challenges from either the imperial courts or the intellectual community. Walking comfortably, even idly in the territory he outlined, philosophers, including those who were usually creative in other issues showed little desire to be iconoclastic, let alone to criticize Zhu's doctrines. A conversation between WANG Yangming and Zhidao 志道, one of Wang's students, exemplifies this scholastic attitude.

> Zhidao asked, "Xunzi said that 'for cultivation of the heart-mind, there is nothing better than *cheng*.' But a former scholar said that he was wrong. Why?"The master said, "He should not be regarded too lightly as wrong. *Cheng* is sometimes interpreted as a moral effort (*gongfu* 功夫) [by classical Confucian writers]. *Cheng* is the original substance of heart-mind (*xin zhi benti* 心之本體). To try to restore this original substance is the work of thinking to be sincere (*sicheng* 思誠).... Though there are many defects in what Xunzi said, one should not a ways find fault with him." (WANG Yangming, 144)

In this conversation, the first position, as the student mentions, is from Xunzi. He holds that *cheng* is the most efficient way for the cultivation of one's heart-mind, and the cultivation will lead to social transformation and change. The "former scholar" seems to be CHENG Yi. Based on the idea of "no irregularity," he insists that *cheng* primarily means the way of Heaven, which is endowed to humans as their nature. It is always perfect and pure, hence the point is not to treat it as a means for the cultivation, but to maintain and preserve it (Cheng and Cheng, 19). The third position that Wang prefers is to integrate the above two to present *cheng* as "moral effort" and "original substance" simultaniously. Despite a slight shift of emphasis to the "moral effort," his interpretation is essentially in tune with

Zhu's definition that *cheng* means both "real principle"/ the "principle of realities" and "sincerity."

Another example of reiterating Zhu's doctrine is in WANG Fuzhi, whom ZHANG Dainian and other contemporary Chinese scholars often praised for having contributed "the most comprehensive description of *cheng*" (ZHANG Dainian 1989, 102). For him, *cheng* is "the principle that Heaven and earth possess." As "the reality of Heaven and earth," it contains no "artificial element (*wei* 偽)" (WANG Fuzhi 1975a, 98, 118). Furthermore, "*cheng* comprises all principles in the world, and penetrates through a myriad of things" (WANG Fuzhi 1975b, 134). It is the ultimate source for all kinds of regular movements in the cosmos. "The flow of material energy is in order, and has never stopped since remote antiquity. This is only because of the existence of such a principle [of *cheng*]" (WANG Fuzhi 1975a, 95). In humans, "it contains all kinds of virtues in the world and stands as the highest good, beyond any interpretation and description" (WANG Fuzhi 1975b, 135). Finally, it signifies a general principle that highlights the commonality between the cosmos and humans. "The principle of *cheng* and no irregularity in the sage is in conformity with that of Heaven which transforms and nurtures a myriad of things" (WANG Fuzhi 1975b, 141). "*Cheng* is the real substance of spirit, and the real function of energy. It is called the 'Way' when referring to Heaven, and the 'nature' when being endowed to humans" (WANG Fuzhi 1975a, 95). As in the case of WANG Yangming's work, almost all the points here, even the phrases themselves can be traced to the four Song masters, especially ZHU Xi. A reader who is looking to him for originality concerning *cheng* must be disappointed.

These repetitions clearly signal the stagnation in the evolution of *cheng*: the idea is too old, even dying; its energy seems to be exhausted in the long journey. The story it tells through the mouths of WANG Fuzhi or WANG Yangming is simply a eulogy of its glory in the past, carrying little fresh inspiration of philosophy. In the broad sense, the repetitions also reflect a general situation in Chinese intellectual life. The vigor that advanced its dynamic evolution in the past is in decline; the traditional way of thinking that proved to be fruitful before no longer meets the needs of its further development. Material life continues, while spiritual energy is weakening. I think that

Chinese culture would have remained in the same state for a quite long time, if there were not intellectual and political challenges from the West.

V. 2. The Contrast

A comparison with what happened in Western civilization will show that *cheng* represents a pattern of thinking that prevailed in both pre-modern China and ancient Greece. However, when the Chinese were still stuck with the old pattern, its Western counterpart developed a new one and actively applied it to various fields. This explains the stagnation in China and the challenges from the West, which it had to face.

V. 2. 1. The Mind and Cheng

In his study of the idea of Nature, Robin G. Collingwood points out an effort to seek for the general principle in Greek thought. It is comparable to the case of *cheng* in China.

> Greek thinkers regarded the presence of mind in nature as the source of regularity or orderliness in the natural world whose presence made a science of nature possible. The world of nature they regarded as a world of bodies in motion....They conceived mind, in all its manifestations, whether in human affairs or elsewhere, as a ruler, a dominating or regulating element, imposing order first upon itself and then upon everything belonging to it, primarily its own body and secondarily that body's environment. (Collingwood, 3)

Two qualifying remarks should be made about this passage. First, the natural world assumed by the Greeks is an entity in ceaseless and orderly motion. Secondly, "mind" is the source of orderliness and regularity manifest in natural phenomena and human affairs. Together they represent a way of thinking: to view Nature and humans as an organic unity, and to grasp the universal principle in the unity. Without any obvious intellectual communication and geographical connection, the Greek thinkers reached a conclusion similar to what we have read in the case of *cheng*. The foundation of this view, as Collingwood indicates, lies in a particular type of analogy.

> The Greek view of nature as an intelligent organism was based on an analogy: an analogy between the world of nature and the individual human being, who begins by finding certain characteristics in himself as an individual, and goes on to think of nature as possessed of similar characteristics. By the work of his own self-consciousness he comes to think of himself as a body whose parts are in constant rhythmic motion, these motions being delicately adjusted to each other so as to preserve the vitality of the whole; and at the same time he finds himself to be a mind directing the activity of his body in accordance with its own desires. The world of nature as a whole is then explained as a macrocosm analogous to this microcosm. (Collingwood, 8)

Despite some dissimilarity in detail, as shown in this study, especially in its first two chapters, a comparable analogy is also applied in Chinese thought. It enables *cheng* to evolve from a simple truth regarding people's everyday life to a complicated philosophical idea, and a general principle close to "mind" in Greece.

In the Chinese case, the notion of such a principle occurred earlier than the final selection of *cheng* as its standard indicator. Historically, Chinese thinkers tried to conceptualize the notion with various terms before and after the formation of *Centrality and Commonality*. As stated in the second chapter, in addition to *cheng*, Xunzi also assigned the term "ritual" to play the same role. Likewise, DONG Zhongshu, a strong advocate for the "common virtue of Heaven and humans," selected "love and profit" to designate the principle. He writes,

> Heaven always takes "love and profit" as its purpose, "nurture and growth" as its mission, and the four seasons: spring, summer, autumn, and winter as its methods. The king also always takes "love and profit" as his purpose, "easiness and happiness of people in the world" as his mission, and the [four feelings:] like, dislike, joy, and anger as his methods. (Dong, 330)

However, it is not by accident that *cheng* was eventually singled out as the proper name for the principle. "Ritual" seems too concrete and complicated, involving not only a large number of human activities and relationships, but also a social hierarchy. It seems difficult to depict convincingly a natural hierarchy as its counterpart. On the other side, "love and profit" is often entangled with human feelings, and therefore is easily associated to an anthropomorphic deity as its agent. This is not likely to accord with the general tendency of religious skepticism in China. In comparison, *cheng* has some remarkable advantages. First, despite a slight difficulty in linking "to be true to oneself" (humans) with "no duplicity" and "ceaselessness" (Nature), it is relatively easy to draw a parallel between the two sides because of the existence of the same "consistency." Secondly, *cheng* has nothing to do with hierarchy in any form. In addition to facilitating acceptance by all ranks and classes, this trait helps to avoid an inextricable problem of matching natural system to human relationships. Finally, *cheng* is more practicable and attainable. Everyone is able to test it in daily life, and observe it in the sequence of the four seasons. It has been a conviction, especially in the Confucian tradition, that human *cheng* fully reflects the entirety of *cheng* as a general principle, so the attainment of the latter demands nothing but a concentration on one's own self-cultivation.

IV. 2. 2. Conservation and Revolution

Incorporating almost all previous thoughts on *cheng*, ZHU Xi created his system. After its prevalence in Chinese society, it seems that philosophers could still develop some original thought from what is contained in its individual components, instead of repeating the ideas framed by the system. For instance, from Xunzi's notion of cosmic *cheng*, it might be further inquired: how do we measure the regularity, persistence, and recurrence in natural phenomena? Is there a quantitative relationship among them? Is it possible to formulate a mathematical structure to generalize all these regularities? Another possibility refers to the treatment of *cheng* as the essential attribute of everything. The questions in this category may include, "How to clarify and classify the relationship among a variety of realities or principles?" "Is it possible to produce a formal logic in regard to them?"

However, as exemplified in the case of Xunzi, those questions have rarely been raised by Chinese thinkers, let alone answered. One of the reasons is that Zhu has reshaped all the ideas about cosmic *cheng* and reality as organic parts of his system for a single purpose—to build up a harmonious society. Consequently, the significance of each of them is defined only through its connection with the purpose; the room in which they can move independently is rather limited. Moreover, the system is not designed for the advancement of the knowledge of Nature and society, but rather for the promotion of the individual's moral effort and the transformation of people. Put differently, after Zhu the question that really interests Chinese thinkers about *cheng* is not "what knowledge of Nature or society do we have?" but "what is the knowledge of them for?" or "what is the social significance of the knowledge?" Corresponding to this basic concern, the thinkers have put their intellectual energy and enthusiasm on the derivation of ethical lessons from the general principle, and on the ensuing arguments for the desirability of moral life and transformation.

In the same fourteenth century, when Chinese were still stagnant at the old pattern signified by *cheng* and its social conclusions, its Western counterpart moved forward to a new phase with a revolutionized view of Nature and humans. Collingwood characterizes the new phase with the following passage.

> The Renaissance thinkers, like the Greeks, saw in the orderliness of the natural world an expression of intelligence: but for the Greeks this intelligence was nature's own intelligence, for the Renaissance thinkers it was the intelligence of something other than nature: the divine creator and ruler of nature. This distinction is the key to all the main differences between Greek and Renaissance natural science. (Collingwood, 5)

Looked at from this point of view, Nature turns to be something similar to a machine, and the divine creator to a clockmaker or millwright. Collingwood continues to write that this view "is equally analogous in its origin, but it presupposes a quite different order of ideas. First, it is based on the Christian idea of a creative and omnipotent God. Secondly, it is based on the human experience of designing and constructing machines" (Collingwood, 8). What it brought is no longer a general principle functioning immanently within an organic structure, or a unity of Heaven and humans, as seen respectively in Greece and China, but a notion of law imposed on Nature by a Creator. Accordingly, humans shifted their focus from adjusting their behaviors in terms of Nature's rhythm, to the discovery of the law.

With the "imposed law" and other related notions, as Whitehead notes, "Galileo, Descartes, and Newton finally launched modern science on its triumphant career. If success be a guarantee of truth, no other system of thought has enjoyed a tithe of such success since mankind started its job of thinking. Within three hundred years it has transformed human life, in its intimate thoughts, its technologies, its social behavior, and its ambitions" (Whitehead, 145). There is no surprise that, with its systematic introduction into China, the Renaissance view clashed with Zhu's system.

V. 3. The Disintegration of Heaven

DONG Zhongshu once stated powerfully that, "the great source of the way comes from Heaven. If Heaven doesn't change, neither will the way change" (Dong 1962, 2518-9). His address on the connection of Heaven and the way is also applicable to that of Heaven and Zhu's *cheng*. Without a thorough change in the notion of Heaven, the validity of his *cheng* will remain, and the repetition of his doctrine will continue. An analysis of Heaven and its modern fate can throw a light on the cause that interrupted the continuation, and the process in which Zhu's system gradually became remote and obsolete.

According to FENG Youlan, "Heaven" in pre-modern China has five interrelated meanings. They are: (1) a material or physical "Heaven" or sky; (2) a ruling and presiding "Heaven," or anthropomorphic deity; (3) a fatalistic "Heaven," equivalent to the concept of fate; (4) a naturalistic "Heaven," equivalent to the English word Nature; (5) an ethical "Heaven," which signifies the highest primordial principle in the universe (Feng 1952, 31). Reading the classic texts in which it occurs, people are often puzzled by the fact that a single "Heaven" may have several meanings at the same time. For example, Mencius talks with King Xiang of Liang that,

> Does Your Majesty not know about young rice plants? Should there be a drought in the seventh or eighth month, these plants will wilt. If clouds begin to gather in Heaven and rain comes pouring down, then the plants will spring up again. This being the case, who can stop it? Now in the world [under Heaven] amongst the shepherds of men there is no one who is not fond of killing. If there is one who is not, then the people in the

> world will crane their necks to watch for his coming. This being truly the case, the people will turn to him like water flowing downwards with a tremendous force. Who can stop it? (*Mengzi*, 1A6)

Mencius makes an analogy between what takes place in "Heaven" and "under Heaven." On the surface, "Heaven" in this context simply means "*sky*." However, sky is part of *Nature*; sometimes, it is even metaphorically used to represent Nature as such. The cloud, rain, lightening, and thunder in the sky may bring various consequences over which people have no control. They signify a *fate* that people have to accept. People may further assume that there may be an *anthropomorphic deity* behind and responsible for all these natural phenomena (Mencius himself may not accept this assumption). Finally, using the analogy of "sky," Mencius plainly addresses the King with an ethical *principle*: Follow the model of "sky" to nurture, rather than kill the people in your state, everyone in the world will be subject to you wholeheartedly. Hence in this single statement, all the five meanings associated with the word "Heaven" are implicitly present. In the time of Mencius, I believe, when hearing the word "Heaven" in this kind of context, a person might immediately associate it with these multiple meanings.

Although this ambiguity is certainly disadvantageous to scientific analysis, it fits the need to maintain Zhu's *cheng*. In the words of Robert Eno, Confucian "Heaven" simultaneously denotes two things: "prescriptive force" and "descriptive role" (Eno 1990, 82-3). Or more concretely, it refers to a conceptual unity with the five components. Among them, "anthropomorphic deity," "primordial principle," and "fate" are more prescriptive. They imply that people should act in accordance with *cheng*, because this is an undeniable command or force from a supreme power over them. In the meantime, "sky" and "Nature" are more descriptive, presenting people with a perfect case of regularity and consistency, which come from cosmic *cheng* and bring favorable consequences to people, such as a good harvest. The consequences, in turn, convince them that a similar regularity and consistency in their activities, which ethical *cheng* causes, will have a positive influence and a desirable achievement as well. The prescriptive force and descriptive role of Heaven are complimentary to each other to the effect that people will learn both

Heaven as command (you should do it) and Heaven as an exemplar (how you do it) at the same time. This is the reason why Zhu and other leading Confucians always treat "Heaven" as the foundation or source of *cheng*.

However, due to two challenges associated with the Renaissance view of Nature from Western civilization, the conceptual unity of "Heaven" began gradually breaking down at the end of eighteenth century. The first challenge is the alteration of world map. Strictly speaking, its direct victim is not "Heaven" itself, but "all under Heaven" (the world). Traditionally, Chinese people had cherished a deep-rooted conviction that their culture possessed a universal validity because it followed the guidance of the way of Heaven and had "Heaven" as its protector and supervisor. Due to this assumed universality, in their lexicon, the world simply meant the Chinese "world," which was mainly a concept of culture and value, rather than that of geography and region. This notion of universality was enforced by the fact that, over a long historical period, Chinese culture always kept its position of dominance, even when Chinese territory was actually occupied by surrounding minorities. The minority rulers normally faced two options: either insisting on preserving their own culture and seeing their regime perish quickly, or shifting toward assimilating themselves with Chinese culture and enjoying a relatively long period of control. In fact, Chinese people's belief in "Heaven" and its prescriptive force was directly related to their experience in the "world." Put differently, the stability of "world" assured them that "Heaven" was always acting in their favor, and its command, such as preservation of *cheng*, should be always revered.

Different from the minorities bordering on China in its history, the Western powers that defeated China in modern times introduced a new concept of world, instead of having to choose between the two options. Consequently, as Levenson points out, "To many Chinese, by the turn of nineteenth and twentieth centuries, China seemed to be losing her title to '*tianxia*' (world), her dignity as a culture. Abandon a hopeless claim, they urged, strengthen political power by changing cultural values, and from a Chinese defeat as '*tianxia*' snatch a victory as '*guo*' (country)" (Levenson, 100).

Due to "China's increasing relations with a bigger and different world," as Munro indicates, the Chinese people gradually realized that "the world was no longer coextensive with Chinese culture" and their culture was no longer a universally accepted one" (Munro 1996, 2). The devaluation of the Chinese "world" inevitably affected the lofty status of "Heaven," its supervisor and protector. The prescriptive force of "Heaven" became doubtful since it seemed incapable of ensuring universality to a culture that had been faithfully subject to it.

The introduction of modern science and technology is the second challenge. It may not be as tangible and fierce as the first, but is more profound in essence. Without any exaggeration, we can say that it effectively deprived "Heaven" of its prescriptive force. When the reason for thunder was unclear to humans, it was easily conceived of as a command from "Heaven," or a message conveying a Heavenly decree. Thus appeared the passage in the *Book of Changes*, which the Song Masters frequently cited, "Under Heaven thunder rolls: all things attain the natural state of no irregularity." However, if it becomes possible for people to explain thunder with scientific theory and evidence, and if they can even bring about artificial thunder and the rain that follows, where does the basis of their conviction in the prescriptive force of "Heaven" lie?

With the two challenges and their triumph, the domain of "Heaven" was reduced to "Nature" and "sky" in which its descriptive role seemingly remains. However, "Nature" and "sky" that are cut off from their original unity also meant something new to Chinese people. They are no longer a reminder for people to act consistently and to cultivate their heart uninterruptedly, but objects of scientific observation and experiment. People know that the knowledge of Nature and sky will practically benefit their physical life, but not necessarily promote their moral conscience. Parallel to this change, the traditional role of the sage becomes irrelevant for modern inquiry of Nature since the perfection in the ethical life has nothing to do with the advancement of people's learning about Nature. In fact, modern science in China is founded entirely on the Renaissance view of Nature, having little connection with the age-old thought of cosmic *cheng* or general principle.

V. 4. Political Distortion

The disintegration of Heaven left Zhu's system as a huge, but problematic legacy with which contemporary people have to deal. Theorists from the two major political forces, the Nationalist Party and the Communist Party, held different stances toward it: one valued it in order to incorporate it within their own doctrine and strategy; while another equated it to feudal ideology and insisted on discarding it completely. Despite the opposition in their stances, they both politicized *cheng*, changing a philosophical and ethical theme into a political issue.

CHEN Lifu 陳立夫, the Minister of Education in the Nationalist government (1938-44), claims that, as an "original substance" (*shengyuan* 生元), "*cheng* of the universe" (*yuzhou zhicheng* 宇宙之誠) is responsible for the existence of a myriad of things. It is an "original motive power" (*yuan dongli* 原動力) that propels things in the universe to move (CHENG Lifu, 150-1). Meanwhile it is manifest in the human world as ethical *cheng*, which he defines this way:

> *Cheng* is the locus of faith, the existence of reality, the source of love, and the original power of action. It is close to what God means to the Western people. The existence of reality is the basis of wisdom; the source of love is the basis of compassion; the original force of action is the basis of courage. Thus, *cheng* is what grants us wisdom, compassion, and courage. (CHEN Lifu, 146)

Although his argument evokes some terms with a flavor of modern science, the notion he holds is still similar to that of Zhu. Beliving that there is a commonality between universal *cheng* ("*cheng* of the universe") and ethical *cheng*, he still strives to derive the legitimacy of the latter from the former. Here, in fact, he makes a historical mistake, arguing without an awareness that his effort is essentially outdated. Put differently, he ignores that the tie of ethical *cheng* and universal *cheng* has already been broken after the disintegration of Heaven and the prevalence of the modern scientific view. To his Chinese contemporaries, an argument for moral consistency on the ground of its conformity with the regularity in the motions of heavenly bodies sounds just as absurd as advocating democracy and freedom on the ground of the mandate of Heaven. It can find few listeners.

Chen's second mistake is even more fundamental, because it goes against the entire tradition of Confucian *cheng*. He defines *cheng* as the "locus of faith." However, "faith" must have its object; it must be a "faith" in something. People need to know *in what* they should be faithful. In Confucian tradition, the answer is unequivocal: the object is humans themselves; *cheng* means to be faithful in our own words and deeds. In contrast, Chen changes this object to be something or someone out of and beyond us. For him, *cheng* means to be faithful in the doctrine of SUN Zhongshan 孫中山 (1866-1925), the founder of Nationalist Party, and sometimes even in the leadership of JIANG Jieshi. This "invention" typically exemplifies how a political consideration distorts an academic discourse.

JIANG Jieshi often interprets *cheng* as a virtue in opposition to falsity (*wei* 僞). He calls on his soldiers, "We should preserve *cheng* and wipe off falsity. We should clean up all hypocrisy (*xujia* 虛假) with our sincerity" (Jiang 1984, 794). Obviously, his *cheng* is in line with CHENG Yi's "secondary" *cheng*, meaning mainly "no deception." Its antagonism with falsity can be traced to a well-known passage from The *Records of Rituals* (*Liji*, 《禮記》). "To highlight *cheng*, while eliminating falsity, that is the essence of rituals" (*Liji*, 1010). As far as this point is concerned, his saying has nothing at odds with Confucian tradition. Nevertheless, trouble occurs when he begins to elucidate its content. "What is *cheng*?" he asks, "*Cheng* means 'diligent practice' (*lixing* 力行) that contains no falsity, no irregularity, pursuing always the perfect" (Jiang 1984, 159). Here the same question will be raised stubbornly: *What* should we diligently practice? *What* is the goal of "diligent practice"? Like what was seen in CHEN Lifu, Jiang's reply is that,

> The revolutionary doctrine (*zhuyi* 主義) is as plain as the sun and moon in the sky. Our founding father [SUN Zhongshan] has already given us perfect works about revolutionary strategy. Moreover, the [historical] facts have already showed us the reason of the successes or failures in the revolution. Today our citizen need only to investigate things and exhaust principles (*gewu qiongli* 格物窮理), and to practice and diligently practice in

> accordance with the doctrine, the strategy, and the thinking line that leads to success. (Jiang 1984, 159)

Now it becomes clear that Jiang's *cheng* means to practice diligently the "doctrine" and "strategy" that Sun formulated. Here Sun fills the traditional position of the sage, whom people should follow sincerely. Jiang promises his audience that, in this way, "we will definitely attain the final success" (Jiang 1984, 159).

However, Jiang neglects a substantial distinction between the Confucian sage and Sun as a particular person. The "sage" is essentially a concept of morality, an embodiment of the highest moral ideal. The sage's doctrine fully reflects the human nature—a commonality shared by everyone, and therefore can be spontaneously understood and indisputably accepted by all of them. On the contrary, Sun's doctrine is mainly a concept of knowledge involving a lot of empirical evidence, reasoning, and discursive thinking, and therefore may cause debates and disputations among people. The Song Confucians denied labeling anyone after Confucius as "sage" because they were clearly aware that this would cause a fatal consequence to their system. For them, entitling a person with whom many people are empirically familiar as "sage" means to hold that his doctrine and conduct, including his way of dealing with some particular issues, are categorically free from any criticisms. For the same reason, if any doubts about the doctrine and conduct do occur, the direct victim must be the legitimacy of the sage, as well as the validity of "sagehood" and "transformation." We will see later that this embarrassing situation actually happened to both Chen and Jiang.

In fact, reading *cheng* as faith and the "faith" as a confidence in a particular person and his doctrine are not an invention of Chen or Jiang, but rather something originated from Sun's theory that "knowing is more difficult than acting" (*zhi nan xing yi* 知難行易). To trace this tradition of the Nationalist Party, we have to examine Sun's theory itself.

Sun starts his doctrine with a criticism of WANG Yangming's "unity of knowledge and action," which I briefly discussed in the second chapter. According to him, Wang has fostered a misconception among Chinese people that "knowing is easier than acting"— an attitude that encouraged lethargy and inaction in intellectual life in general, and philosophical thinking in particular. Now, to cure the social illness that Wang has caused, we need to think in reverse. Despite the fact that the logic of Wang's doctrine doesn't allow for the conclusion as made by Sun, and Sun himself actually contributes nothing to clarify the philosophical issues involved in the relation of knowledge and action, his theory becomes a common idea among his students in the Party.

In brief, his theory consists of two points. First, "With the growth of modern science one's knowledge and one's action are set further apart. One who knows does not have to act, and not only that, but one who acts does not have to know" (Sun, 785). It is his position that there must be a division of labor among people, where one party are the thinkers, and another just the doers. This social separation is so deep that the thinkers do not need to act, while the doers do not need to know. His second position directly explains why "knowing is more difficult than acting" or thinkers are more valuable than doers.

> The advance of civilization is achieved by three groups of people: first, those who see and perceive ahead, or discoverers; second, those who see and perceive latter, or promoters; and third, those who do not see or perceive, or practical workers. From this point of view, China does not lack practical workers, for the great mass of people are of this kind. (Sun, 785)

Knowing is more difficult because it can be undertaken only by a handful of social elite, like Sun himself. On the contrary, the Chinese majority, or the "great mass of people" as he phrases, need only to be faithful or confident in what the elite has already known. Their job is not to question the correctness of the elite's discovery, but rather to act in accordance with what the elite have already discovered. In the final analysis, the advocacy of Chen and Jiang for practice or diligent practice is simply a footnote to Sun's above idea.

Due to his interpretation of *cheng* as diligent practice of Sun's doctrine, and his replacement of the sage with Sun, Jiang's promotion of *cheng* meets wide ridicule and fierce criticism from Chinese intellectuals. Among his critics is Ai Siqi 艾思奇 (1910-1966), a leading Communist theorist. On Jiang's claim that "both diligent practice and extension of knowledge originate from perfect *cheng*," Ai inquires, "What is *cheng*? Plainly speaking, what is called *cheng* here is simply a synonym of superstition" (Ai, 936). His comment and criticism deserve a close examination, because it mixes keen observation with wrong conclusion. Ai is correct in pointing out that Jiang's *cheng*, which means a readiness to follow Sun's doctrine sincerely, even blindly, represents a "superstition" that denies people's right to inquire into its correctness. However, in a further move, he confuses Jiang's *cheng* with the idea of *cheng* itself. "The term *cheng* in China is simply applied as a sign of superstition. People can read such a phrase in many temples and many fortune-telling books, 'If [one is in] *cheng*, then a lucky omen will come'" (Ai, 938). He goes so far as even to claim that *cheng* is "an ideology of the Chinese feudal age" (Ai, 936).

The history of *cheng* proved two mistakes in his statement. First, the meaning of *cheng* that Ai mentions is just a relatively unimportant component in the entire system of the idea of *cheng*. Historically, it is mainly popular in folk society, having little influence on Chinese intellectuals. Equating this particular use with the idea of *cheng* itself means an irresponsible neglect of many valuable components in the idea that are still relevant to modern life. Secondly, *cheng* is primarily a philosophical concept, although it originated and was developed mainly in a historical period which Ai and his comrades habitually call "feudal society." As with other major concepts, such as "substance," "function," "ritual," "emotion," and "nature," it goes far beyond merely reflecting the features of the society from which it emerged. In this sense, a political label like "feudal ideology" is obviously misleading and even absurd. Ai's interpretation of *cheng* exhibits another form of the politicization of a philosophical idea, and exemplifies a Communist stance toward traditional Chinese thought in general, and *cheng* in particular. It has been propagated in China since 1949 when the People's Republic of China was established.

V. 5. In Praise of *Cheng*

With the disintegration of "Heaven," the unity of Zhu's *cheng*, which is composed of three elements—ethical *cheng*, cosmic *cheng*, and universal *cheng*—is also broken up. Now the laws of Nature that natural sciences investigate have replaced the cosmic *cheng*. The universal *cheng* that reflects the thinking pattern of human civilizations in their early stage turned out to be obsolete. As for the domain of ethical *cheng*, the concepts of the sage and his transforming power became invalid, and even the term *cheng* itself was devalued due to its politicization by the two Parties. Then, are there still elements in the system that validate *cheng*'s modern relevance, and ensure that it will still serve as a positive value for humankind? If so, where does this remnant stay after the disintegration of "Heaven" and the disunity of the system? These are the questions we now try to answer.

V. 5. 1. Go Back to Community Life

In the first chapter, I outlined a deep-rooted notion by analyzing three meanings of "*xin*" (trustfulness, trustworthiness, and faithfulness), and the four interrelated concepts: self-cultivation, sincerity, consistency, and trust. I believe that what these terms convey constitute the core meaning of *cheng* in the systems that we examined so far. Roughly, we can compare it to a robust child, and the other parts in the systems to some colorful, even extravagant outer garments that succeeding thinkers continuously put on it. After the upheaval in the Chinese world of thought, all the decorative garments are stripped off; all the sophisticate gifts the child received are taken away. But, all and all, the child is still a vigorous being, healthy and strong. As the "lost son" in the *Bible* and in the Buddhist *Lotus Sutra*, he finally comes back to the community life from which he was born and in which he has been whole-heartedly welcomed. Put philosophically, the validity of the core meaning lies in community life, and its applicability can be proved only by investigating its connection with this life.

In pre-modern China, DAI Zhen (1724-1777) seems to be the only major thinker trying to de-link *cheng* from "Heaven" and to justify its validity on a materialistic basis. Compared with what his predecessors held, this certainly represents a modern vision of the time-honored topic of *cheng*. In general, we can ascribe its acquisition to both Dai's personal interest and the special education and training he took. Unlike most Chinese thinkers in the history, what attracted Dai were not only classic studies, but also certain issues pertaining to mathematics, astronomy, hydraulic engineering, phonetics, collation of texts, and textual criticism. Consequently, as Wing-tsit Chan observes, he "was better known as a great master of 'Investigation-Based-on-Evidence' (*kaoju* 考據) than as a philosopher. But his investigations and philosophy are really inseparable, for they reinforce each other" (Chan, 709). The following elucidation of the *Mencius* and *Centrality and Commonality* typically reflects his position on *cheng*.

> *Cheng* means reality. According to *Centrality and Commonality*, what it realizes (*suo shi zhe* 所實者) are wisdom, compassion, and courage; what make it as reality (*shi zhi zhe* 實之者) are humaneness, rightness, and ritual. We speak of wisdom, compassion, and courage in terms of a person's blood-material energy and knowing mind (*xieqi xinzhi* 血氣心知), because aside from them there are no wisdom, compassion, and courage. And we speak of humaneness, rightness, and ritual propriety in terms of humanrelationship and daily affairs (*renlun riyong* 人倫日用), because without them humaneness, rightness, and ritual do not exist. (Dai, 50)

In terms of Dai's interpretation, *cheng* as reality is composed of humaneness, rightness, and ritual propriety; meanwhile it ensures the presence of wisdom, compassion, and courage. Hence, we need to understand *cheng* in its relation to the two groups of virtue—"wisdom-compassion-courage" and "humaneness-rightness-propriety." Furthermore, "wisdom-compassion-courage" is directly related to a person's physiological and psychological qualities, while "humaneness-rightness-ritual" to his social life. Put differently, the specific composition of "blood-material energy and knowing mind" decides whether or not one is a person with or without "wisdom-compassion-courage," while the "human relationship and daily affairs" explains what "humaneness-rightness-propriety" is and why it is valuable. In light of this analysis, *cheng* is basically an ethical concept, which contains "humaneness-rightness-propriety" within, and enables a person to act with "wisdom-compassion-courage" without.

It should be noted that, unlike ZHU Xi and his followers, Dai doesn't appeal to Heaven for the legitimacy of *cheng*, but rather taking a radical step to interpret both Heaven and human nature from a naturalistic approach. He comments on two passages from *Centrality and Commonality* that,

> Blood-material energy and knowing mind are allotments from *yin* and *yang* and the five elements, and they constitute human nature. Therefore *Centrality and Commonality* says, "What is endowed by Heaven is called nature." Human relationships and daily affairs are all matters referring to our blood-material energy and knowing mind. Therefore *Centrality and Commonality* says, "To follow our nature is called the Way." (Dai, 50)

Two points are noteworthy in this passage. First, standing mainly as the source of material factors—"*yin* and *yang* and the five elements," "Heaven" in Dai seems short of a prescriptive force. In correspondence, the human nature that Heaven endows turns to be something composed of those factors. Although Heaven and human nature are still in a parallel relationship, the commonality they share changes. Now, instead of being still an ontological entity, it becomes a material object, accessible to scientific research. Secondly, Dai reads the "Way" primarily as a proper course regarding "human relationship and daily affairs," which is consistent to humans' "blood-material energy and knowing mind." In my view, this allows us to infer that Dai is looking for a well designed social policy that comes with a correct understanding of human nature, and goes well with its tendency. Like the first point, although the harmony between the Way and human nature is still the final goal to pursue, its reference is restricted to a harmonized relation between the social policy and human nature. Also, this relation should be released from its entanglement with the way of Heaven, and redefined as the object on which ethics and social sciences investigate.

Today we need to continue Dai's effort, defining *cheng* unambiguously as a sheer ethical-moral-social concept with a connotation that the core meaning conveys. It still possesses both a descriptive role and a prescriptive force—to describe an admirable psychological state and its external expression and influence, and to command people to preserve this state for their own benefit and for the prosperity of their community. Meanwhile, we should make it clear that the source of its prescriptive force is no longer in "Heaven," but in people's community life.

As social animals, we humans have to live a communal life, dealing with people around us, and working with them for the attainment of our common goal. Life itself has taught us that a trust from and among people is the condition for our success and for the survival of our community. One of the great contributions that Chinese thinkers made to humankind is that they not only identified *cheng*—"to be true to oneself" as the final assurance for the acquisition of the trust, but also explored deeply its content. In addition, they designed a systematic program for the preservation of *cheng*, and for the promotion of its core meaning. It helped to formulate a moral imperative that "you should be true to yourself if you want to make your mind at ease and earn the trust from others." Of course, this doesn't mean that the imperative has been consistently practiced by all the members in a community, or that all Chinese people act in accordance with the principle of *cheng*. Instead, it tells only that, thanks to their efforts, people become conscious that to accept the imperative and act correspondently is the best way to earn the trust from their fellow members and to fulfill their responsibility to the community. Particular views of Nature may come and go, and different civilizations may rise and decline, but it is predictable that the truth epitomized by this imperative will be constantly valid and relevant to each individual and each community.

V. 5. 2. The Restoration of Cheng

In this study of *cheng*, I have always avoided using words like "destruction" or "demolition" to describe the contemporary fate of Zhu's system. This comes with two concerns. First, these terms cannot accurately reflect the nature of the alteration that the system undergoes. It is true that the fundamental crisis in the turn of the nineteenth and twentieth centuries brought to China a variety of problems to which the system failed to answer. Also, this failure reflects a kind of social and theoretical irrelevance, which diminished its intellectual value, causing people to doubt on its correctness. However, I would like to argue that Zhu is not necessarily wrong, although his system as a whole is actually abandoned today. Isaiah Berlin's comment on the "turning-point" in European history may throw a light on this issue. He writes,

> By a turning-point I mean a transformation of outlook..., a radical change in the entire conceptual framework within which the questions had been posed; new ideas, new words, new relationships in terms of which the old problems are not so much resolved as made to look remote, obsolete and, at times, unintelligible, so that the agonizing problems and doubts of the past seem queer ways of thought, or confusions that belong to a world which has gone. (Berlin 1997, 168)

As a "conceptual framework" in Berlin's sense, Zhu's system was rooted in the pre-modern Chinese life, signifying a special thinking pattern, a moral goal, and an ideal relationship in humans. It satisfied the theoretical needs of people in that time, and therefore was widely accepted and practiced by them. There is no doubt that his system has never lacked of critics then and now, and these criticisms often hit the marks. However, none of them was able to "destroy" or "demolish" the entire system, just as no criticisms can fundamentally overthrow the systems of Plato or Aristotle, Kant or Hegel. Zhu's system, as well as these Western systems, is essentially a static reflection of people's life in a particular period, whereas life itself is dynamic, like a river moving forward uninterruptedly. With Chinese life entering into a new historical phase, the system itself is inevitably left behind, gradually losing its contemporary significance. This is the reason why it becomes "remote," "obsolete," and even "unintelligible." In actuality, it is not "destroyed" or "demolished" by any modern cultural "hero," but "forgotten" by Chinese people who enter a new period, and have to face new challenges.

The second concern about the words "destruction" or "demolition" is related to the universal validity and applicability that the core meaning of *cheng* possesses. Since the core meaning implicitly centers in Zhu's system, it is essentially inappropriate and misleading to phrase its modern fate with such words. Nowadays, we have to be more careful when exploring this intellectual heritage. It is wrong to persist in some of his doctrines, such as the parallelism of the way of Heaven and human nature, and the identity of ethical and cosmic *cheng*. Meanwhile, it is also wrong to demote or ignore the truth that the core meaning signifies. In today's world, as shown by the current situation in China, what may be more harmful to a society is the second mistake.

In contemporary China, despite the devaluation of Zhu's system, what the core meaning of *cheng* delivers has still been appraised as a true virtue. Two phrases "*chengshi*"誠實 (honesty) and "*chengxin*" 誠信 (trustworthiness), which remain active in Chinese discourse, have evidenced its great vitality. Speaking roughly, the former refers to a person's character of sincerity, while the latter to a trustable quality that a person's words and deeds represent. Thus, we can apply the term *chengshi* to a person, and the term *chengxin* to the person's behavior. Nevertheless, especially from the middle of the 1990's, along with the rapid economic development in China, a term "the crisis of sincerity and trustworthiness" has accelerated its frequency of use in both mass media and people's daily conversation. It indicates unmistakably a worrisome fact in Chinese society that a relatively large number of institutions and individuals have compromised sincerity and trustworthiness for some short-term profits. Consequently, it seeds doubt on the validity and applicability of the two virtues, and even generates a wide distrust among the people. Without any exaggeration, this crisis has already threatened the cohesion of Chinese society.

It is tragic to see that ethical *cheng* becomes a stranger to a great number of residents in its own birthplace. Today, its opposite, "deception" or "self-deception," against which CHENG Yi repeatedly warned, has remarkably polluted many walks of life in China. The two fields that have been specified prone to deception are commerce and academia. Habitually, Chinese observers name all kinds of deceptive conducts in economic activities as "corruption in commerce" (*shangye fubai* 商業腐敗). It includes, but is not limited to, marketing knowingly phony products, selling goods at an unfair price, and treating customers differently because of their age and status. In parallel, the deceptive conducts in scholarly and educational contexts are generally called "corruption in education" (*jiaoyu fubai* 教育腐敗). Examples of corruption in education range from bogus diplomas conferred by accredited institution, plagiarism, to writing and saying things contrary to one's knowledge for the sake of personal gains. Due to the crucial role of fostering the next generation that education plays, the corrupt activities in this field are particularly alarming.

A diagnosis of the crisis in general, and the deception or corruption in particular, reveals its two practical causes. First, Chinese society is undergoing a period of transition in which the new market economy is flourishing, while the old planning one remains dominant. The gray area between the two economies often tempts the people without a strong sense of social responsibility to act deceptively for some immediate gains. This phenomenon has occurred in almost all former Communist states. As thinkers in the world generally agreed, one of the cures is for the government to speed up its process of legislation and to strengthen its enforcement of law.

Secondly, and the more profound, the crisis is directly related to the long-time negligence of promoting ethical *cheng*, to which the Chinese government should be held accountable. As exemplified in AI Siqi's work, communist propaganda has labeled *cheng* as "feudal ideology" since the 1940's. In accordance, the cluster of virtues that constitute *cheng* as a conceptual unity, such as sincerity, honesty, integrity, consistency, trustworthiness, and faithfulness are not strongly advocated. More than often, they are not treated as fundamental values that characterize humankind itself, but rather a kind of expedient means subject to certain economic or political purpose. As a result, a great number of people in several generations who grow up with this ill education fail to internalize ethical *cheng* as a principle of autonomy to restrain their conducts, and to cultivate their heart so as to act naturally with the guidance of ethical *cheng*. For its cure, there may be no better method than encouraging people to rediscover the core meaning of *cheng* and rethink its relation with the well-being of themselves and their community.

Conclusion

The introduction of Western notions, ideas, and theories into China positioned the idea of *cheng* that Zhu's system represents in the context of world civilization. Now it is no longer an outlook of the universe developing and effecting lonely in a relatively enclosed land, but one which has to compete with its Western counterpart for its legitimacy and validity. In reference with the Western view that gradually took shape since the Renaissance, Chinese intellectuals painfully realized that, despite its glory in the past, Zhu's system as a whole has lost its direct relevance to modern life. To this historical legacy the two political parties adopted two sharply contrasting stances: one strove to reshape it with modern terms and notions, another planned to dump it completely. However, they both failed because of a twofold reason: Zhu's system as a whole is not compatible to the modern spirit of Nature and society, but the core meaning of *cheng* that is central to the system represents a universal truth whose validity is beyond any particular time period. In fact, this twofold reason also underlines the modern fate of *cheng*: all the pre-modern systems have become obsolete, but the core meaning that roots in community life and centers in these systems will keep its vitality so long as there are still humans living in this planet.

REFERENCE

Ackrill, J. L. 1981. *Aristotle: the Philosopher.* Oxford: Clarendon Press.

Ai, Siqi 艾思奇, 1988. "*The Destiny of China*— An Utterly Idealistic and Deceptive Philosophy," "《中國之命運》—極端唯心論的愚民哲學." In The *Selected Materials for the History of Contemporary Chinese Philosophy* 《中國現代哲學史教學資料選集》, vol. 2. Beijing: Beijing daxue chubanshe 北京大學出版社.

Ames, Roger T., and David L. Hall, 2001. *Focusing the Familiar.* Honolulu: University of Hawaii Press.

Aristotle, 1941. *The Basic Works of Aristotle*, Richard Mckeon ed. New York: Random House.

______. 1976. *Ethics.* Thomson, J. trans. New York: Penguin books.

Berlin, Isaiah, 1996. *The Sense of Reality.* New York: Farrar, Straus and Giroux.

______. 1997. *The Proper Study of Mankind.* New York: Farrar, Straus and Giroux.

______. 1999. *The Root of Romanticism.* Princeton: Princeton University Press.

______. 2000. *The Power of Ideas.* Princeton: Princeton University Press.

Berthong, John, 1993. "Master ZHU Xi's Self-Realization: the Role of *Cheng*." *Philosophy East and West*, 43/1. Honolulu: University of Hawaii Press.

Bodde, Derk, 1976. "Harmony and Conflict in Chinese Thought," in *Studies in Chinese Thought*, Chicago: University of Chicago Press.

Bruce, J. P., 1923. *Chu Hsi and His Masters: An Introduction to Chu*

Hsi and the Sung School of Chinese Philosophy. London: Probsthain.

Chan, Wing-tsit, 1969. *A Source Book in Chinese Philosophy*. Princeton: Princeton University Press.

Chen, Chun 陳淳, 1990. *CHEN Chun's Analysis of Philosophical Terms* 《北溪字義》. Beijing: Zhonghua Shuju 中華書局.

Chen, Kenneth, 1973. *Buddhism in China*. Princeton: Princeton University Press.

Chen, Lifu 陳立夫, 1964. *The Philosophy of Life* 《生之原理》. Taipei: Zhengzhong shuju 正中書局.

Chen, Tingchuo 陳廷綽, 1959. *A Criticism on Lyric Poetry from CHEN Tingchuo* 《白雨齋詞話》. Beijing: Renmin wenxue chubanshe 人民文學出版社.

Cheng, Hao 程顥 and CHENG Yi 程頤, 1981. *The Collected Works of Cheng Brothers* 《二程集》. Beijing: Zhonghua Shuju 中華書局.

Cihai, 《辭海》, 1979. *The Sea of Words*. Shanghai: Shanghai cishu chuban she 上海辭書出版社.

Collingwood, R. G., 1945. *The Idea of Nature*. Oxford: Clarendon Press.

Dai, Zhen 戴震, 1961. *An Explanation in Terms and Meanings of* the Mencius, 《孟子字義疏證》. Beijing: Zhonghua shuju 中華書局.

Daxue 《大學》. In Zhu, 1983.

de Bary, Wm. Theodore, Wing-tsit Chan, and Burton Watson comp., 1999. *Sources of Chinese Tradition*, vol. 1. New York: Columbia University Press.

Dilthey, Wilhelm, 1981. *Der Aufbau der geschichtlichen Welt in den Geisteswissenschaften*. Frankfurt and Main: Shuramp.

Dong, Zhongshu 董仲舒, 1992. *Luxuriant Gems of the Spring and Autumn Annals* 《春秋繁露》. Beijing: Zhonghua shuju 中華書局.

______. 1962. *The History of Han Dynasty* 《漢書》. Beijing: Zhonghua shuju 中華書局.

Enker, E. trans., 1927. *Geschichte der Chinesischen Philosophie*, 2 vols. Rechenberg: Stiepel.

Eno, Robert, 1990. The *Confucian Creation of Heaven*. New York:

State University of New York Press.

Feng, Youland 馮友蘭, (also, Feng, Yu-lan). *A History of Chinese Philosophy*, vol. 1 (1952) & 2 (1953). Derk Bodde trans. Princeton: Princeton University Press.

______. 1960. *A Short History of Chinese Philosophy*, Derk Bodde ed. New York: Macmillan Company.

______. 1982. *A New Edition of the History of Chinese Philosophy* 《中國哲學史新編》, vol. 3. Beijing: Renmin chubanshe 人民出版社.

Foriers & Perelman, 1973. "Natural Law and Natural Rights," in *Dictionary of the History of Ideas*, vol. 3. New York: Charles Scribner's Son.

Gadamer, Hans-Georg, 1994. *Truth and Method*, Weinsheimer and Marshall trans. New York: Continumm.

Geach, Peter, 1997. *The Virtues*. Cambridge: Cambridge University Press.

Graham, A.C. 1958. *Two Chinese Philosophers*. London: Lund Humphries.

______. 1989. *Disputers of Tao*. La Salle: Open Court.

Guanzi 《管子》, 1996. *The Guanzi*. In YAN Changyao 顏昌嶢 ed. *An Annotation and Commentary on the Guanzi* 《管子校釋》.Changsha: Yuelu shushe 岳麓書社.

Guo, Xiang 郭象, *A Commentary on the Zhuangzi* 《莊子注》. In the *Zhuangzi*.

Guoyu 《國語》, 1998. The *Conversations of the States*. Shanghai shifan daxue guji zhengli yanjiu suo 上海師範大學古籍整理研究所. Shanghai: Shanghai guji chubanshe 上海古籍出版社.

Hanfeizi 《韓非子》, 1959. *The Hanfeizi*. In CHEN Qiyou 陳奇猷 ed. *The Collected Commentaries on the Hanfeizi* 《韓非子集釋》. Beijing: Zhonghua shuju 中華書局.

Hegel, G. W. F., 1974. *The History of Philosophy*, vol. 1. Halden and Simons trans. London: Routledge and Kegan Paul.

Huainanzi, 《淮南子》, 1989. *The Huainanzi*. In LIU Wendian 劉文典 ed. *The Collected Commentaries on the Huainanzi* 《淮南鴻烈集解》. Beijing: Zhonghua shuju 中華書局.

Hughes, E. R., trans., 1924. *The Great Learning and the Mean in Action*. London: Dent.

Hui Jiao 慧皎，1992. *Biography of Eminent Buddhist Monks* 《高僧傳》. TANG Yongtong 湯用彤 ed. Beijing: Zhonghua shuju 中華書局.

Hui Neng 慧能, 1983. *The Platform Sutra*, 《壇經》. In GUO Peng 郭鵬 ed. *A Commentary on the Platform Sutra*, 《壇經校釋》. Beijing: Zhonghua shuju 中華書局.

Jiang, Jieshi 蔣介石, 1937. *The Complete Works of JIANG Jieshi* 《蔣介石全集》. Shanghai: Wenhua bianyi guan 文化編譯館.

_______. 1984. *The Complete Works of Late President JIANG Jieshi* 《先總統蔣公全集》, vol. 1. Taipei: Zhongguo wenhua daxue chubanbu 中國文化大學出版部.

Kang, Youwei 康有爲, 1987. *Subtleties of* the Mencius《孟子微》Beijing: Zhonghua shuju 中華書局.

Kant, Immanuel, 1964. *Groundwork of the Metaphysics of Morals*. J. P. Paton, trans. New York: Harper & Row.

Lunyu 《論語》. In Zhu, 1983. Arthur Waley trans. *The Analects of Confucius*, New York: Vintage Books, 1989.

Laozi 《老子》, 1984. *The Laozi*. In ZHU Qianzhi 朱謙之 ed. *An Annotation and Explanation on the Laozi* 《老子校釋》. Beijing: Zhonghua shuju 中華書局. D. C. Lau, trans. *Lao Tzu: Tao Te Ching*, New York: Penguin Books, 1963.

Levenson, J. R., 1966. *Confucian China and Its Modern Fate*. Berkeley and Los Angels: University of California Press.

Li, Ao 李翱, 1963. *Recovery of the Nature* 《復性書》. In *The Selected Philosophical Works from the History of China: the Period from the Two Han Dynasties to the Sui and Tang Dynasties* 《中國歷代哲學文選：兩漢隋唐編》. Beijing: Zhonghua shuju, 中華書局.

Liang, Su 梁肅, 1983. *The General Rules of Cessation and Contemplation of Tiantai School* 《天台止觀通例》. In *The Selected Materials concerning the Thought of Chinese Buddhism* 《中國佛教思想資料選編》, vol. 2, bk. 1. Beijing: Zhonghua shuju 中華書局.

Liezi 《列子》. *The Liezi*, 1979. In YANG Bojun 楊伯峻 ed. *The Collected Commentaries on the Liezi* 《列子集釋》. Beijing: Zhonghua shuju 中華書局. A. C. Graham, trans. New York: Columbia University Press, 1960.

Liji 《禮記》, 1989. In SUN Xidan 孫希旦 ed. *The Complete Explanations of the Record of Rituals* 《禮記集解》. Beijing: Zhonghua shuju 中華書局.

Liu, Xiaogan 劉笑敢, 1994. *Classifying the Zhuangzi Chapters*. Ann Arbor: Center for Chinese Studies, the University of Michigan.

Lukes, Steven, 1973. *Individualism*. New York: Harper and Row.

Lüshi chunqiu 《呂氏春秋》, 1984. *Mr. Lü's Spring and Autumn Annals*. In CHEN Qiyou 陳奇猷 ed. *An Annotation and Commentary on Mr. Lü's Spring-Autumn Annals* 《呂氏春秋校釋》. Shanghai: Xuelin chuban she 學林出版社. Knoblock and Riegel trans. *The Annals of LÜ Buwei*, Stanford: Stanford University Press, 2000.

MacIntyre, Alasdair, 1984. *After Virtue*. Notre Dame: University of Notre Dame Press.

Mengzi 《孟子》. *The Mencius*. In Zhu, 1983. D. C. Lau, trans. *The Mencius*, New York: Penguin Classics, 1970.

Metzger, Thomas A., 1977. *Escape from Predicament*. New York: Columbia University Press.

Mou, Zongsan 牟宗三, 1986. *The Heart-Mind and Nature* 《心體與性體》, vol. 1. Taipei: Zhengzhong shuju 正中書局.

Mouzi 牟子, 1983. *Disposing of Error* 《理惑論》, in *The Selected Materials concerning the Thought of Chinese Buddhism* 《中國佛教思想資料選編》. SHI Jun 石峻 et al., eds. vol. 1. Beijing: Zhonghua Shuju 中華書局.

Munro, Donald, 1969. *The Concept of Man in Early China*. Stanford: Stanford University Press.

______. 1988. *Images of Human Nature*. Princeton: Princeton University Press.

______. 1996. The *Imperial Style of Inquiry in Twentieth Century China*. Ann Arbor: Center for Chinese Studies, University of Michigan.

______. ed. 1982. *Individualism and Holism: Studies in Confucian and Daoist Values*. Ann Arbor: Center for Chinese Studies, the University of Michigan.

Needham, Joseph, 1956. *Science and Civilization in China*, vol. 2. Cambridge: Cambridge University Press.

Qian, Mu 錢穆, ND. *The Collected Works of Mr. QIAN Mu* 《錢賓四先生文集》, vol. 18. Taipei: Lianjing chuban gongsi 聯經出版公司.

Rousseau, Jean Jacques, 1953. *The Confessions*. J. Cohen trans. New York: Penguin Classics.

Sartre, Jean-Paul, 1977. *No Exit and The Flies*. S. Cilbert. trans. New York: Alfred A. Knopf.

Schwartz, Benjamin, 1985. *The World of Thought in Ancient China*. Cambridge and London: Harvard University Press.

Shijing 《詩經》. *The Book of Poetry*. In Zhu, 1980.

Simmel, Georg, 1950. "Individual and Society in Eighteenth and Nineteenth Century of Views of Life." In K. H. Wolff, trans. and ed. *The Sociology of Simmel*. Illinois: Glencoe.

St. Augustine, 1943. *The Confessions*, Pilkington trans. New York: Liveright Publishing Corp.

Sun, Zhongshan 孫中山, 1960. In de Bary et al., eds. *Sources of Chinese Tradition*. New York: Columbia University.

Tang, Yongtong 湯用彤, 1997. *The History of Buddhism in Han, Wei, Two Jins, and the South and North Dynasties* 《漢魏兩晉南北朝佛教史》. Beijing: Beijing daxue chubanshe 北京大學 出版社.

Taylor, Rodney, 1990. *The Religious Dimension of Confucianism*. Albany: State University of New York Press.

Trilling, Lionel, 1972. *Sincerity and Authenticity*. Cambridge, Massachusetts: Harvard University Press.

Tu, Wei-ming, 1976. *Centrality and Commonality*. Honolulu: University of Hawaii Press.

Wang, Bi 王弼, 1980. "A Simple Exemplification of the Principle of *the Laozi*," "老子志略." In Lou Yulie 樓宇烈 ed. *The Collected Works of WANG Bi* 《王弼集》. Beijing: Zhonghua shuju 中華書局.

Wang, Fuzhi 王夫之, 1975a. *A Commentary on Master Zhang's Correcting Youthful Ignorance*, 《張子正蒙注》. Beijing: Zhonghua shuju 中華書局.

_______. 1975b. *Discussions after Reading the Great Collection of the Commentaries on the Four Books* 《讀四書大全說》. Beijing: Zhonghua Shuju 中華書局.

Wang, Yangming 王陽明, 1986. In Chan, Wing-tsit comp. *WANG*

Yangming: the Instruction for Practical Living and the Inquiry on the Great Learning 《王陽明傳習錄及大學問》. Taipei: Liming wenhua shiye gongsi 黎明文化事業公司. Wing-tsit Chan trans. *Instruction for Practical Learning and other Neo-Confucian Writings by WANG Yangming*. New York: Columbia University Press, 1963.

Weber, Max, 1951. *The Religion of China: Confucianism and Daoism*. Hans H. Gerth trans. New York: Macmillan Company.

Wenzi 《文子》, 2000. *The Wenzi*. In WANG Liqi 王利器 ed. *An Explanation of the Meaning of the Wenzi* 《文子疏義》. Beijing: Zhonghua shuju 中華書局. Thomas Cleary trans. In *The Daoist Classics*, vol. 1. Boston: Shambhala Press.

Whitehead, A. N., 1954. *Adventures of Ideas*. New York: Macmillan Company.

______. 1978. *Process and Reality* New York: Macmillan Company.

Wieger, L., 1917. *Histoire des Croyances Religieuses et des Opinions Philosophiques en Chine despuis l'origine jusqu'a nos jour*. Hsienhsien: Mission Press. E. T. C. Werner trans. 1927. Hsienhsien.

Xiong, Shili 熊十力, 1962. *New Consciousness-only Theory* 《新唯識論》.Taipei: Guangwen shuju 廣文書局.

______. 1976. *Essentials of XIONG Shili's Philosophy* 《十力語要》, vol. 1. Taipei: Guangwen shuju 廣文書局.

Xu, Shen 許慎, 1963. *Explanation of Script and Elucidation of Characters* 《說文解字》. Beijing: Zhonghua shuju 中華書局.

Xunzi 《荀子》, 1988. *The Xunzi*. In WANG Xianqian 王先謙 ed. *The Collected Commentaries on the Xunzi* 《荀子集釋》. Beijing: Zhonghua shuju 中華書局. Burton Watson trans. New York: Columbia University Press, 1964.

Yang, Xiong 揚雄, 1987. *The Aphorism* 《法言》. In WANG Baorong 王葆榮 ed. *An Explanation of the Meaning of the Aphorism* 《法言義疏》. Beijing: Zhonghua shujiu 中華書局.

Yijing 《易經》, 1979. *The Book of Changes*. In Gao Heng 高亨 ed. *A Modern Explanation of the Ancient Commentaries on the Book of Changes* 《周易大傳今注》. Shandong: Qilu shushe 齊魯書社. Wilhelm/Baynes trans. Princeton: Princeton University Press, 1990.

Yu, Ying-shih, "Individualism and the Neo-Daoist Movement in Wei-Jin China." In Munro, 1982.

Zhang, Dainian 張岱年, 1983. *An Introduction to the Methodologies for Studying the History of Chinese Philosophy* 《中國哲學史方法論發凡》. Beijing: Zhonghua Shuju 中華書局.

______. 1989. *A Brief Discussion on the Concepts in the Pre-modern Chinese Philosophy* 《中國古代哲學範疇要論》. Beijing: Zhongguo shehui kexue chuban she 中國社會科學出版社.

Zhang, Heng 張亨, 1992. "The Origin and Evolution of the Idea of the Unity of Heaven and Human 天人合一觀念的原始與變化." In *The Collection of International Conference on the Values in Chinese People* 《中國人的價值觀國際討論會論文集》. Taipei: A Research Series from the Center for Chinese Studies, No. 3.

Zhang, Hengshou, 張恆壽, 1989. *The Chinese Society and Its Thought and Culture* 《中國社會與思想文化》. Beijing: Renmin chuban she 人民出版社.

Zhang, Zai 張載, 1978. *The Collected Works of ZHANG Zai* 《張載集》. Beijing: Zhonghua shuju 中華書局.

Zhao, Qi 趙岐, ND. *A Commentary on* the Mencius 《孟子注釋》, vol. 7.

Zheng, Jingwang 鄭景旺, 1978. The *Writings of ZHENG Jingwang* 《夢齋筆談》. In ZHANG Mantao 張蔓濤 ed. *Buddhism and Chinese Culture* 《佛教與中國文化》. Taipei: Dasheng wenhua chubanshe 大乘文化出版社.

Zheng, Xuan 鄭玄. *A Commentary on Centrality and Commonality* 《中庸注》. In QIAN Mu.

Zhongyong 《中庸》. In Zhu, 1983. James Legge trans. *Confucius' Analects, the Great Learning, and the Doctrine of the Mean*, New York: Dover, 1971.

Zhou, Dunyi 周敦頤, 2000. *Penetrating the Book of Changes of Master Zhou*, 《周子通書》. Shanghai: Guiji chubanshe 古籍出版社. Chan, Wing-tsit, trans. 1969.

Zhu, Xi 朱熹, 1980. *The Book of Poetry with ZHU Xi's Commentary* 《詩集傳》. Shanghai: Guji chubanshe 古籍出版社.

______. 1983. *The Collected Commentaries on the Four Books* 《四書集

注》. Beijing: Zhonghua shuju 中華書局.

______. 1986. *Recorded Conversations of Master Zhu* 《朱子語類》. Beijing: Zhonghua Shuju 中華書局.

______ ed. 2000. *Reflection on Things at Hand* 《近思錄》. Shanghai: Guji chuban she 古籍出版社. Wing-tsit Chan trans. *Reflections on Things at Hand.* New York: Columbia University Press.

______. 2001. *The Completed Works of Master Zhu* 《朱子全书》, vol. 13. Shanghai: Guji chuban she 古籍出版社.

Zhuangzi, 《莊子》, 1961. *The Zhuangzi.* In GUO Qingfan 郭慶藩 ed. *The Collected Commentaries on the Zhuangzi* 《莊子集釋》. Beijing: Zhonghua shuju 中華書局. Burton Watson trans. New York: Columbia University Press 1964.

Zuozhuan, 《左傳》, 1984. In YANG Bojun 楊伯峻 ed. *The Collected Commentaries on Zuo's Commentary on the Spring and Autumn Annals* 《春秋左傳集釋》. Beijing: Zhonghua Shuju 中華書局, 1981. James Legge trans. *The Chinese Classics*, vol. 5. Hong Kong: Hong Kong University Press, 1960.

Index

E

F

G

H

I

J

K

L

P

Q

R

S